ISBN 978-1-333-31890-1
PIBN 10489244

H. B. Irving.

Trial of

EDITED BY

H. B. Irving, M.A.(Oxon.)

With an Appreciation of the Editor

BY

SIR EDWARD MARSHALL HALL, K.C.

EDINBURGH AND LONDON

PRINTED BY
WILLIAM HODGE AND COMPANY, LTD.
GLASGOW AND EDINBURGH
1920

CONTENTS.

CONTENTS.

ILLUSTRATIONS.

The Late H. B. IRVING.

By Sir Edward Marshall Hall, K.C.

Owing to the lamented death of Mr. H. B. Irving, while this volume was still in the hands of the publishers, I have been asked to write a few words in memory and appreciation of him as a criminologist. Harry Irving, as his friends always knew and called him, first came into my life many years ago when I was engaged at the Central Criminal Court in a case which attracted a great deal of attention at the time. It was known as the Grafton Street or " Box " murder, the victim having been put into a large trunk and left at the cloak room of a railway station. The case took a very dramatic turn at the trial, and the prisoner, a woman, was acquitted of murder and convicted of manslaughter only, though, until all the facts were elicited, it had seemed a hopeless case to defend. Even at that time Irving was keenly studying criminal trials and procedure, and he maintained that this case illustrated very forcibly his view that in the French system the lack of effec- tive cross-examination of hostile witnesses often worked grave hardship to the accused. This view he repeats more than once in his books on French criminals, and he often told me that he considered that this and the hostile interrogation of the prisoner by the presiding judge were the great blots on the French method. From that time onwards I saw a good deal of him, and he took the greatest interest in the criminal cases in which I was briefed.

Even at Oxford, as I learn from mutual friends who were undergraduates with him, that bent had declared itself. The essay and discussion societies, without which youthful Oxford seemed unable to exist in the early nineties, had no attractions for him otherwise than as meetings where he could listen to or read papers on criminology. That, with the O.U.D.S.,

The Late H. B. Irving.

monopolised his attention, somewhat to the detriment of his "schools." It was the same, I understand, while he was reading for the bar. At Oxford he used to attend the Assize Courts, and one of his New College contemporaries has told me how his recital of what passed in those somewhat sordid present-ments of life would enthral Junior Common Room afterwards. It was always stated amongst his contemporaries in those days that even then he had started on his "Life of Judge Jeffreys," a work which certainly might have come from a far more mature pen. One has only to go through the books that he has produced, either as author or editor, to realise what care and attention he must have given to criminology; but if I may be allowed to express my personal opinion, it was his keen sense of drama, his great dramatic instinct, that made him study criminals and their trials in search of the drama that he knew he was sure to find.

It is somewhat remarkable, but none the less true, that crime and the history of criminals have a great attraction for very many people who would not be suspected of such an interest. In the introduction to his "Remarkable Criminals," Irving recalls how his father, Sir Henry Irving, told him that one night, when he sat up late with Tennyson, the latter said he had not kept such late hours since a recent visit he had paid to Jowett when the absorbing subject of conversation was "Murders," and on this topic the poet and philosopher had talked till the early morning.

In his preface to his Studies of French Criminals, Irving opens with this quotation from Edmund Burke—"The annals of criminal jurisprudence exhibit human nature in a variety of positions, at once the most striking, interesting, and affecting. They present tragedies of real life often heightened in their effect by the grossness of the injustice and the malignity of the prejudices which accompanied them. At the same time, real culprits, as original characters, stand forward on the canvas of humanity as prominent objects for our special study." In the first lines of the book itself, dealing with the history of Lacenaire, he quotes from "Les Miserables" of Victor

xii

An Appreciation.

Hugo—"Every human society has what is called in theatres a third sub-stage. It is the grave of the depths. It is the cave of the blind. Man there becomes dragon. Hunger and thirst are the point of departure; Satan is the point of arrival."

From these two quotations, taken together, may be gathered the real reason of Harry Irving's great interest in criminology. For a man so strongly imbued with the dramatic instinct, he possessed a very keen sense of justice and was intolerant of persecution or tyranny in any form; while he was a great believer in the old-fashioned precision of our criminal procedure and a great stickler for the observance of its technicalities. He was not alone in deploring the somewhat haphazard way in which indictments are now drawn under the present Act, and he regarded the abolition—or shall I say suspension?—of the grand jury as a great blot on our administration of the criminal law. Called to the bar, as he was, when quite a young man, he might have had a great career in the criminal Courts, where a sense of drama is never wasted and a good actor has advantages which others lack. No counsel is allowed by the rules of the profession to express his opinion upon the guilt or innocence of an accused person, but if an advocate for the defence can legitimately, in his advocacy, convey to the jury the impression of his belief in his client's case, he has gone a long way towards securing their verdict. Alas, how many verdicts have been lost by clever men for the want of this one little touch of the actor! I well remember listening in a case to a fine speech by a man who was a great speaker without being a great advocate. The speech was perfect in composition and logic, but it left one cold; whereas the speech in reply, badly as it might read in the reports, was a human speech on the level of its audience, and it won the verdict. A few days later I happened to meet one of the jury and asked him how they failed to be convinced by the other speech, "Oh," said he, "the speech was right enough, but he didn't believe a word of it himself; he had his tongue in his cheek all the time."

What a difference between that and the wonderful speech that Sir Edward Clarke made in defence of Mrs. Bartlett! No

The Late H. B. Irving.

one who had the good fortune to hear it had any doubt that Clarke knew when he made it that he would secure a triumphant acquittal. I am not sure if Irving actually heard that speech or not; I rather think he did, but we often discussed it and he always said it was the best of the many fine speeches that great advocate ever made.

Another thing that attracted Irving to the study of crime and criminals was the accuracy of his mind, his love of lucid and chronological arrangement of facts, and his devotion to the development of a theory. Some of his theories, as to motive, were rather fantastic; but once he had started a theory, he was not satisfied until he had explored it by every avenue. In some of the so-called " unsolved mysteries " of crime, he formed very shrewd ideas as to the identity of the criminal, although the police may not have felt justified in acting on the evidence that was available. Please note that I say *evidence*, for under our system there may be, and often are, many things known to the police which could not be proved in a Court of justice, and this is where the great difference comes in between our system and the French. In France and other foreign countries the police almost always arrest on suspicion and trust to the cross-examination or interrogation of the accused by the magistrate to convert that suspicion into a practical certainty. This is one reason why Irving found the study of French criminal trials so much more interesting and so much more dramatic than the British. The two systems start from a different point of view, and the methods adopted to carry out the process are wide as the poles asunder. In France every accused person is presumed to be guilty, and every kind of trick is resorted to in the hope of securing a confession or of proving the presumption, whereas in England every accused person is presumed to be innocent until the verdict of the jury of " Guilty." So jealous are our Courts of this principle that a statement by an accused person in custody is not admissible in evidence unless it is proved that the accused has been properly cautioned by the person to whom this statement is made. It was this well-

An Appreciation.

known principle of our criminal administration that aroused Irving's enthusiasm, and he was never slow to notice and condemn any attempt to weaken it or whittle it down.

My space will not allow me to attempt to refer to, much less to analyse, the fascinating records of crime that he dealt with so fully and so ably in "Studies of French Criminals," published in 1901, and the "Book of Remarkable Criminals," published so recently as in 1918. His "Life of Judge Jeffreys" is a monument of industry and research and I doubt if I ever read a more unanimous consensus of praise than the reviews of this book, which appeared in practically every journal of importance. In addition to the present volume, he has edited with great skill and care two others—(i.) The Trial of Franz Müller, the North London murder of 1864, which he dedicates to that ever-young man of ninety-seven, Lord Halsbury, who, as Mr. Hardinge Giffard, appeared in the case as one of the juniors for the prosecution ; (ii.) The Trial of Mrs. Maybrick, which is dedicated to Lord Sterndale, Master of the Rolls, who, as Mr. Pickford, was junior to the late Lord Russell of Killowen for the defence of that most unfortunate woman. Irving was fortunate in his selection for dedication, as I doubt if there are two more popular personalities to be found in the estimation of the profession to which they belong.

One trait in Irving's character must not be overlooked— sometimes he was so impressed with the methods and conduct of different criminals that he came almost to respect their ability, and whilst he had and expressed the greatest contempt for some of the criminals whose records he unearthed, he undoubtedly admired the misplaced and misused talents of men like Lacenaire and Peace. In recent times he expressed sympathy with the famous Dr. Crippen, and though, from circumstances over which I had no control, I was personally unable to conduct his defence, I too always felt some inexplicable sympathy for him. Of one thing both Irving and I felt convinced, that if Crippen had cared to throw over the companion who was eventually arrested with him, he might have made good his escape.

The Late H. B. Irving.

In the preparation of this volume dealing with the trial of the Wainwrights, Irving had taken the keenest interest and often had we talked over the points together. I remember the trial well, though I was only a schoolboy at Rugby at the time, and Irving was much interested in hearing my personal reminiscences of this case, which was tried at the Old Bailey in 1875, eight years before I was called to the bar. Five of the counsel engaged in the case I knew well, and three of them, Sir Harry Poland, Sir Douglas Straight, and Mr. Charles Gill, I hope I may claim as intimate personal friends.

By a somewhat curious coincidence, I was brought into close touch with two other criminal cases which were very notorious before I came to the bar. As a small boy, I found my way into the Police Court at Brighton, where I saw Christiana Edmunds in the dock, charged with the murder of a little boy by poison at Brighton, a crime for which she was afterwards convicted and sentenced to death at the Old Bailey; but, being found insane, she was sent to Broadmoor, where she died only a few years ago. There were many very interesting incidents in connection with this case, which Irving and I often discussed, not the least amusing of which was the one which occurred at the trial between verdict and sentence. The prisoner had pleaded, in bar of sentence of death, that she was *enceinte*, and a jury of matrons was empanelled. This jury desired the assistance of a medical man who happened to be in Court, and he required a stethescope. A message was sent into Court, and the presiding judge asked one of the police to fetch one from one of the shops on Ludgate Hill; after a time the officer returned, bringing a naval telescope, and apologised by saying it was the smallest he could get.

The other case of which I have a personal recollection and in which Irving took a keen interest, was the Lefroy case. On Monday, 27th June, 1881, I was at Brighton Station, about to proceed to London, when I noticed a considerable commotion. Going to inquire the cause, I saw a man, looking very ill, who was being taken to the Sussex County Hospital, and was told

An Appreciation.

that he had been injured during his journey in the train which had just arrived from London. This man was Lefroy, who had in fact murdered Mr. Gold in that train and who must have had at that time, partly hidden in his shoe, the watch and chain of the murdered man, the presence of which was afterwards detected and led to his arrest. I proceeded to London, and the dead body of Mr. Gold must have been lying in the tunnel through which we passed. I talked over this case with Irving, who, as usual, had all the details at his finger-ends, and he was most particularly interested in my telling him of a long conversation I had had with Henry Labouchere on the last day of the trial, when he criticised the tactics adopted by Montagu Williams who led for the defence.

No notice of Harry Irving in this connection would be in any sense complete which did not contain some reference to the club in which he took so much interest and helped to found. The " Crimes Club," as it was nicknamed, or, more properly, " Our Society," was intended to be an association originally of twelve, and later of forty, members interested in criminology, who were to meet periodically at dinner and after dinner debate cases and matters connected with that subject. It has been very successful, and the meetings have been all the more interesting because members and their guests are pledged to absolute secrecy, thus giving free play to unfettered discussion. Nowhere will Harry Irving be more missed than at the meetings of this club. I little thought when, only a short while ago, I was considering with him the details of the Wainwright case, that before the volume was published he would have " gone west." If it had not been his fortune to be the son of a great actor and a great actor himself, he might have earned fame as a great advocate, but his was the better rôle. There was one subject on which he and I were in complete accord, and that was the improvement of the status of the police and detective force of this country. We both advocated the centralisation of the detective organisation in London, with branches in direct communication all over the country. If men of education and ability could be attracted

The Late H. B. Irving.

by remunerative salaries to this work, then there would have been, and would be, more chance of dealing successfully with the clever fraternity who live by their wits, and I know of no class of man who could do better work of this kind than men who possess those abilities which were so noticeable in Harry Irving.

Many affectionate notices of him have appeared, and all the kind things that have been said of him he richly deserved. Honest, upright, courageous, generous to a fault, he was the soul of chivalry and old-world courtesy. To know him was to love him, and once you gained his friendship you were sure of a champion at all times and on all occasions. A sure way to draw him was to attack some one who was absent. They who write his life will have an easy task where they want to praise him, but it is with a keen sense of my own insufficiency that I pen these few lines to his memory as a criminologist.

THE WAINWRIGHTS.

INTRODUCTION.

At the beginning of the year 1874 there was probably no more popular or respected individual among the principal inhabitants of that long and broad thoroughfare, the Whitechapel Road, than Mr. Henry Wainwright, brushmaker, carrying on his business in partnership with his brother William at Nos. 84 and 215 Whitechapel Road. Henry Wainwright's father, a respectable tradesman, churchwarden of his parish, had died some ten years before, leaving a fortune of £11,000 to be divided between his four sons and a daughter. Henry Wainwright, described as "gentleman," had married, in 1862, the daughter of a "merchant," by whom he had had four children. At the time this narrative opens he was living with his wife and family in Tredegar Square.

Genial, hospitable, always ready to "stand treat," rather showy and assertive in his *bonhomie*, Wainwright had all those gifts that make for popularity. Nor was he without intellectual interests, unusual in a man of his position. As early as 1860, when he was twenty-two years of age, Wainwright was a prominent member of the Christ Church Institute, St. George's-in-the-East, and a particular supporter of its musical and elocutionary classes. About the same time we find him giving an entertainment in an East-End school, described as "An Evening with Thomas Moore," and taking an active part in private theatricals. He appeared, among other parts, in that of Tom Cranky in "The Birthplace of Podgers," made famous by J. L. Toole, and gave occasional readings in Dickens, Barham, and Tom Hood. In 1867 Wainwright delivered a lecture at the Leeds Mechanics' Institution on "The Wit and Eccentricity of Sydney Smith." He had at one time figured as a temperance lecturer, but in later life would seem to have departed from those principles.

The Wainwrights.

In appearance Henry Wainwright is described as moderately tall, thick, and broad-shouldered in build. There was a Jewish cast in his countenance, accentuated by a large nose and his dark brown hair and beard, waved and curly. His beard and moustache concealed a heavy and sensual mouth. His blue eyes were full and prominent, but with the curious dusky, sleepy look associated with those of Orientals. The whole effect of the face was by no means displeasing, and to women Mr. Henry Wainwright was anything but unattractive.

Among no class of people in the Whitechapel Road at that time was Wainwright more popular than with the actors at the Pavilion Theatre. The theatre was situated next door to Wainwright's shop at No. 84. Wainwright was on good terms with the management, supplied them with brushes and mats, evinced great interest in all things connected with the drama, and enjoyed practically the free run of the theatre. He was always lavish in entertaining, and to actors getting very humble salaries it was a much-desired privilege to be asked out to sup with Mr. Wainwright. Vanity played no small part in Wainwright's character. After one of these suppers a recitation by the host was accepted as a recognised feature of the entertainment. Curiously enough, in the light of subsequent events, his favourite piece on these occasions was Hood's " Dream of Eugene Aram.'' He is said by one of those who heard him to have recited the poem with force and vigour, but without that peculiar sense of horror which makes its recitation so vivid in the hands of a great actor.

In public affairs Wainwright took an occasional part. He was an ardent supporter of the Conservative party. In one instance his interest in the burning questions of the day made him figure prominently in a dramatic scene. During 1872 and 1873 Arthur Orton, the Tichborne claimant, was stumping the country holding meetings to raise funds for his defence in his approaching trial for forgery. A meeting of his East-End supporters, of whom Wainwright declared himself one, was held on the stage of the Pavilion Theatre. At the conclusion of the claimant's speech the heavy drop curtain was lowered unexpectedly, and, had it fallen on the head of Orton, who was immediately beneath it and unconscious of its descent, might

Henry Wainwright.

Introduction.

have terminated that impostor's career and saved his country a
considerable expenditure of public money. But Wainwright
sprang forward at the critical moment, and, before the catas-
trophe could happen, pulled back the claimant out of all danger.
Loud applause greeted this dramatic incident, and Orton and
Wainwright appeared hand in hand before the curtain to receive
the congratulations of the audience—a strange association of
the criminal that was with the criminal yet to be.*

A pleasant account of the home life of Wainwright at this
time, and an instance of his natural friendliness and geniality
are given by J. B. Howe, an East-End tragedian of the day, in
his book, " A Cosmopolitan Actor "—

> A few days after my arrival, I left my house in Tredegar
> Terrace, Bow, to proceed westward, and as I crossed Tredegar
> Square I saw a hansom cab drawing up to the centre house of
> the row. A gentleman of medium height jumped out, and
> approaching me exclaimed: "Bless me, I can't be mistaken.
> It's Mr. Howe." "You have the advantage of me," I replied,
> and yet your face is familiar!" "Oh, yes, I've seen you often
> at the East London; come into the house if you have a moment
> to spare, I can give you a good glass of sherry."
>
> After having addressed the cabman and rung the bell, the
> door was opened by a smart slavey, and he led the way to an
> elegantly furnished parlour. Wine was brought on the table,
> with biscuits, and while we were chatting about my travels, the
> door was gently opened and a pretty, dark lady entered with two
> lovely children. The gentleman merely said: "My wife, Mr.
> Howe."
>
> The lady took a seat and seemed greatly pleased with the
> interest her husband evinced in the hurried explanation I gave
> of my voyage home, and, amongst other remarks, I elicited from
> him the fact that he was in some sense an actor himself. "That
> is," said he, "I play for charitable purposes sometimes, and also
> give lectures at the Bow and Bromley Institute and other places."
>
> All this time I did not like to put the somewhat rude ques-
> tion, "What might be your name?" thinking, of course, that
> he would divulge it in the course of the glib conversation; but,
> however, he did not, and after a lapse of perhaps thirty-five
> minutes, he left the room to make some explanations to his wife,
> and, re-entering, exclaimed—
>
> "Were you going towards the city?"
> "I was going to the West End when I encountered you."

---

* This scene is described by the late Arthur Williams, the
comedian, who was present at it, in his " Reminiscences," which
appeared in the *Stage* newspaper in 1914.

The Wainwrights.

"Oh, then, you can come in my cab as far as Whitechapel, if you have no objection."

"None in the least," I rejoined.

"All right, jump in; good-bye, my dears." Then kissing the children and his wife he joined me, and we turned into the Bow Road towards Mile End. As we drove along, I thought I had never in my life encountered a nicer man. A fine head, firmly balanced on square shoulders; raven locks, and large penetrating blue eyes, short whiskers just tinged with a red sandy hue, and a power of conversation really wonderful. He asked me where I intended to open in London. I told him I really did not know, as I had not as yet shown myself. By this time we were at Mile End. "Well," he exclaimed, "as I am so near my shop, I'll just jump out and leave you."

He alighted, shook hands with a friend, and walked away arm in arm towards the London Hospital.

"Who was that gentleman?" I asked of the cabman, "I did not like to ask him his name, he seemed to know me well enough." "You must have seen him often," said the cabman, "it's Mr. Henry Wainwright, the brushmaker."

But underneath this apparent domestic happiness, the prosperity and respectability of Mr. Henry Wainwright, the brushmaker, there lurked a story of intrigue, hitherto a secret from the world, which was fated to ruin the good name of Wainwright and destroy the esteem in which he was held by his fellow-men, an esteem which to a man of his temperament was a constant source of self-congratulation. Unknown to all, the respectable and respected Mr. Henry Wainwright was clandestinely a *coureur des femmes*, and, if his own account is to be believed, an eminently successful one. In the course of his surreptitious adventures he was led into forming a connection of a more lasting character than attaches usually to incidents of this kind, the consequences of which were to threaten the exposure to that double life which Mr. Wainwright had hitherto concealed so cleverly from his family and friends.

In the course of the year 1871 Wainwright had met at Broxbourne Gardens, a favourite pleasure resort of Londoners at that time on the banks of the river Lea, a girl about twenty years of age, named Harriet Lane, daughter of John Lane, a gas manager employed in the Royal Gunpowder Mills at Waltham Abbey, living at Waltham Cross. Harriet Lane herself was apprenticed to a milliner and dressmaker at Waltham Abbey.

Introduction.

She is described as a lively little woman with pleasing manners and a love of finery. If certain letters found in her possession, written in the years 1871 and 1872, are to be accepted as having come from Henry Wainwright, their intimacy would appear to have commenced under assumed names, Wainwright passing as "George Williams," and Harriet Lane as "Miss L. Varco." In July, 1871, Williams writes—

> "Darling creature, off to Paris—for God's sake don't write, etc. Drop me a line in about a fortnight (if you don't in that time thoroughly forget me) to P.O., Whitechapel Road. Oceans of love."

On August 25th he makes an appointment to meet Miss Varco in the first-class waiting room at Bishopsgate Station.

In September he writes to her from Germany, this time signing himself "George Varco"—

> "It is very uncertain how long I shall stay away from England, perhaps for ever, God knows, so think no more of me, and quite forget you ever saw me. I have told P.O. to send me only letters received in name of
> "Yrs most affectionately,
> "GEO. VARCO."

A letter from Strasburg follows this—

> "My little Beauty, not home till December, drop me a line to P.O. by Dec. 1st, if you don't forget me, as in all probability you will."

If these letters were written by Henry Wainwright to Harriet Lane—and there seems no reason to doubt it—the intimacy had ripened quickly after the return of "George Varco" from Germany. In the February of 1872 there appeared in the *Waltham Abbey and Cheshunt Weekly Telegraph* an advertisement, sent to the newspaper in a woman's handwriting, to the effect that on the 22nd instant, at St. Mary's, Percy King, Esq., of Chelsea, had been married to Harriet, ninth daughter of John Lane, of Waltham Cross, Herts. Percy King was Henry Wainwright, and henceforth Harriet Lane was to be known as Mrs. King. In July Mr. and Mrs. King were living together in St. Peter's Street, Mile End, and there on August 22nd a daughter

The Wainwrights.

was born to them. After moving to Alfred Place, Bedford Square, and Cecil Street, Strand, Mrs. King, in 1873, returned to St. Peter's Street, where, in December of that year, a second daughter was born. There Mrs. King remained until the May of 1874, when she went to lodge at the house of a Mrs. Foster, 3 Sidney Square, Mile End Road.

Thus, unknown to his wife and to the world at large, Henry Wainwright had for three years been leading this double life. His relationship with Harriet Lane had been kept a profound secret, known only to the one or two persons who had been brought into close contact with Mrs. King. Among these was a Miss Wilmore, for whom Harriet Lane had worked at one time as a dressmaker. Miss Wilmore would seem to have had a very real affection for Harriet Lane, and, when she learnt of her connection with Mr. King, had, with Wainwright's approval, taken care of the elder of the little girls. But beyond Miss Wilmore few, if any, knew of the identity of Mr. Percy King with Henry Wainwright, and, had things prospered with Wainwright as in the past, he would have had no difficulty in fulfilling his responsibilities towards his clandestine family, and so rendering unlikely that the exposure of his misconduct which above all things he sought to avoid.

Unfortunately for him, to a great extent, no doubt, through his own neglect and extravagance, his business affairs had been going steadily from bad to worse, until in 1874 they had reached a crisis. His brother William, to whom he owed a considerable sum of money, dissolved their partnership. An attempt of Wainwright to carry on the business with a new partner ended disastrously. His debts, irrespective of that to his brother, amounted to over £3000. In May his creditors met and agreed to accept a composition of 12s. in the pound, of which, however, Wainwright never paid more than 9s. In July he was so hard put to it for cash that he is found unsuccessfully trying to pawn a revolver.

These financial embarrassments had reacted most unhappily on the relations between Wainwright and Mrs. King. At the beginning of their intimacy her lover had allowed her the generous sum of £5 a week; in fact, as Harriet Lane said herself, Mr. Wainwright " kept her like a lady." But as his

Introduction.

financial position grew more insecure, Wainwright could not continue to keep Mrs. King on this scale. With ever-increasing liabilities, he found the tie of his mistress and her family more and more irksome. His payments to her diminished steadily, and it was at last with considerable difficulty that Mrs. King could get any money out of him at all. She was herself obliged to pawn a number of her things. Under these trials Mrs. King developed a certain hastiness of temper and a tendency to drink more than was good for her. She took to going to Wainwright's shop at 84 Whitechapel Road and making unpleasant scenes. On one occasion Wainwright would appear to have used physical violence towards her. Under the influence of drink, she had created a disturbance outside her lodgings, and, in the summer of 1874, was under notice to quit from her landlady. But through all her troubles Harriet Lane remained constant to Wainwright. Nothing on earth, she said, should ever part her from Henry. Her constancy was to cost her dear.

To Wainwright the situation had become intolerable. Not only had Harriet Lane become dangerous to his reputation and peace of mind, but he had no doubt tired of her. To this clandestine Don Juan of the Whitechapel Road the jealousy and importunity of Harriet Lane promised to be serious obstacles to the enjoyment of other amorous adventures. Owing to her inconvenient devotion to him, he could see no prospect of palming her off on another man. On September 10th, 1874, Wainwright ordered half a hundredweight of chloride of lime, which was packed in a box and sent to No. 84 Whitechapel Road. On the following day, Friday, the 11th, Mrs. King left her lodgings at four o'clock in the afternoon, taking with her a nightdress done up in a small parcel. She told Miss Wilmore that she was going to meet Henry Wainwright at his place in the Whitechapel Road. From that hour Mrs. King was never seen again alive, and, in the course of the same day, the chloride of lime at No. 84 had disappeared.

Besides the shop at No. 84, Wainwright had a warehouse, No. 215, on the opposite side of the Whitechapel Road. Three men working next door to this warehouse swore that, on an evening about this time in September, between half-past five and six o'clock they had heard three pistol shots fired in rapid succes-

The Wainwrights.

sion, which sounded as if they came from Wainwright's premises.
This warehouse was a long, narrow building some 40 yards in
depth. A good deal of the flooring was stone, but at the extreme
end was a raised portion, called the paint room, the floor of
which was of wood. Since Friday, September 11th, 1874,
Harriet Lane, Mrs. Percy King, had been lying in chloride of
lime, shot through the head and her throat cut, under the floor
of the paint room at 215 Whitechapel Road.

To explain the mysterious disappearance of Harriet Lane,
Wainwright told Miss Wilmore and such of her relations as
inquired about her that she had gone off with a man named Teddy
Frieake, with whom she was living on the Continent, and Miss
Wilmore received a letter purporting to come from Mr. Frieake,
addressed from the Charing Cross Hotel, in which the writer said
that Mrs. King had promised to have nothing more to do with
Mr. King or her family and friends. On these conditions Mr.
Frieake was going to marry her, and they were about to start
for Dover. From Dover Henry Wainwright and Miss Wilmore
received telegrams from Frieake saying that he and Harriet
were off to the Continent for a spree. According to Henry
Wainwright, Edward Frieake was a friend of his, and on more
than one occasion during 1873 and the early part of 1874 Wainwright and a person calling himself Edward Frieake had visited
Harriet Lane at her lodgings. It was true that Henry Wainwright had a friend called Edward Frieake, an auctioneer, but
this was not the Edward Frieake who had visited Harriet Lane
and taken her away to marry her on the Continent. There
was evidence to suggest that this Edward Frieake had been
impersonated on his visits to Harriet Lane by Henry Wainwright's brother Thomas, and the letter purporting to come
from Frieake, written from the Charing Cross Hotel, was undoubtedly in the handwriting of Thomas Wainwright. When
in the course of their inquiries the friends of Harriet Lane
lighted on the real Edward Frieake, the auctioneer and friend of
Henry Wainwright, and he had satisfied them that he knew
nothing of, and had never had any dealings with, Harriet Lane,
Wainwright explained the awkward fact by saying that it was
not this Edward Frieake who had gone off with Harriet, but
another man of the same rather uncommon name, a young

Introduction.

fellow of three- or four-and-twenty, whom he had met at some billiard rooms in Fenchurch Street. In spite of the apparently singular coincidence of Henry Wainwright having two friends of the uncommon name of Frieake combined with the Christian name of Edward, and the unsatisfactory character of his explanation of Harriet's disappearance, it is to the credit of his plausibility and self-assurance that he succeeded in convincing the friends of Harriet Lane of the truth of his story. After the beginning of the year 1875, her friends would appear to have accepted the situation, and no further inquiries were made as to her fate. The two children of Mr. and Mrs. King were left in the care of the faithful Miss Wilmore, who received from Wainwright the money necessary for their maintenance.

Wainwright was now on the way to experience those feelings of terror and remorse which he had been so fond of portraying in his recitation of "The Dream of Eugene Aram." But such are not the emotions usually felt by murderers. It is difficult to believe that any one as imaginative as Hood's Aram would ever have committed a murder; he is certainly utterly unlike the Aram of real life, who would seem to have been very little troubled at any time by feelings of acute horror or remorse. Apprehension would better describe, as a rule, the feelings of the murderer who has an awkward secret buried in, as he hopes, some unsuspected and inaccessible place. At the same time, the change in the Henry Wainwright of ante-murder and post-murder days was unmistakable, and impressed itself on many of those who had known him during both periods.

My friend, the late Frank Tyars, for many years a member of my father's company, was engaged as an actor at the Pavilion Theatre at different times during 1874 and 1875. He described Wainwright, as he first knew him, as a man of a very self-assured and confident bearing, who walked down the Whitechapel Road as if it belonged to him, hail-fellow-well-met in his manner, cordial and friendly towards all those associated with the theatre. Before the summer of 1874 Tyars left the Pavilion, but returned there later to fulfil another engagement. It was then that he noticed an extraordinary change in the demeanour of Wainwright. He first saw him coming down the street. Instead of the breezy, self-confident gentleman he had known, he saw a

The Wainwrights.

man walking slowly along in a furtive, hang-dog way, and, to his astonishment, recognised him as Henry Wainwright.

J. B. Howe had also observed the change in the man. He had become nervous, impatient, and irritable. He had taken to visiting public-houses, where he would sit drinking more than was good for him, and nervously cracking and eating walnuts, of which he was very fond.

Fortunately for Wainwright, men put down this marked change in his manner and disposition to the pressing nature of his financial difficulties, which were constantly increasing. On November 27th, 1874, the shop at No. 84 Whitechapel Road was burnt down, its contents completely gutted by the fire. Wainwright claimed £3000 insurance money from the Sun Fire Office, but the company disputed his claim. He brought an action against them, which had not yet come on for trial at the time of his arrest. Wainwright was in the habit of speaking with great excitement and bitterness of the conduct of the company in resisting his claim, so much so that J. B. Howe found himself very nearly involved in a row in the bar of the " Royal Oak " owing to some expression he had used in trying to calm Wainwright's too outspoken indignation against the Fire Office.

In September, 1874, Wainwright had been obliged to raise money by a mortgage on the warehouse at 215 Whitechapel Road. In June, 1875, Wainwright had been declared a bankrupt. In the July of that year the mortgagee of No. 215 foreclosed and took possession of the premises, including that portion known as the paint room, under which were lying the remains of Harriet Lane. Wainwright about this time had given up his business as a brushmaker, and was employed as manager by a Mr. Martin, a well-to-do corn merchant in the New Road, Whitechapel. Mr. Martin had taken over Wainwright's brush business in a friendly way, and advanced him £300. He paid Wainwright a salary of £3 a week, and intended when the money he had advanced had been paid off to restore to him his business. Wainwright was in the habit of calling for his letters at No. 215, and would seem to have had access to the premises. Was it safe to leave the proof of his guilt under the floor of the paint room. Many persons had noticed at different times an unpleasant smell in the warehouse, and an

Introduction.

inquisitive dog that nosed about too frequently in the neighbour-hood of the paint room was said to have disappeared suddenly.

In November, 1874, Thomas Wainwright, the brother who had been mixed up so mysteriously in the history of the legendary Edward Frieake, had started an ironmongery business at a place called the Hen and Chickens, in the High Street, Borough. The business had failed, and, in June, 1875, Thomas' principal creditor put in an execution. A sale was held on June 28th. After the sale the premises were locked up, the key being in the possession of Thomas Wainwright. The foundations of the building known as the Hen and Chickens were deep and solid, and down in its cellars were some very remote and inaccessible corners, convenient hiding-places for inconvenient relics.

The anniversary of the disappearance of Harriet Lane was approaching. It was an anniversary on which Henry Wain-wright might with some reason congratulate himself as a hitherto successful murderer. His victim had been dead a year, and no one was troubling any further about what had become of her. If he could only transfer successfully her remains from the Whitechapel Road, where it was no longer safe to leave them, to the convenient hiding-place in the Borough, he had every reason to hope that they might remain undiscovered for an indefinite period. He had made only one mistake. Chloride of lime preserves rather than destroys human remains. The removal would be therefore a difficult and extremely unpleasant task. But with the help of his brother Thomas it had to be done, and on September 10th, 1875, the two brothers purchased between them a quantity of American cloth, some rope, a chopper, and a spade.

Next morning, Saturday, September 11th, the very day on which Harriet Lane the year before had left her lodgings in Sidney Square to go to meet Henry Wainwright, a friend of Thomas Wainwright remarked that he was not looking well. The work that had been done the night before, the making up of the two parcels in American cloth that were waiting at No. 215 Whitechapel Road to be taken to the Borough, cannot have been a pleasant occupation. But so far everything had been carried out successfully. It was left to Henry Wainwright to make the final journey.

The Wainwrights.

About four o'clock that afternoon Wainwright asked a youth of the name of Stokes, who had at one time been in his employment, and was now a fellow-manager with him at Mr. Martin's, in the New Road, if he would help him to carry a parcel. Stokes assented, and together he and Wainwright went to 215 Whitechapel Road. There Wainwright produced two large and heavy parcels done up in American cloth. He carrying one and Stokes the other, they walked as far as Whitechapel church, where Wainwright told Stokes to mind the parcels while he went to a cab-rank a little way off to fetch a four-wheeler. Stokes was by this time suspicious of the two parcels. They smelt offensively, and he had an idea that Wainwright might be trying to remove surreptitiously a quantity of human hair, used by brushmakers, which had been already sold to Mr. Martin as part of the stock of the business. Later Stokes declared that a supernatural voice had called to him distinctly three times, saying, "Open that parcel." Whatever his reason, Stokes did open the parcel, and saw, to his horror, a human hand. By this time Wainwright had returned with the cab. Stokes said nothing. Wainwright put the parcels in the cab and drove off. The voice then spoke again to Stokes, saying with some sense, "Follow that cab!" This he did, as hard as he could go. Once the cab stopped, and Stokes concealed himself in a doorway. A lady of Wainwright's acquaintance had just come out of a public-house at the corner of Greenfield Street. She was Miss Alice Day, a ballet dancer at the Pavilion Theatre. She had known Wainwright about five years, but the acquaintanceship was, she said, " an ordinary one," free of any improper intimacy. Wainwright got out of the cab to meet her, and asked her if she would like a drive with him over London Bridge. He was now smoking a large cigar. She accepted his invitation on condition that he promised to get her back in time for her work in the theatre. They started off in the cab, with the two parcels on the front seat. Wainwright gave her a paper to read, and said, " Don't speak to me, I'm thinking." The cab passed over London Bridge, Stokes still in pursuit, and endeavouring vainly to interest one or two sceptical policemen in his breathless chase. At last the cab reached the Hen and Chickens, in the High Street, Borough. Wainwright got out and went into the build-

Introduction.

ing with one of the parcels. In the meantime Stokes had succeeded in attracting the attention of a policeman, who came up
to the cab, and was waiting there when Wainwright returned.
Wainwright had already taken the other parcel out of the cab
when the constable interposed, and the following dialogue took
place : —

P.C.—Do you live here?

W.—No.

P.C.—Have you got possession of this place?

W.—I have, and you haven't.

P.C.—Well, go inside.

W.—No, perhaps you had better go in.

P.C.—I want to see what's in that parcel you have just
taken in.

W.—Ask no questions and there's £50 for each of you.

By this time another constable had come up. The officers
said that they did not want Wainwright's money, and took him
along with them into the Hen and Chickens. There they opened
one of the parcels and found the remains of a human body.
Wainwright said desperately, " I'll give you £100, I'll give
you £200, and produce the money in twenty minutes if you'll
let me go." But it was all of no avail. The game was up.
Wainwright and Miss Alice Day were taken to the Stone's End
Police Station, and the remains to the St. Saviour's mortuary.

Wainwright had failed as a criminal. On this fatal day,
September 11th, he had made two simple blunders which had
ruined a plan that seemed on the verge of complete success. He
should not have waited to light his large cigar till he got into
the cab; he should have lit it before he began to handle the
offensive parcels with Stokes; he might even have offered one
to his companion. He should not have gone to fetch the cab
and left Stokes with the parcels; he should have looked after
the parcels while he sent Stokes to fetch the cab. These were
strange oversights in one who had come so near to hiding his
guilt perhaps for ever. The anniversary had been as surely
fatal to Henry Wainwright as a year before to Harriet Lane.

The fuller details of the evidence collected against Henry Wainwright and his brother Thomas will be found in the report of the
trial along with the medical evidence, by means of which the

The Wainwrights.

remains found in Henry Wainwright's possession were identified as those of Harriet Lane. It only remains to trace the course of events from the arrest of the chief culprit to his execution.

On 'September 13th. Henry Wainwright, aged thirty-six, described as " manager of a school " at Chingford, Essex, and Alice Day, aged twenty, dressmaker, were charged at Southwark Police Court " with having in their possession the mutilated body of a woman at present unknown, and supposed to have been murdered." At the time of his arrest Wainwright's wife and family had left Tredegar Square, and were living at School House Lane, Chingford. The evidence of Stokes and the constables was taken. Wainwright asked no questions. Alice Day clutched hold of him and said, " For God's sake tell them what I know of the matter—I know nothing." Wainwright answered, " I met her Saturday. She knows nothing." Both prisoners were remanded. The inquest on the body opened before the Southwark coroner on September 15th.

At the next hearing at the Police Court, on September 21st, Wainwright was charged with the wilful murder of Harriet Lane. Mr. (now Sir Harry) Poland appeared to prosecute for the Treasury, and Mr. Besley for the defence. Early in the proceedings Alice Day was discharged. The case had by this time aroused great public interest. Among those present in Court as spectators was Mr. Hawkins, Q.C., afterwards the well-known judge. One fact damaging to his client's case was elicited by Mr. Besley in the course of an over-eager cross-examination. The father of Harriet Lane had been called to speak to the identity of the remains. He said that they were those of his daughter, but could give no very specific reason for saying so. The body was so far decomposed as to make any recognition of the features out of the question. Mr. Besley, anxious to emphasise the vagueness of Mr. Lane's evidence, pressed him as to the impossibility of his having any more definite reasons for his statement. Suddenly the witness, under the stress of cross-examination, recollected that Harriet had been scalded on the leg as a child, and that the scar of the burn had remained. Mr. Poland was quick to avail himself of this unexpected piece

Introduction.

of information. He had the body re-examined, and below the right knee a distinct scar, about the size of a two shilling piece, was found.

At the resumed inquest on October 1st an important witness, Miss Wilmore, the friend of Harriet Lane, was called for the first time. She was asked as to the circumstances under which Harriet Lane had left her lodgings in Sidney Square on the afternoon of Friday, September 11th, 1874. Miss Wilmore said that Harriet told her not to mind if she did not see her on the following Sunday, as she might go out with Percy, that is, Wainwright, otherwise Mr. Percy King. When she left she said she was going to 215 Whitechapel Road, and that she was going to live there. "She had told me," said Miss Wilmore, "she was going to have——" At this point Mr. Besley objected, and the witness was not allowed to say any more. At the trial the whole of the evidence of Miss Wilmore as to these statements made to her by Harriet Lane before she left her lodgings was excluded, following a decision of Chief-Justice Bovill in the Pook case, tried at the Central Criminal Court in 1871. In this case a charge of murder against a man called Pook, a statement made by the murdered woman as to where she was going on the evening of her death was disallowed, and in Wainwright's case Chief-Justice Cockburn gave a similar decision. The statements made to Miss Wilmore by Harriet Lane were, said the judge, "no part of the act of leaving, only an incidental remark. It was only a statement of intention, which might or might not have been carried out."*

On October 1st Thomas Wainwright was arrested and charged as an accessory after the fact.

The last two hearings of the case at the Police Court took place on October 12th and 13th, when both prisoners were committed for trial to the Central Criminal Court.

On October 14th the coroner's jury returned a verdict to the effect that the mutilated remains were those of Harriet Lane, otherwise King, and that she was wilfully murdered by Henry Wainwright.

---

* Cox's "Criminal Law Cases," XIII., p. 171.

The Wainwrights.

In the *Times* report of the last two days' proceedings at the Police Court, the name of Mr. W. S. Gilbert is given as being instructed with Mr. Besley for the defence of the prisoner Henry Wainwright. This Mr. W. S. Gilbert was no other than the famous humorist and dramatist, afterwards Sir W. S. Gilbert, the collaborator with Arthur Sullivan in the Savoy operas. Though a barrister, Gilbert had at this time given up practice and devoted himself to writing. To his annoyance, he found himself summoned on a jury. Unfortunately for him, only practising barristers are exempted from jury service. As he was hard at work on a play, it was extremely inconvenient for him to obey the summons. If, however, he could make a fugitive reappearance as a practising barrister, he would be able to claim exemption. In order to do this he persuaded a friend to give him a nominal brief for two days in the Wainwright case, and thus it is that his name appears as counsel for the defence in the reports of these two days' proceedings at the Police Court.

Gilbert told the present writer a peculiar story with regard to his connection with the case. Henry Wainwright, in his later years, had developed a strong and remarkable likeness to Tom Robertson, the dramatist, the author of "Caste" and other well-known comedies of that day. Robertson died in 1871. Gilbert attended the funeral, and noticed among those standing near the grave a man who bore a strange resemblance to the deceased dramatist. Some short time after Gilbert got into a carriage on the Underground Railway, and saw sitting in the corner of the carriage this same man, whose likeness to Robertson had struck him so forcibly at the grave side. The resemblance was so startling that Gilbert forgot for the moment that his friend was dead, and was almost on the point of speaking to the stranger. When he attended at Southwark Police Court and Henry Wainwright came into the dock, Gilbert recognised at once in his occasional client the man who had twice surprised him by his curious likeness to Tom Robertson.

At the October Sessions of the Central Criminal Court the grand jury returned true bills against Henry and Thomas Wainwright, but, on the application of the defence, the trial was postponed until the November sittings.

Introduction.

It commenced at the Old Bailey on November 22nd. The presiding judge was the Lord Chief Justice of England, Sir Alexander Cockburn. The career of Cockburn at the bar had been brilliant, and his success in Parliament conspicuous. A gifted and accomplished man, remarkable for his eloquence of speech and quickness of apprehension, vanity played no small part in his character. As a judge he delighted to try cases that had attracted the public attention, and in his conduct of them did nothing to minimise their importance or the prominence of his own part in the proceedings. The result was that he showed a strong tendency, very conspicuous in the Tichborne trial, and in lesser degree in that of Wainwright, to prolong unnecessarily the length of a case and exaggerate unduly its importance. In the opening of his summing up in Wainwright's trial he speaks of " the magnitude and importance of this great trial." This is the language of exaggeration. The Wainwright trial was sensational in character and remarkable in many of its features, but it was not a great case, nor one of magnitude. The facts against Henry Wainwright were on the whole fatally clear, the proof of his guilt overwhelming. And yet the case took nine days to try. The Attorney-General devoted a whole day, from ten to three o'clock, to his closing speech, and the Chief Justice another day, from ten to four, to his summing up. These two efforts might well have been for all practical purposes compressed into one day. But forty years ago the law was less expeditious, and public time and money were of little account in the eyes of judge and counsel, who were enjoying the long-drawn-out pleasures of a *cause célèbre*. One of the outstanding features of the Wainwright case was the very clever defence of Thomas Wainwright by his counsel, Mr. Moody, and there were those who felt that Cockburn, in his anxiety to shine himself, showed a rather unworthy want of appreciation of Mr. Moody's success. The Chief Justice's charge to the jury was no doubt an impressive performance. One listener has described how Henry Wainwright was visibly moved when Cockburn described in graphic language the murder of Harriet Lane as he conceived it to have taken place.

The Attorney-General, Sir John Holker, came down to the Old Bailey to prosecute Wainwright. In these days the prose-

The Wainwrights.

cution in such a case would have been left in all probability
to the counsel for the Treasury, but forty years ago it was
usual for one of the law officers to conduct the prosecution in
an important murder trial. "Sleepy Jack Holker," as he was
called, was an enormously successful advocate. He was at this
time reckoned to be making professionally about £22,000 a
year. He is described as "a tall, plain, lumbering Lancashire
man, who never seemed to labour a case nor to distinguish
himself by ingenuity or eloquence, but through whom the justice
of his cause appeared to shine as through a somewhat dull but
altogether honest medium." No man at the bar has ever com-
mended himself so thoroughly to the confidence and affections
of a British jury as did Holker by the plain and unvarnished
character of his advocacy. With the Attorney was Mr., now
Sir Harry, Poland, than whom, in his day, there was no fairer
and at the same time more deadly prosecutor of criminals. Had
the trial taken place at the present time, the conduct of the case
would no doubt have been left in his hands.

Mr. Besley, who defended Henry Wainwright, was a well-
known member of the criminal bar, but he was not an advocate
of remarkable ability, nor did he ever attain to any great place
in his profession. Two of his colleagues in the case were to
make their mark, Mr. (afterwards Sir) Douglas Straight, then a
rising member of the junior bar, and Mr. C. F. Gill, the well-
known K.C. of to-day. Mr. Moody, whose defence of Thomas
Wainwright was an outstanding feature of the trial, had been
for many years the *Times* reporter at the Central Criminal
Court, the Middlesex Sessions. He was a man of considerable
ability, but as an advocate lacked that "Court manner" which
is such an important element in success at the bar.

The trial concluded on the 1st of December. Henry Wainwright was found guilty of wilful murder and sentenced to death,
Thomas to seven years penal servitude as an accessory after the
fact. The Frieake episode, which the Chief Justice described
as mysterious and incapable of definite solution, was not considered to afford evidence strong enough to constitute Thomas
Wainwright an accessory before the fact, and so render him
liable to the extreme penalty of the law.

Henry Wainwright, when called upon before sentence, swore,

Introduction.

standing on the brink of eternity and in the presence of God, that he was not the murderer of the remains found in his possession, a statement which the Chief Justice stigmatised as a "rash assertion." In the *Times* of December 21st, the day of Wainwright's execution, the substance is given of a document, stated to have been drawn up by Henry Wainwright and sent to the Home Secretary. In this he says that he had grown weary of the importunities of Harriet Lane and her threats of exposure, and that he confided his trouble to his brother Thomas. The latter replied that he was confident that for a sum of £20 some one could be found to marry Harriet and take her away. Henry gave his brother the money on the understanding that Harriet was to be got rid of in this way. One day Thomas came to him at 84 Whitechapel Road and told him that he had got rid of Harriet. Asked how, he replied that he had shot her, and that her body was lying at 215 Whitechapel Road. "Good God, Tom!" exclaimed Henry, "what have you done?" He at once threatened to inform the police, but Thomas answered that if he did so he would swear that Henry had done it, and, as Harriet Lane was his paramour and her body on his premises, the case would look very black against him. This reasoning apparently convinced Henry of the wisdom of silence, and "in a moment of excitement" the brothers decided to bury the body, a task performed by the ever ready Thomas.

Thomas Wainwright was said at the time to have made a statement in a directly opposite sense, according to which Henry was the sole murderer of Harriet Lane.

It is impossible to say what were the actual circumstances of Harriet Lane's death. To the last, though he admitted the justice of his sentence, Henry Wainwright never confessed to having killed her himself. On the other hand, Major Arthur Griffiths, in his "Chronicles of Newgate," says that a conversation overheard in that prison between the two brothers satisfactorily exonerated Thomas from the guilt of the murder.

The accounts of the mental attitude of Henry Wainwright during his last hours on earth are conflicting. After his execution the governor of Newgate read a statement in which the condemned man expressed penitence and faith in God and the

The Wainwrights.

mercy of the blessed Saviour. Major Griffiths, however, in the book already quoted, states that Wainwright's demeanour was one of reckless effrontery to the end, and that he died impenitent. The night before his execution he was allowed as a special favour to smoke a cigar. This he did, walking up and down the prison yard with the governor, boasting of his extraordinary successes with women, and recounting his many adventures. "The only sign of feeling he showed," writes Major Griffiths, "was in asking to be allowed to choose the hymns on the Sunday the condemned sermon was preached in the prison chapel, and this was probably only that he might hear the singing of a lady with a magnificent voice who generally attended the prison services. During the singing of these hymns Wainwright fainted, but whether from real emotion or the desire to make a sensation was never exactly known."

On the Friday before his execution Wainwright saw his wife and his brother William, who had assisted him in his defence.

The accounts of Wainwright's demeanour on the scaffold are as conflicting in some respects as those of his mental attitude at the last. On one thing they all agree, the firmness with which he met his death. "The prisoner," wrote the *Times* reporter, "who had apparently been dressed with scrupulous care, bore himself at this awful crisis with conspicuous fortitude; and as he stepped upon the drop, his handsome features were lighted up with an expression of resignation, unmixed with anything approaching bravado." According to the account of another spectator, however, Wainwright was not in quite such a resigned frame of mind nor oblivious to his surroundings. By the invitation of the Lord Mayor and Sheriffs, though public executions had been abolished, about sixty persons had been invited to the yard of Newgate Prison to witness Wainwright's execution. A friend of the writer who was present describes the scene as "absolutely Hogarthian and horrible," the cold December morning, the waning moon, the rope dangling to and fro in the shed awaiting its victim, a gaslight that flared noisily, the well-dressed crowd of privileged visitors come to see the show, the Sheriffs' footmen, who had some of them obviously fortified their spirits for the occasion; the whole scene seemed to him ghastly and sickening in the last degree. When Wain-

Introduction.

wright came to the scaffold, said one reporter who was present, he looked round on the assembled spectators with a glance of infinite scorn, and then, with a contemptuous movement of his head, muttered, "Come to see a man die, have you, you curs!" "Villain though he was," added the narrator, "he did die like a man, and I have felt sick and mean and ashamed of myself ever since."*

Wainwright was not the first nor the last man to commit murder in order to preserve a respectable character. For that and no other reason, John Tawell, the Quaker, murdered, in 1845, his mistress, Sarah Hart. His sole motive for the crime was, he said, to prevent his wife, with whom he had been for four years living as a highly respected and respectable gentleman, from discovering his infidelity. Tawell had as a young man been transported from England for forgery. In Australia he soon obtained a good conduct ticket-of-leave, and set up business in Sydney as a chemist. There always forward in good works, he soon came to be looked on as a "very saintly personage." He made a comfortable fortune and returned to England. After his first wife's death he had formed an illicit connection with Sarah Hart, a servant in his house, by whom he had two children. On his marrying again, his mistress left his house and went to live at Slough, Tawell's second wife being kept in complete ignorance of her existence. At Berkhampstead, where Tawell lived, he acquired a considerable reputation for piety, generosity, and benevolence, and, though after his conviction for forgery he had been expelled from the Quakers, and they had refused on his return to England to receive him again into their society, he always wore their characteristic dress. At the time of Sarah Hart's death Tawell's fortune had considerably diminished, so that, apart from any fears he may have had of his intrigue becoming known to his wife, the expense of keeping Sarah Hart and her children had begun to be burdensome. After attempting, some months earlier, to poison her with morphia, he killed her by giving her prussic acid in a glass of stout.

---

* "The Spice of Life," by Thornmanby, p. 122.

The Wainwrights.

In a manner similar to that of Wainwright, by shooting her and then cutting her throat, John Beale, a manservant, in the year 1857, murdered in Leigh Woods, Clifton, a woman whom he had seduced and promised to marry, though he was in fact a married man. And two years after Wainwright's trial, a seemingly pious, chapel-going young Welshman, named Cadwallader Jones, murdered at Dolgelly, under circumstances of great ferocity, a woman of light character with whom he had carried on a clandestine intrigue. She had become with child by him, and threatened to reveal her condition to his wife. At the end of a violent scene between them Cadwallader Jones beat her to death with a heavy stone, cut up her remains, and threw the pieces into the river. A week later a young man fishing in the river brought up a human hand. This discovery led to the finding of the rest of the remains, and Cadwallader Jones, who from the first confessed his guilt, was tried and executed.

Of these murderers to save appearances Wainwright was undoubtedly the most successful. For a whole year his crime was concealed, and everything pointed to the efficacy of the new hiding-place which he had chosen for the remains of his victim. There is something inexplicable in his want of judgment at the last in the handling of the parcels. Whether it arose from over-confidence or want of nerve, his mistake in leaving Stokes with the parcels appears to be a neglect of the most obvious precaution under the circumstances. In the stress of an actual murder such carelessness, even in the matter of an essential detail, is intelligible. But with no excuse for hurry or trepidation, with everything in favour of the carrying out of a plain and simple scheme, it is difficult to understand Wainwright's lapse. It looks like over-confidence, for he seems to have been calm enough that afternoon. He betrays no sign of uneasiness to Stokes; he meets Miss Day and invites her to drive with him; he sits in the cab smoking and thinking. Perhaps he underrated the intelligence of Stokes, which does not appear to have been very great. This failure of Wainwright's at the last moment remains one of the mysteries of the case.

The dual nature of the man is remarkable. Externally, to the world, Wainwright was a kind, genial, generous sort of fellow, vain, caring much for the regard of his fellow-men, no

Introduction.

doubt amiable and pleasant at his home. He seems to have had a sense of the dramatic in life. Who knows if the peculiar situation of a Eugene Aram had some strange attraction for him? But under his pleasing exterior Wainwright concealed dangerous qualities. He was strongly sensual in his appetites. He was fond of good food; he had the physical well-being of a certain type of *l'homme à femmes*. He seems to have looked on women as his natural prey, and with such a temperament as this cruelty and a want of sensibility are often found associated. But he had kept the secret of this baser side of his character well hidden from the world, and great was the surprise of Henry Wainwright's many friends when he stood suddenly revealed to the world as a deliberate and heartless murderer. It may be that Wainwright killed Harriet Lane as much because her obstinate attachment to him promised to be a hindrance to his pleasures as from the desire to preserve his reputation before the world. The double motive expresses the man's character, his desire to stand well in the eyes of his fellow-men, and, unknown to them, to indulge to the full in the gratification of his passions.

A shock, somewhat similar to that occasioned to his friends by Wainwright's sudden appearance as a murderer, was felt by the friends of his namesake, Thomas Griffiths Wainewright, when he stood revealed to them as a forger and secret poisoner. Though Thomas Griffiths, artist and man of letters, the friend of Hazlitt and Charles Lamb, would deeply resent comparison with Henry Wainwright, brushmaker in the Whitechapel Road, being in the same category of crime he cannot avoid it. In various circles in life both these criminals imposed successfully on their fellow-men by their attractive and showy qualities, and were looked on as harmless, good fellows in whose society it was pleasant to find one's self. "Kind, light-hearted Waine-wright!" was Charles Lamb's regretful comment on the disappearance from society of his criminal friend. No doubt similar expressions of regret were heard in the Whitechapel Road during the September of 1875. Thomas Griffiths wrote art criticism and painted pictures; Henry Wainwright lectured on books and recited poetry. Literature appealed to them.

The Wainwrights.

Thomas Griffiths " wept tears of gratitude and happiness " over Wordsworth; Henry Wainwright was an admiring expounder of the art of Sydney Smith and the poetry of Tom Moore. But the influence of such elevating pursuits had in neither case any effect on character; it did not save Thomas Griffiths from being one of the most wicked and heartless poisoners that ever lived, nor Henry Wainwright from the guilt of a cruel murder. Both men were sensualists, both spendthrift and extravagant. There comparison ends. " Janus Weathercock " was no doubt a very superior person in many respects to the brushmaker in the Whitechapel Road; he was at the same time unquestionably the greater villain of the two.

Leading Dates in the cases of Henry and Thomas Wainwright.

1862.		Henry Wainwright is married.
1871.		He first meets Harriet Lane.
1872.		
February	10	Henry Wainwright and Harriet Lane advertise a marriage as Mr. and Mrs. Percy King.
August	22	Harriet Lane gives birth to a child.
1873.		
December	3	A second child is born.
1874.		
March		Wainwright compounds with his creditors.
May		Harriet Lane moves to lodgings in Sidney Square.
September		Wainwright executes a mortgage on his premises in the Whitechapel Road.
	10	Wainwright purchases chloride of lime.
	11	Harriet Lane leaves her lodgings to go to meet Wainwright, and is never seen again alive.
October	17	"Edward Frieake" telegraphs from Dover that he has gone on the continent with Harriet Lane.
November		Thomas Wainwright starts an ironmongery business at the Hen and Chickens in the Borough.
	27	Wainwright's premises at No. 84 Whitechapel Road are destroyed by fire. His claim against the Insurance Company is disputed.
1875.		
June	30	Wainwright is declared bankrupt.
July		The mortgagee takes possession of the premises at 215 Whitechapel Road.
September	10	Henry and Thomas Wainwright buy some American cloth, a spade and chopper.
	11	Henry Wainwright is arrested in taking the remains of Harriet Lane from the Whitechapel Road to the Hen and Chickens.

LEADING DATES.

13   Wainwright and Alice Day charged at Southwark Police Court with having in their possession the mutilated body of a woman unknown, supposed to have been murdered.

15   Inquest opened at the Vestry, St. Saviour's, Southwark.

21   Wainwright charged with wilful murder of Harriet Lane, Alice Day discharged.

October   1   Thomas Wainwright arrested.

3   He is charged at Southwark Police Court, as accessory after the fact.

13   Henry and Thomas Wainwright committed for trial.

14   Coroner's jury return verdict of wilful murder against Henry Wainwright.

26   Grand jury at Central Criminal Court find true bills against Henry and Thomas Wainwright.

27   Trial postponed to November sessions.

November 22   Trial commences.

December 1   Henry Wainwright sentenced to death, Thomas Wainwright to seven years penal servitude.

December 21   Henry Wainwright executed at Newgate.

THE TRIAL.

CENTRAL CRIMINAL COURT.

MONDAY, 22ND NOVEMBER, 1875.

The Court met at Ten o'clock.

Judge—

HE LORD CHIEF-JUSTICE OF ENGLAND (*Sir James Alexander Cockburn, Bart.*).

Counsel for the Crown—

THE ATTORNEY-GENERAL (*Sir John Holker, Q C.*).
Mr. H. B. POLAND.
Mr. BEASLEY.
Instructed by Mr. POLLARD on behalf of the Treasury.

Counsel for Henry Wainwright—

Mr. EDWARD BESLEY.
Mr. DOUGLAS STRAIGHT.
Mr. TICKELL.
Mr. C. F. GILL.
Instructed by Mr. PELHAM.

Counsel for Thomas George Wainwright—

Mr. MOODY.

B

The Wainwrights.

HENRY WAINWRIGHT (thirty-seven), brush manufacturer, and
THOMAS GEORGE WAINWRIGHT (thirty), ironmonger,
remanded from last session, were indicted for the wilful
murder of Harriet Louisa Lane. In a second count Henry
Wainwright was alleged to have committed the murder,
and Thomas George Wainwright was charged as an accessory after the fact. A third count stated the deceased to
be a woman unknown.

The Jury having been duly empanelled and sworn,
The ATTORNEY-GENERAL, in opening the case for the prosecution, referred to the relationship between the two prisoners, and
then touched upon Henry Wainwright's introduction to and
acquaintance with Harriet Lane, which ripened into a close
intimacy, the woman ultimately becoming the mistress of the
prisoner under the name of Mrs. King. In August, 1872,
Mrs. King had a child by Henry Wainwright, and in October,
1873, he took lodgings for her at 70 St. Peter Street, where
she lived until April, 1874, another child being born there.
Whilst she was in St. Peter Street, the prisoner used to visit
her, and letters passed between them, some of which showed that
Henry Wainwright, or "Mr. King," and Mrs. King were not
on very good terms. In one letter he strongly requested her
not to write to him again. However, in April, 1874, Mrs. King
left the house, 70 St. Peter Street, and she was taken by him,
with her two children and a nurse, to Mrs. Foster's, 3 Sidney
Square, he telling Mrs. Foster that he wanted apartments for
his wife and his children and nurse. During the time Mrs.
King was residing at Mrs. Foster's, Miss Wilmore, who had
known Mrs. King at Waltham, used to go and see her. Whilst
this woman was paying her visits—after April, 1874—Henry
Wainwright must have got into very embarrassed circumstances,
for in June he was declared a bankrupt. He had a wife and
four children at this time living at Tredegar Square; and he (the
Attorney-General) thought he should be able to show that he
had an entanglement with another woman, if not other women.
From the evidence they should also gather that the prisoner had
lost some of his affection for Mrs. King; for during the time
she was living at Mrs. Foster's she was very seldom visited by
him, and although he sent people to her, he gave her very little
money. When he did call upon her. angry words were heard
proceeding from the apartment in which the prisoner and Mrs.
King were. Wainwright was no doubt worried by Mrs. King
very considerably, by her making demands for money, and
perhaps she accompanied these demands by threats, declaring

2

Mr. H. B. Poland.

Opening Address to Jury.

that she would go to Mrs. Wainwright if he did not meet her requests. It would be proved that the prisoner became so embarrassed that he sent some one to pawn a revolver. This showed that the prisoner was in embarrassed circumstances, and also that he had a revolver.

Now, during the time Mrs. King was living at Mrs. Foster's, there came to see her a man known by the name of Edward Frieake. In reference to this individual, the following letter was received by Mrs. King from Wainwright:—"Dear Pet,— E. F. is coming down at seven to-night, and will give you a call with a message from me.—P. K." He (the Attorney-General) read this for the purpose of showing that he did not come of his own accord to see Mrs. King, but was sent there. Besides this man Frieake, Henry Wainwright had a friend also named Edward Frieake, but to him, as the evidence would show, Mrs. King was unknown.

The Attorney-General then proceeded to allude to the occasion on which Mrs. King came home intoxicated with the prisoner Henry and the man who had been introduced to her as " Teddy Frieake." Up to this time Mrs. King's conduct had been exceedingly good, and she was very much liked by those with whom she was brought in contact. In consequence of this piece of bad conduct, however, Mrs. Foster gave Mrs. King notice to leave, which would expire on Wednesday, 9th September, 1874. He would here pause to draw attention to the position of affairs. At this time Henry Wainwright and Mrs. King did not seem to be on very good terms. It was clear that Henry Wainwright was very considerably embarrassed, that he was very much harassed by Mrs. King by demands for money, which he had not the means of satisfying. It was clear, after this notice to quit had been given, he would have to provide apartments for Mrs. King somewhere else. He would therefore have been put to considerable expense and trouble. It was probable—he would say no more—that Wainwright was entangled at this time to some extent with other women; so that altogether he had an adequate motive, if anything could be considered an adequate motive, to desire to get rid of Mrs. King. On behalf of the prosecution he (the Attorney-General) charged that the prisoner had at this time formed a plan to enable him to get rid of the woman, that he had laid the scheme, and that he intended to get rid of her, was making his preparations for it, and that when she had disappeared, he intended to attribute her disappearance to Edward Frieake, and induce Mrs. King's parents and friends to believe that she had gone away with some one of that name.

The Wainwrights.

The Attorney-General. To continue the narrative, Mrs. King asked Mrs. Foster to be allowed to remain in her lodgings two days over her time, and permission was given to her, so that the day for leaving would be Friday, the 11th. As she had to leave Sidney Square, it was of course necessary that she should make some fresh arrangements, and she was met by Miss Wilmore and Henry Wainwright for the purpose of discussing the question. It was then decided that Miss Wilmore should take some apartments of her own and take charge of the children, whilst Mrs. King went to some place provided for her by Henry Wainwright. At that time Mrs. King received a sum of money from Henry for the purpose of paying her debts and getting her things out of pawn. She got these things on 11th September. But he must draw attention to what took place the previous day. On 10th September Henry Wainwright bought half a cwt. of chloride of lime, which was sent to No. 84 Whitechapel Road, and subsequently found its way to No. 215. That might strike them at this stage as an unimportant fact, but their attention would be called to it more than once before they had done. Mrs. King, having redeemed her things from pawn, made arrangements to leave the house where she was then living. It was arranged that Miss Wilmore was to leave on the same day, but later, for the new lodgings at Grove Street, Stratford. About four o'clock on 11th September Mrs. King left, taking only a night-dress with her. She bade good-bye, kissed her children, and bade them farewell—a long farewell, for after that the poor woman was never seen. On the same afternoon three work-men were making some repairs on the premises next door to 215 Whitechapel Road, between five and seven o'clock. This warehouse was immediately adjoining those of Wainwright. Well, these workmen heard three pistol shots fired in rapid succession, and after that all was still. At first they thought the shots had been fired by a person named Pinnell, who, they knew, had such a weapon, which he occasionally fired. They went down, but not seeing any one, they returned to their work. He should have other evidence to bring before the jury, from which they might possibly conclude that these shots killed the woman, that her body was stripped and laid in a grave prepared for the purpose on the ground floor of the workshop of Henry Wainwright. The body having been laid there, was covered with a layer of chloride of lime. Any one who was not ignorant would have known that chloride of lime would keep a body, but an ignorant person might have supposed either that it would prevent the exhalations consequent upon decomposition, or would destroy identity altogether.

4

Opening Address to Jury.

Now he had already told them that when Mrs. King went away on the 11th September she was not prepared for any lengthened stay, having only a nightdress in a parcel. Miss Wilmore certainly expected she would return. After a few days, not hearing anything further about the missing woman, Miss Wilmore and Mrs. Taylor, sister of Harriet Lane, went to see Wainwright. In answer to the inquiries of Mrs. Taylor about her sister, he said he did not know, but he had given her £15 before she left, and as she had no outfit, he gave her £10 more to buy clothes with. He understood that she had gone to Brighton with a person named Frieake, an auctioneer, who had lately come into a lot of money, and no doubt when it was spent they would come back. He added, however, that if she did come back they could not expect him to receive her again, but he promised to do something for the education of the children. A few days afterwards she received a letter purporting to have come from Frieake, to the effect that he was very much surprised at not having received a reply to his last letter, in which he had given all particulars as to the arrangements he had made with Mrs. King. The writer said she had solemnly promised never to see or speak to King or any of her own friends, and on these conditions, and on condition that she kept her promises, he would marry her in a few weeks. He wished them distinctly to understand that she was never to see her friends; and he added in a postscript, " We are just off to Dover." Miss Wilmore saw Mrs. Taylor, had an interview with Henry Wainwright, and in the course of the conversation told him of the letter. He said he had received a similar one. He read portions of it, and it agreed with that received by Mrs. Taylor. He paid Miss Wilmore a sum of money to keep the children.

The father of Harriet Lane was very anxious to hear about his daughter, and, through Mr. Eeles, he set inquiries about her on foot. This person saw Henry Wainwright, and the prisoner told him that Mrs. King had gone off with Teddy Frieake, who had come into a lot of money. Mr. Eeles at once went to Mr. Frieake, and in consequence of what the latter said, Eeles and he went to Wainwright, and the prisoner said, " Oh, it is not you; it is another Frieake." Mr. Frieake, however, remembered having got a letter the previous September from Mrs. King. He searched, found it, and he and Eeles again went down to see Wainwright. Old Mr. Lane was there at the time. Erieake showed the prisoner the letter. He read it, put it down, and reiterated the statement that it was another Frieake, not the person then present. They then went away. From time to time the prisoner said Mrs. King had been seen, and no doubt she would turn up in course of time.

5

The Wainwrights.

The Attorney-General then proceeded, by the aid of models
in Court, to describe to the jury the premises at 84 .and 215
Whitechapel Road. Rogers, Henry Wainwright's manager,
removed from 84 to 215 in October, 1874, and remained till
April, 1875, and at the time they went in they were annoyed
by a smell which he suggested did not come from ashes, as they
thought, but from the body of the murdered woman, which was
covered with a thin layer of earth and chloride of lime. Towards
the end of January the inquiries for Mrs. King ceased, and her
boxes were given up to old Mr. Lane on 21st January. But
though the inquiries ceased, the danger of the discovery of the
body increased.

About the beginning of 1875 the prisoner Thomas obtained
a sum of money from Mr. Lewis by a bill of exchange, with
which he re-established himself at the sign of the Hen and
Chickens in the Borough. He had been making arrangements
for it, and got it in February. In June, Mr. Lewis took possession of the premises in lieu of his money, also the stock that
Thomas had put into the shop. It was necessary for Lewis
to keep possession of the premises, and in order to do so he put
a new lock on the door, and kept the key himself.

After reading a letter sent by Henry Wainwright to Miss
Wilmore, stating that he " could do nothing until November,"
the Attorney-General went on to state that Mr. Behrend, Henry
Wainwright's mortgagee, took possession of the premises, 215
Whitechapel Road, and advertised them for sale. A woman
named Mrs. Izzard was put in occupation of the house, and it
thus became necessary for the prisoner Henry Wainwright to
dispose of the body, he still having access to the premises.
On 10th September, 1875, Henry Wainwright purchased a piece
of American cloth, and Thomas purchased a chopper and a
shovel. On the morning of 11th September both the prisoners
were seen talking together outside Mr. Martin's shop (where
Henry was a manager), and the young man spoke to them.
Thomas then seemed ill, and he had shaved off his moustache.
About four o'clock that afternoon Stokes and Henry Wainwright
left Mr. Martin's shop to go to 215 Whitechapel Road.

The Attorney-General then described the removal of the
packages containing the parts of the deceased's body in a cab
from Whitechapel Road to the Hen and Chickens.   Stokes,
having seen the hand of a woman, followed the cab over London
Bridge, and attracted the attention of a policeman. When the
police constables were about to open the parcels, the prisoner
Henry, who was accompanied by a young woman named Alice
Day, said, " For God's sake don't touch it, and I will give you

6

Opening Address to Jury.

£200, and produce the money in twenty minutes." On being removed with Alice Day to the police station, a key was found in the possession of the prisoner Henry, which fitted the padlock which was attached to the door of the Hen and Chickens, and which Thomas had obtained in June from Mr. Lewis' office. In a cellar at the Hen and Chickens a grave was already prepared for the reception of the remains, just such a place as a person would wish to conceal a murdered body in. The police went to the premises, 215 Whitechapel Road. They found a chopper, a spade, and a knife, and also that the flooring had been cut through, and a shallow grave about 3 feet in depth had been made; something had evidently recently been taken out of the grave, which, besides articles belonging to the deceased, contained a considerable quantity of chloride of lime. In the fire-grate certain discoveries were made which showed that clothes had been consumed there.

Harriet Lane seemed to have been of attractive appearance. She had a quantity of light golden hair, which she made into the form of a pad, fastened by a number of hairpins. In the pad the police found a conical bullet which fitted the pistol belonged to Henry Wainwright. The woman's head had been penetrated by two shots, one behind the ear and the other immediately in front. The surgeons also found that either before or immediately after death, when the circulation was still, the windpipe had been severed almost to the vertebræ. Either this wound itself or any one of the shots fired would have caused death.

The prosecution asserted that from the examination of the body there was sufficient evidence that the body was that of Harriet Lane, for the following reasons:—The body had been hacked by an unskilful hand in about ten pieces. The body had been put together, and found to be that of a woman 5 feet high. Harriet Lane was 5 feet high. The hands were very small; so were those of Harriet Lane; and the same thing might be said with regard to the feet. The hair, a good deal of which was left, was of the same colour as that of Harriet Lane—a light auburn or golden. The hair was attached to a pad, such as Harriet Lane wore, and to which it was attached by innumerable hairpins. The surgeons also found a decayed tooth which had been visible when the deceased spoke or smiled. Harriet Lane had such a tooth. The surgeons were of opinion that the deceased was of the age of Harriet Lane. They found a scar of a remarkable character on the right leg just below the knee. It was about the size of a two-shilling piece. Harriet Lane had such a scar. Some years before a red-hot poker from

The Wainwrights.

the fire had fallen on her leg, and produced a severe burn, which,
when it healed, left a scar about the size of a two-shilling piece.
Besides these personal appearances, rings were found in the
grave such as Harriet Lane had worn, and such as she had got
out of pawn prior to 11th September, 1874. There were also
buttons which had been worn by Harriet Lane. From all these
circumstances he should ask the jury to come to the conclusion
that this was Harriet Lane. Thus he had touched upon the
evidence which affected Henry Wainwright in the main. Some
of the details were very shocking and revolting, but he besought
the jury not to allow the character of such details to unsteady
their minds, and prevent their coming to a right, a dispassionate,
and calm conclusion.

The learned Attorney-General then briefly called attention to
the evidence that affected the prisoner Thomas, and explained
the two counts in the indictment—one charging the prisoner
with being accessory to the murder before the fact, and the
second with having been accessory after the fact. There was
no doubt Thomas did purchase the hammer and chopper, and
he confessed to doing it in the statement which he had made
to the police, and which had been taken down in writing. The
evidence of Mrs. Foster as to the identifying of the man who
had called with Henry Wainwright to see Mrs. King was not very
strong, nor could it be called conclusive, but he (the Attorney-
General) would strengthen it in this way. A bottle of champagne
was brought in on one occasion, and Frieake and Mrs. King
drank it. Mrs. Foster had no champagne glasses, and Thomas
Wainwright went to a neighbouring public-house to borrow
some. The landlord at the public-house would be called, and
he would say that on a particular date about the first week in
September (and he would give a good reason for remembering
the period) the two brothers were in his house for a considerable
time discussing some affair or other between themselves, that
one of them got a bottle of champagne; that they went out
together; and that shortly afterwards Thomas returned and got
another bottle of champagne, some glasses having been previously borrowed. Although the evidence of Mrs. Foster could
not be considered as conclusive as to identity, still that, taken
with the evidence of the publican, became strong.

The question then arose, why was the prisoner Thomas there?
That Mrs. King believed the man to be Frieake was perfectly
clear, and if the prisoner Henry had formed the plan which had
been alluded to, then it would be necessary to introduce a person
named Frieake on the scene. This was the reason, he submitted,
why Thomas had represented Edward Frieake. The Attorney-

8

No. 215 Whitechapel Road

(Where Henry Wainwright carried on business as a brushmaker).

Opening Address to Jury.

General quoted the letter that purported to have been written by E. Frieake, about the promise said to have been made by Harriet Lane, and said if there was any desire to get rid of the woman this was just such a letter as would have been written for the purpose. Then there were the telegrams and the key of the premises of Lewis, which must have been handed by Thomas to Henry. Then on 10th September both prisoners were found buying implements together which were necessary for the murder. The only remaining portion of the evidence was that he was seen with his brother in a public-house the previous evening. Some one must have been engaged for a long time, for the business transacted could not have been despatched at once. Some one was there, either alone or in company with some one else, and it would take some time to dig the grave, hack up the body in the way that was done, and bury it. Next morning Thomas was seen looking haggard and pale, with his moustache shaved off, and was spoken to on the subject by those who had noticed it. He said he had been at this place, and that on the previous day he had spent a long time in the Surrey Gardens. They were not going to bring any evidence, either to rebut or confirm the statement made before the magistrates. If any explanations for these facts were given, which were consistent with innocence, if any explanations which would satisfy any reasonable mind that they were consistent with innocence were given, well and good. But if no such explanations could be given, they would be entitled in the face of the proof of guilt to act upon them.

Evidence for the Prosecution.

JOHN BUTLER, examined by Mr. POLAND—I am deputy-surveyor of the Metropolitan Police Board. I know the premises 215 Whitechapel Road. They are on the right-hand side going from London. The model of the building produced is an accurate one. It embraces Mr. Pinnell's premises, and Mr. Wiseman's next, and extends back to the back of Mr. Pinnell's premises, and goes beyond at the back into Vine Court. I also produce the ground plan showing the exit by Vine Court. I also produce a plan of the neighbourhood in which these houses are situated. It includes the premises at No. 215, No. 84 on the other side of the road, and Sidney Square on the left. I produce a model of the cellar at the Hen and Chickens, which I made myself. The only entrance to the cellar is down these steps, and when you get into the cellar there is no window or light, or any access

The Wainwrights.

John Butler except down the steps. At the bottom of the steps there is an inner cellar of brickwork, and a hole in the brickwork 2 feet 6 to 3 feet, which I believe has been always there. I got through it. There was a quantity of loose earth. I also produce the ground plan and a plan from London Bridge to the back at the corner, showing the Hen and Chickens.

Cross-examined by Mr. BESLEY—There is no door at the top of the stairs leading to the cellar.

By the LORD CHIEF JUSTICE—What do you mean by "loose earth," which you say you found there?—When the props were put up to support the flooring above they excavated some of the loose earth to make the foundations for the props, and did not remove it afterwards.

A. P. Stokes ALFRED PHILIP STOKES, examined by Mr. POLAND—I live at 34 Baker's Row, Whitechapel, and I am a brushmaker. In September of the present year I was in the service of Mr. Martin as manager at 78 New Road, Whitechapel. The prisoner Henry Wainwright was also in Mr. Martin's employment as a manager. I had been in this service about five or six weeks before the particular Saturday, and Henry Wainwright had been in service about eleven weeks. I have known Henry Wainwright for seventeen or eighteen years. He carried on business formerly at 84 Whitechapel Road, the shop at which the articles were sold. He was a brushmaker. I did work for him, but away from the premises, and when I had finished I took it to 84 Whitechapel Road. I had worked for him between seventeen and eighteen years. I knew the premises No. 215 Whitechapel Road as a packing place. West, his chief clerk, who lived there first, left some time in July, 1874, and from that time no one lived there until Mr. Rogers went to occupy them in November of the same year. They were shut up at night, but were used for packing purposes. I believe the keys were always left in the counting-house at No. 84 until the fire. Henry Wainwright went out of business about a month before he went into Mr. Martin's service. He told me he was living at Schoolhouse Lane, Chingford, but I never went there. In September of this year, on Thursday or Friday, the 9th or 10th, I believe, but I cannot say which, I had some conversation with Henry. I told him I had bought a chain for the scales. He said, "Oh, yes! it is very useful," and then he said, "I have a chopper and a shovel to sell likewise which will be very useful." I said, "Yes, so they will, sir, as we require them for the place." I next saw him on the Saturday morning, but nothing happened till about half-past four, when, in Mr. Martin's presence, he said, "Will

10

Evidence for Prosecution.

you carry a parcel for me, Stokes?" I said, "Yes, sir, with **A. P. Stokes**
the greatest of pleasure." We then went together to 215 Whitechapel Road, in through Vine Court to the back premises.
Henry took a key out of his pocket and opened the door. We
both went in, and he told me to go upstairs and fetch down a
parcel. I went upstairs, and through by the skylight into the
dwelling-room, 80 or 90 feet from the point where we came in,
but did not find the parcel. I came downstairs and told him
I could not find it; he said, "Never mind, Stokes, I will find
them where I placed them a fortnight ago, under the straw."
I saw some straw up in a corner, and two parcels wrapped in
black American cloth, and tied up with rope. He said, "These
are the parcels I want you to carry, Stokes." I lifted them
up, and I says, "They are too heavy for me," and put them
down. He said, "Wait a bit, Stokes. Here is the shovel and
chopper I want you to sell for me." He had told me that he
wanted me to sell them to Mr. Martin, my employer. I saw
a shovel and chopper and a hammer lying near. I said, "All
right, sir," and I picked up the chopper, and said, "What's
this on it? It stinks." I saw some mess on it. He said, "It
is only cat's or dog's dirt." He took it in his hands, and wiped
it off, and then wiped it on a piece of newspaper, and laid it
on the floor.

When you made the observation you saw something on the
chopper—some mess?—Yes. He afterwards said, "Come
along, Stokes." I picked up both parcels and followed him.
I then said, "I can't carry them; they stink so bad, and the
weight of them is too heavy for me." He said, "I will take
one off you at the bottom of Vine Court." As I walked to the
door he said, "Wait a bit, Stokes. Let me see if old Mr.
Johnson is watching us."

Who is Johnson?—A decorator living somewhere in the Mile-
End Road.

By the Lord Chief Justice—Why should he be watching?
Did his premises overlook those of the prisoner?—Oh, no; but
I have often seen him watching.

Examination continued—Prisoner said to me, "All right,
Stokes, no one is looking. Come on." I noticed a hammer
in the place, but nothing else. I carried the two parcels out of
the premises from Vine Court into Whitechapel Road. He took
the lightest of the parcels from me, and we walked to Whitechapel Church, which would be about a quarter of a mile. As
we were going on I said, "I shall have to rest, sir. It's too
heavy for me. I cannot carry it." He replied, "For God's
sake don't drop it, or else you will break it." When we got

11

The Wainwrights.

A. P. Stokes to Whitechapel Church he said to me, " Stokes, mind these parcels while I go and fetch a cab." I said, " All right, sir," and he went for the cab.

Did he put the parcel down?—Yes, alongside of mine, opposite Blyth's, the wireworker, and he went towards a cab-stand.

Whilst he was away what did you do?—I looked into the parcel, the one I carried myself. I felt as I must do it.

By the LORD CHIEF JUSTICE—Never mind what you felt you must do. You were asked what you did?—I looked into the largest parcel. I opened the top of the parcel, and the first thing I saw was a human hand. Then proceeding further I saw a hand, which had been cut off at the wrist.

Examination continued—Then I had the presence of mind to cover the parcel up again quick. I then waited until Wainwright returned with the cab, which was in about five minutes. It was a four-wheeled cab. When he came with it he asked me to help him to put the parcels in, and I did so with a little hesitation. I put one in the bottom of the cab, and he put the other there also.

Did he say anything to you?—He said he would see me at seven o'clock in the evening. I answered, " All right, sir," and then he got into the cab, and drove off up Church Lane towards East India Docks.

Where were you to see him?—At my place. He did not say why.

Did you follow the cab?—Yes.

Did you notice whether he was smoking?—He was not smoking when he got into the cab, but was when he got out. The prisoner told the cabman to drive up Commercial Road, " round to the left," and the man did so—down Church Lane to the Commercial Road.

By the LORD CHIEF JUSTICE—You saw them to the corner, did you not?—Yes; the cab went so far as the chemist's shop in Commercial Road on the left, and I followed, running. At the chemist's shop, close to Greenfield Street, the cab stopped. Greenfield Street would be about 70 yards from Church Lane.

Examination continued—Did Wainwright get out?—Yes; he walked towards the West India Dock away from the city. He was there met by a young woman called Alice Day.

Do you know her?—Yes, I do. He talked with her for about one minute, and then came back with her to the cab.

Did you notice where she had been?—Yes; she was at the corner of the street, waiting.

Where were you at this time?—Hiding in a doorway opposite.

12

Evidence for Prosecution.

He said to the cabman, "Drive on as fast as you can over A. P. Stokes London Bridge to the Borough." The cab turned round and went in the direction of the City. I ran after the cab until I saw two constables by Leadenhall Street. I was very exhausted, and called their attention to the cab. But they laughed, and said, "Man, you must be mad." I called to them to stop the cab, but did not tell them why. I could scarcely speak at the time. The cab was then 30 yards at least ahead from me. I ran after it, and followed it by Leadenhall Street and Fenchurch Street over London Bridge. It stopped beside the factory, on the right-hand side of the Borough, which is part of the premises of the London Joint Stock Bank. From the place where it stopped, by standing a little on one side, one can see the Hen and Chickens. It stopped close to the pavement. There were two police constables close behind me. I saw Henry Wainwright put out his hand, which caused the cab to stop at the entrance; he got out, took the lightest parcel, and went towards the Hen and Chickens. The names of the constables are Turner and Cox, No. 48 and No. 290. I said, "For God's sake, run after that man with the high hat, with the parcels in his hand. There is something wrong." Turner went instantly, and on my telling Cox what I had seen he went to the cab. I told Turner not to touch him, but to follow him and see where he was going. Alice Day was in the cab, and Cox spoke to her, but I did not hear the words. I saw Turner follow Henry Wainwright to the Hen and Chickens on the other side. In a short time Wainwright returned. He went to the cab to get the other parcel. I did not notice what he did then. I went back to my employer, Mr. Martin, knowing that they were in good hands. I was so exhausted that I felt I should drop if I stayed any longer.

When Henry Wainwright had the conversation with me about the chopper and the shovel, he said, "Ask Mr. Martin to buy them in the presence of me, and I will say they are very useful. Will you call for them on Monday morning, Stokes?" I said, "How much shall I ask for them?" He replied, "I will leave that to you." I was to say they were my own, and sell them in my own name. I had known Alice Day for three or four years. She was engaged at the Pavilion Theatre as a ballet girl. The front entrance of the theatre is next door to 84 Whitechapel Road. I had seen her many times with Henry Wainwright before this Saturday, in public-houses and walking out in the street together. I had seen the two together in Commercial Road about a fortnight or three weeks previous to this Saturday. I had seen Thomas Wain-

13

The Wainwrights.

A. P. Stokes wright coming to the shop in Whitechapel Road when he was only a young man, and I knew him as the brother of Henry. He kept the Hen and Chickens, in the Borough, but I don't know where he lived in September, 1874 or 1875. I have been outside the door many times waiting for Mr. Wainwright. A few months before September, in July, I noticed a smell in No. 215 Whitechapel Road. It appeared to come from the rubbish in the corner close to the paint-room under the warehouse. The rubbish was dirt and cabbage leaves which had been lying there for months. I spoke about it to the clerk and the porter. The rubbish was not removed till after this was found out. I was not in Wainwright's service. I was employed by him. I made up the work and took it home.

Cross-examined by Mr. BESLEY—I have done work, I and my father, for Wainwright for seventeen or eighteen years, working out of the house. I knew he lived in Tredegar Square. He lived at Chingford nine or ten months—he went there from Tredegar Square. When I was in Henry Wainwright's employment I always did my work at home, but I used to go frequently to 84 and to 215 Whitechapel Road. For the last three months I went three times a day. After the fire took place, on the 27th November, 1874, I always went to No. 215. I went there at all hours. I am familiar with the warehouse premises, No. 215. When the place is open there is a glass front, an ordinary shop front. You would see from the street back to the end of the warehouse, if the warehouse door were open—on entering the shop you could see direct to the back of the warehouse. It was not fitted up like a shop, but was all shelved. It was fully 80 feet from the Whitechapel Road to the back of the house. In the daytime, owing to the circular skylights at the back of the warehouse, you could see all over it, except at the side where the stone flagging is, but you cannot see that because it went in a nook, and you cannot see into the paint-room. The stonework which was raised up was by the paint-room. There is a recess like a fireplace there. You cannot see where the stones were raised, from the street. From the glass skylight it would be exceptionally light at that part; there are three skylights, and they have gasaliers; the first had a two-branch burner, and the next the same, and one had an eight-branch burner, but only six of them admitted lights, so that you may call it a six-light burner. There is also one gas light in front of the shop as you go in. There is most light at the furthest end of the warehouse. I have not the least doubt I was there in September in 1874 about twice a day. The gas lights were lighted every evening when the

14

Evidence for Prosecution.

place was open, but sometimes it used to be closed at dusk— A. P. Stokes the ordinary time of closing was eight. There were usually two men at work on the premises, the clerk, Vostius, and the porter, Titienes, and sometimes Mr. Rogers, the traveller. I did not go as much to the back part of the warehouse after September as before. I ceased to work for Henry Wainwright in June, 1875, and a short time afterwards went to Mr. Martin's. I left Mr. Martin's about eight weeks before the particular Saturday. Henry Wainwright was manager at Mr. Martin's at the same time as I was. He looked over one side of the warehouse, and I the other. I was present when Mr. Martin took away the fixtures. I believe it was the latter end of July or the beginning of August.

Did you take notice of the disagreeable smell there?—No; because I had very often smelt a disagreeable smell before, and thought it came from the rubbish, which I knew was there.

When you were giving your evidence on the 13th September you mentioned the name of Mr. Johnson?—No, I don't think I did. Neither did I at my first examination say anything about Henry Wainwright speaking to me about the chopper and hammer. I believe I did mention about the prisoner saying to me as we were leaving the premises, " All right. No one is looking. Come on."

By the Lord Chief Justice—When did you first mention Mr. Johnson's name?—It was at the Treasury, I believe.

The Attorney-General (in answer to the Lord Chief Justice as to why Mr. Johnson's name should have been mentioned) said Mr. Johnson had been appointed one of the trustees in the bankruptcy.

By the Lord Chief Justice—You don't seem to have mentioned before that you were to wait until he looked to see whether Mr. Johnson was watching?—Perhaps not.

Perhaps not. Do you mean to say you said one thing one day and another thing just now?—No; I am telling the truth.

The Lord Chief Justice (after a pause, during which the depositions were scanned)—Looking at this shows the importance of good writing. It seems to me to be, " I wonder Johnson is not watching us, as he always is."

Mr. Besley—He says, " I wonder if any one is watching us —if Johnson is watching us, as he always is."

The Lord Chief Justice—These are two different statements. You have said one thing before the coroner, and another here.

Cross-examination continued—I am not sure that I have ever attributed the words, " All right; no one is looking, come on," to Wainwright before. It is true, however.

15

The Wainwrights.

A. P. Stokes Did you ever say before, " The weight is so heavy, and the stink so bad " ?—Yes, I did.

By the LORD CHIEF JUSTICE—Was the smell bad?—Yes; it was very bad. I thought it was hair till I got up to Whitechapel Road, because we had been talking about hair on the way to No. 215.

Cross-examination continued—When did you say the parcels were heavy and you could not carry them?—I don't know when or where, but I know that I have said it before, either at the inquest or before the magistrate.

You said to him, "I shall have to have a rest; it is too heavy; I can't carry it "?—Yes, I did, and have said it before.

Have you been to the Treasury since the committal for trial, or have they sent any one to you?—No. I have not had any writing put into my hand, and I have never seen the models produced until to-day.

Cross-examined by Mr. MOODY—I was seventeen or eighteen years in the service of Henry Wainwright and his father when the prisoner Thomas was quite a young chap and Henry was a young man. There is not as much as ten years' difference in age between the brothers.

Re-examined by the SOLICITOR-GENERAL—The prisoners' father died about thirteen years ago. After that William and Henry carried on the business as partners; after they ceased to be partners Henry and Mr. Sawyer carried it on. They dissolved partnership in July, 1874. After that Henry had the place to himself, and carried on the business in both places until the fire. There are gates or folding doors at the front of No. 215, with a sort of fanlight over the top. When you get in at the front there are no doors to go through; it is all open space right to the end. At the end of the warehouse, where the skylights are, there was formerly a paint shop or paint room partitioned off from the rest of the room. The flooring of the paint room was a little raised from the rest of the floor, one step; it was not used to keep paints in, but for storing painting brushes in. There was a door in the partition leading from the body of the warehouse into the paint room. On the right as you go in there is a door leading into Vine Court. A little way in front of that doorway the place was flagged. The partition was there when I worked for Henry Wainwright, but it was pulled down in June or July last, I believe, when Mr. Rogers was there. When the fixtures were sold to Mr. Martin the remainder of the fixtures were left, and the gas fittings. There were two lots of fixtures taken away; the last lot were taken away about August, and the first late in June or the beginning of July. The parti-

16

Evidence for Prosecution.

tion was there then, but not at the time the last lot was taken away; it had been removed. What had been the paint room was open to the rest of the room. The flooring of the paint room was boarded, and so was the rest of the warehouse, except the part that was flagged. That was at the furthermost end. The floor of the paint room was raised a little, and then the stonework of the other place was raised higher still. On entering from Vine Court you would first place your foot upon some flagging which extends a few feet from the entrance. That flagging is a little above the floor of the warehouse. There is a fireplace in the warehouse, about the centre, on the right. When I spoke about hair I was referring to hair that we use in our trade, pigs' bristles. If they are not cleaned and dressed they smell rather peculiar, but not quite so bad as that did. We do not use size; we use pitch or glue. I thought the parcels contained hair.

By the LORD 'CHIEF JUSTICE—Was anything said to you by Henry Wainwright with reference to those parcels that led you to think they contained hair?—Yes; as we were going on the road to 215 he said to me, '' We want some hair for so-and-so.'' I said, '' Yes, we do, sir.'' He said, '' Well, we must get it on Monday, or else the men won't be able to finish the work.'' That had no reference to the hair at No. 215, but I thought it was hair for all that.

HENRY TURNER (policeman M 48), examined by Mr. BEASLEY —I am an officer in the Metropolitan Police Force. At four minutes past five on the afternoon of 11th September of the present year I was on duty in the High Street, Borough, at the corner of St. Thomas Street. I saw the witness Stokes then; he seemed rather excited, and very much exhausted; he had his hat in his hand, and perspired very much in the face. He made a communication to me, in consequence of which I went up to a cab which had just drawn up. The cabman was just beginning to rein up at the corner of Southwark Street. The prisoner Henry Wainwright got out of it really before it had stopped, with a parcel in his right hand, and, in consequence of what Stokes told me, I followed him to the Hen and Chickens. He put the parcel down on the footway, took a key from his pocket, unlocked the padlock, and went in. I returned to the cab, which was about 40 yards from the Hen and Chickens, and saw another parcel there on the front seat, wrapped in American cloth, 18 inches long and 9 or 10 inches wide. Constable Cox, M. 290, was there. I spoke to the young woman in the cab, whom I now know to be Alice Day, and had some

c   17

The Wainwrights.

Henry Turner conversation with her. Cox stood behind the cab. I joined him, and waited. Henry Wainwright, on coming out of the house, came and walked straight to the cab. He was smoking a very large cigar. I did not observe whether he was smoking before; his back was towards me. He put the bolt on the door, but did not lock it. He took the other parcel out of the cab with his left hand when I spoke to him. I said, "What have you got there, sir?" He said, "Why do you interfere with me? I am only going down to an old friend of mine?" I walked alongside of him under the Town Hall till we got to the Hen and Chickens. The door was shut, but the padlock off. He seemed to want to pass by, but I caught hold of him, and he stopped. I said, "Do you live here?" He said, "No." I said, "Have you got any business here?" He replied, "Yes, and you have not." I said, "Go inside." He seemed disinclined to do so, and when Cox joined me we pushed him in. When we got inside I said, "How came you in possession of this place? I thought it belonged to Mr. Lewis?" He answered, "So it does now." He added, "Say nothing, ask no question, and there is £50 each for you." Cox then barred the door on the inside (there was a bar inside, there was no fastening), and we walked a few steps down the shop together. The prisoner Henry had a parcel in his left hand all the time. I said to him, "What did you do with the first parcel you brought here?" He said, "It is only on the first floor." I told Cox to go and look for it. I had hold of the prisoner then.

We walked down the shop together about half a dozen steps when I saw the parcel in a dark corner on the cellar steps. I called Cox aside and said, "Get hold of this man, and I will see what is in the parcel.". Cox took hold of him. I put the parcel on an old counter, on the left-hand side of the shop, and then perceived what a dreadful stench proceeded from it. Wainwright said, "Don't open it, policeman; pray don't look at it, whatever you do; don't touch it." I then pulled the cloth over, and my fingers then came right across the scalp of a head, across the ear. I found it contained part of the remains of a human body. I got hold of the prisoner, and Cox went to get the cab. Wainwright then said, "I'll give you £100, I'll give you £200, and produce the money in twenty minutes, if you will let me go." He said nothing more.

The cab was then brought to the door by Cox, and I put the first parcel into the cab. The prisoner had been holding the second parcel all the time in his left hand. Cox came back for it. The prisoner threw himself round as if to throw the parcel away from him, but he was put into the cab; the woman was

18

Evidence for Prosecution.

still in the cab, and we were driven to the station.   Near where Henry Turner
the cab was standing you could see to the Hen and Chickens,
which was between 40 and 45 yards off.   On the way to the
station the female who was in the cab said, " Mr. Wainwright,
you have done a fine thing for me," to which he did not reply.

At the station the parcels were put down in the yard, and
found to contain the remains of a female body, much decomposed; the features were not recognisable; the hair on the head
was very much clotted with blood, lime, and dirt.   Mr. Larkin,
the surgeon, saw them, and they were taken to St. Saviour's
dead-house the same evening.   Henry Wainwright and Alice
Day were charged about eight o'clock the same evening.   The
charge was that they had in their possession a human body,
decomposed, and supposed to be murdered.   Both prisoners
then made a statement, which was taken down by Inspector
Fox in writing.   I found a black leather bag in the cab, an
ordinary travelling bag; it was empty.   I did not notice
whether there was a newspaper in it.

Cross-examined by Mr. BESLEY—When Wainwright took the
second parcel out of the cab, I said, " What have you got
there?"   He laughed, and said, " All right, policeman, I am
only going down to a friend of mine."   When I mentioned Mr.
Lewis' name, he offered to go with me to Mr. Lewis.

ARTHUR COX (policeman M 290), examined by the SOLICITOR- Aurthur Cox
GENERAL—I was on duty in the High Street, Borough, on 11th
September, a few minutes after five o'clock.   I saw Stokes, who
drew my attention to a cab.   I went to it and saw a woman in
it, and a parcel on the front seat wrapped in American cloth.
There was also a black leather bag.   Turner spoke to the
woman, but I did not hear what he said.   A short time afterwards I saw Henry Wainwright come from the direction of the
Hen and Chickens, smoking a cigar.   He opened the door of the
cab nearest the pavement, and took out the parcel lying on the
front seat.   Turner asked him what he had got in the parcel.
He took the cigar from his mouth and said, " All right, policeman.   I am only going to a friend of mine."   He then turned to
me and said, " Why do you interfere with me."   I was standing
on his left side, Turner on his right.   I said, " We have
received information that what you have got in the parcel is
wrong."   Turner, he, and I went towards the Hen and Chickens,
but about 50 yards off I went back to the cab.   I left police
constable 310 in charge, and went back to the Hen and
Chickens.   Wainwright seemed to have some altercation with
Turner, and I heard him say, " No, perhaps you had better."

The Wainwrights.

Arthur Cox We then pushed him inside the shop door, a little wicket door, and Turner said, "How did you come in possession of this place; it used to belong to Mr. Lewis?" He said, "Come with me to Mr. Lewis, and you'll find it's all right. Say nothing, and ask no questions, and there's £50 for each of you." I said, "No, we are going to do our duty, and we don't want your money." I then said, "Wait, Turner, while I fasten the door," as there was a crowd outside. I then took up an iron bar and placed it against the door. Turner said, "Will you tell me where the other parcel is which you brought in here," and the prisoner said, "It's only on the first floor." I went up five or six steps, when Turner said, "Come down, Cox; here it is in the corner." I came down, took hold of the prisoner, and Turner, lifting the parcel, put it on an old counter. The prisoner repeated twice, "For goodness sake don't touch it." Turner partially pulled the oilcloth open, and found it contained the remains of a dead body. I sent for a cab, and the prisoner was put in, and he and Alice Day were taken to the station with the parcels, which I ultimately conveyed to St. Saviour's deadhouse.

Cross-examined by Mr. BESLEY—The head of the cab horse was pointing down the Borough. The cabman was not on the box then; he was standing on the pavement near the horse's head.

Adjourned till to-morrow.

Second Day—Tuesday, 23rd November, 1875.

WILLIAM ANDREWS, examined—I am a cabman, living in W. Andrews
Pearl Street, Spitalfields. On 11th September I was on the
rank in High Street, Whitechapel. Whilst there a gentleman
beckoned me. It was the prisoner Henry Wainwright. I followed him. I pulled up at the corner of Church Lane. I saw
a young fellow there, but did not take notice of him. The
gentleman put the parcels in; there were two parcels and a
bag. This gentleman got in after the parcels and told me to
go on till he told me to stop. He stopped me in the Commercial Road and got out; he came back shortly with a
female. They both got in, and he told me to go over London
Bridge till he told me to stop; he stopped me at the corner of
Southwark Street, in the Borough, got out, took a parcel out,
and walked away. I did not see where he went. Two policemen
came up and looked in the cab. Afterwards the parcels were
put in, the prisoner, the female, and the policemen, and I drove
them all to the station.

Cross-examined by Mr. BESLEY—I did not know what the
charge was when the parcels were put into the cab in Whitechapel Road. I was on my box. When they were taken out
in the Borough I was standing by my horse's head.

ALICE DAY, examined by the ATTORNEY-GENERAL—I live at Alice Day
No. 8 Queen's Court, Greenfield Street, Commercial Road.
Prior to 11th September last I was in the ballet at the Pavilion
Theatre. I had been there for some years. I know Henry
Wainwright, and have known him about five years. I first
became acquainted with him at the Pavilion Theatre, behind
the scenes. I have often been with him to public-houses and
to theatres—sometimes alone, but oftener with other ballet
girls. I remember 11th September last. In the afternoon of
that day, about ten minutes to five, I saw Henry Wainwright
at the corner of Greenfield Street. He was walking. I did not
meet him by appointment. He asked if I would go for a ride
with him as far as London Bridge. I replied, "Yes; if he
would bring me back by a quarter-past six, as I had then to be

21

The Wainwrights.

Alice Day at the theatre"; and he said he would. We got into a four-wheeled cab, which he had waiting. I noticed that there were some bundles in American leather and a black bag on the front seat. We then drove away and passed over London Bridge. We were not talking as we went along. We did not stop. He gave me a newspaper off the black bag to read. He was smoking a cigar. When he gave me the paper he said, "Don't speak to me, I'm thinking." The cab stopped in the Borough. I did not notice anything peculiar about the parcels. I perceived a smell, but I thought it was the American leather. When the cab stopped he got out and took one of the parcels. He said, "I'm going round the corner with this parcel to a ware-house, and if it's open I will come back for the other." He then went away. After he had gone away, some policemen came up to the cab, and they afterwards took us to the station, and the parcels also, and the black bag. Henry knew where I lived. He had been to see me many times. I knew Thomas, but only for about twelve months.

Cross-examined by Mr. Besley—The acquaintanceship between myself and Henry Wainwright was an ordinary one. There never was the slightest impropriety between us during the whole of the five years. I earned my living by going to the Pavilion Theatre and by dressmaking. Wainwright's shop, No. 84, was next to the Pavilion Theatre. In the five years it has happened more than half a dozen times that I have been present with him, with other ballet girls. There were business transactions between the profession and Henry Wainwright. He supplied brushes and mats, and he was in and out of the theatre continually on those occasions. When I and the ballet girls had refreshments with him we were never together more than a quarter of an hour.

By the Lord Chief Justice—Where did you have refreshments?—In the theatre and outside at the public-house in Baker's Row, near the stage door.

Cross-examination continued—I suppose some of the young ladies were so bold as to ask him for refreshments?—Yes, very often.

But these occasions never occupied more than a quarter of an hour?—No.

By the Lord Chief Justice—Either with these girls or when you were alone?—Not more.

Cross-examination continued—On 11th September I was standing outside the public-house at the corner of Greenfield Street, and could be seen some distance off. The smell was so slight that the American leather seemed to me to account for

22

Evidence for Prosecution.

it. I had not the slightest suspicion of anything being wrong. **Alice Day**
Wainwright was a great favourite with the actors in the theatre,
and the proprietors and lessees.

Re-examined by the ATTORNEY-GENERAL—To what theatre
had you been with him?—Covent Garden. We were alone
then. On another occasion I went to the Grecian Theatre, but
then I had a young lady from the theatre with me. I forget
the other theatre I went to with him; it was not the Pavilion.

By the LORD CHIEF JUSTICE—What were you doing outside
the public-house?—I had just left it with one of the people of
the theatre. I had not been there a minute. I had only just
come out, and was going to cross the road.

MATTHEW FOX, examined—I am an inspector of the **Matthew Fox**
Metropolitan Police. I was on duty on 11th September last at
Stone's End Police Station, in the Borough. I was there when
Henry Wainwright and Alice Day, and the two parcels and a bag
arrived. When they were first brought in Constable Turner,
addressing me, said, "Mr. Fox, here are a man and woman
with two parcels, and I think they are wrong." Not knowing
what was in the parcels, I asked the prisoner Henry Wainwright
what they contained and where he got them. He replied, "I
don't know what they contain; a gentleman gave them to me to
carry." I then took them to the yard adjoining the station,
opened them, and saw the contents. I found they contained
portions of a body. Alice Day had not then said anything.
I sent for the surgeon, Mr. Larkin, and after he had examined
them he made a statement to me. I then directed the prisoners
to be put into the dock. I said, "I will charge you with having
the remains of a female in your possession, believed to have
been murdered." I asked him his name and address, and he
gave me it as "Henry Wainwright, 78 New Road, Whitechapel."
Next he said, "If you send for my friend Mr. Martin at 78
New Road, I will tell you in his presence how I became possessed of those parcels." I went myself to Mr. Martin, but he
arrived at the station before I got back, not having been at
home when I called. Stokes had fetched him. The prisoners
were then again placed in the dock, and charged as before.
Henry Wainwright then said—and I took his statement in
writing—"Yesterday week, I think, a gentleman, known to
me for some time by meeting him at public-houses, asked me
if I wished to earn a pound or two. I said, 'Yes, I am
always willing to make money,' or something of that sort. He
said, 'I can put a sovereign or two in your way.' I then
inquired how, and he said, 'By taking two parcels over to the

23

The Wainwrights.

Borough.' I said it was a big price for so small a job. He said, 'Take them over and ask no questions, and here's a couple of sovereigns for you.' I said, 'If you make it five pounds I will take them.' He agreed to make it three pounds, and gave me a key, and told me to take them over to the Hen and Chickens, an empty house in the Borough. He brought them to me, and put them on the pavement, and I brought them over; and that is how I came into possession of them." At that time Stokes was in the station, but the prisoner had not seen him. Alice Day afterwards made a statement in Henry Wainwright's presence, which I took down. [This statement being objected to, it was not pressed by the Attorney-General.] After that I searched Henry Wainwright, and found upon him twenty-seven keys.

On the same evening I went with Stokes to 215 Whitechapel Road, to the back entrance in Vine Court. Stokes took me there, and pointed out the door, and with one of the keys taken from Henry Wainwright I opened the door. When I got in I saw on the stone-flagged floor a small chopper, wrapped up in a piece of newspaper; a spade, a hammer, and an open pocket knife, a common pocket knife. On the chopper, which I produce, I noticed a deal of matter which smelled strongly—similarly to that of the body. This is the spade (produced), a new one. It was covered and marked with lime and clay, and some hairs.

At the extreme end of the warehouse the floor was raised a few inches higher than the rest; that was the original construction of the floor. I found some boards loose; I took them up and found that some of the joists had been cut. I was induced to look there by finding the boards loose, and also by a smell which attracted my attention to the spot. I took up three of the flooring boards, and found that four of the joists upon which they rested had been cut. The joists rested on the earthen floor, they were not fastened to the boards. I saw then that the earth underneath was mixed with chloride of lime. I did no more on that occasion. I put the boards back again, locked the door, put a policeman in charge, and left; it was then light.

Next morning, Sunday, the 12th, I went to the place again and made a further examination. I had all the loose earth removed, and found that earth had filled a grave 5 feet long, 2 feet wide, and 2 feet deep, and I found the mould in that grave to be very largely mixed with chloride of lime. I picked up one lump amongst a number of others as a specimen. I found some hair amongst the earth, and took a specimen of that. It was human hair of a light colour.' I have part of it here.

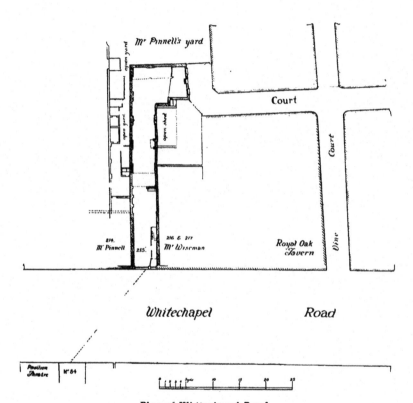

Plan of Whitechapel Road

(Showing the premises at Nos. 84 and 215 occupied by Henry Wainwright).

Evidence for Prosecution.

I saw the hair that was on the body, and it seemed to be exactly **Matthew Fox** the same colour. I have some of the hair here which I took from the body (producing it). That portion has been washed since by the surgeon. I noticed that on the flags as you entered by the back door there was a large amount of rubbish on one side and straw on the other. On the part where the straw was it was raised; it had the appearance as if something had been concealed, or as if some person had slept in it, or as if some person had been covered with it. On the other end of the flagged portion was about a cart load of ashes and other rubbish. I had the rubbish cleared away from the stones, and underneath I found red, irregular blotches, which appeared to me to be blood. On the ledges of the stone I found marks as if done with this small axe in chopping. There were cuts or indentations in the stone, and a small part was broken away. It had been recently broken, quite fresh. I found a piece of rope underneath the boards on the grave, on the loose earth. It was an ordinary piece of rope with a loop at the end, which was cut. That was all I noticed at that time. I gave directions to have the place properly searched. I was there about two hours on Sunday morning. Inspector M'Donald and Detectives Forster and Newman were with me. I have two rings which I received from Detective Newman, also two jet buttons which I received from Inspector M'Donald, and two earrings. I have also two jet buttons that I received at the police station from Mrs. Allen in Mrs. Taylor's and John Lane's presence; I have also a pair of boots which I got from a box in Mr. Lane's house at Waltham. I produce a pad which I got from Mr. Larkin; and also three bullets, one from Mr. Larkin and two from Mr. Bond. I also produce a padlock which I took from the door of the Hen and Chickens by direction of the magistrate, and I produce a key of that padlock which I got from Turner on the night of 11th September. I went to the Hen and Chickens and went down to a cellar below. I found a quantity of loose earth there, I should say at least three cart loads, in the inner cellar; that was after I crept through the hole.

Cross-examined by Mr. BESLEY—The first words Turner said in Henry Wainwright's presence were, "I think this man and woman have got parcels, something wrong." The parcels were there. It was then that Henry Wainwright said, "I don't know what they contained, a gentleman gave them to me to carry." It was after Mr. Larkin made a communication to me that I asked Wainwright's address, and he gave me his address, "78 New Road, Whitechapel, where you will find Mr. Martin." I was absent two hours before I came back to the station. I

The Wainwrights.

Matthew Fox waited at No. 78 to search the premises. Stokes was not at the station before I went to No. 78; I found him there when I got back.

I have a list of the things I found on Henry Wainwright (produced). Among them I found a pocket knife. It was an ordinary pocket knife. I have not said before to-day that my attention was directed to the loose boards by the smell. I was examined three or four times at the Police Court, beginning on 13th September and ending on 13th October. I gave my principal evidence as to my visit to 215 Whitechapel Road on 13th September. An ordinary constable was placed outside the premises. Newman and Forster were to be in the neighbourhood, and to assist in searching. The hair I have produced was found by myself in the grave. I have not shown the stone to any stone mason; I showed the stains on the stones to the doctors after we had cleaned and swept the rubbish off; they had dried up, and were trampled upon, and were then scarcely perceptible. I attended all the examinations both at the Police Court and the inquest. I showed the earrings to Mrs. Taylor, Miss Wilmore, Mrs. Rogers, and to Mrs. Izzard at the last examination before the magistrate; Mrs. Izzard turned out to be the owner of the earrings. They had been shown to the previous persons for the purpose of identifying them as the earrings of Harriet Lane. I was present when M'Donald found the buttons. I believe the burnt ashes in the grate in the house have been microscopically examined; I gave Mr. Bond specimens of what I found there. M'Donald searched the ashes. There was only one grate in the house that had the appearance of having had a recent fire in it.

Have you heard any suggestion made that Henry Wainwright has made a confession to you?—No, I have not.

Have you seen it so stated in the *Weekly Despatch* newspaper, or elsewhere?—No, I have not.

There is no truth in any such statement?—Oh, no, none whatever.

The LORD CHIEF JUSTICE—Do you mean to say that any such statement has appeared in a newspaper?

Mr. BESLEY—Yes, my lord. I was asked to call your attention to it, but did not think it worth while.

The LORD CHIEF JUSTICE—It is most improper.

[Mr. Besley then read a paragraph from the paper referred to, stating that Henry Wainwright had made a confession to the police, from which it appeared that Thomas Wainwright had really committed the murder, and that Henry had cut up the body afterwards.]

26

Evidence for Prosecution.

The LORD CHIEF JUSTICE—It is a very great pity that any Matthew Fox such statement should be made.

Mr. BESLEY said the paragraph went on to declare that, owing to these circumstances, a change would be made in the indictment, and that Thomas Wainwright would be charged with the murder, while Henry would only be charged as an accessory.

The ATTORNEY-GENERAL—I need hardly say, my lord, that had any statement been made to the police, my learned friend would have been communicated with.

Mr. BESLEY—I have no doubt of that.

The LORD CHIEF JUSTICE—It is very evident that that must not be further circulated.

Cross-examined by Mr. MOODY—The axe is a small one, such as might be used for cutting firewood, a cheap one; there are the trade-marks on it of the person who sold it, and on the spade as well.

Re-examined by the ATTORNEY-GENERAL—This is the list of the things I found on Henry Wainwright—£3 10s. in gold, 12s. 8d. in silver, some copper money, a foreign coin, some pawnbrokers' duplicates, twenty-seven keys, a silver watch and metal chain, a tape measure, spectacles and case, a knife, rule, pencil case, two cigars, a pair of eyeglasses, a pocket handkerchief, and a memorandum book. The knife was an ordinary pocket knife.

There was only one grate that I saw in which there were ashes; that was on the first floor, in a room that appeared to be used as a kitchen. I don't recollect a grate in the warehouse. I went there first between eight and nine o'clock on 11th September; it was very dark then; I had to procure lights. I did not light the gas; there was no gas there then, the fixtures had been removed. I had police lanterns and candles. A piece of velvet ribbon was handed to me by Mr. Larkin, and I have it here. I got about 2 lbs. of chloride of lime from the grave; it was in a kind of cake. I could have picked up more; in one part of the grave it was nearly all pure chloride of lime. There are windows at that part of the premises looking into Vine Court, but they were always closed, made up with shutters; when I went there the shutters had every appearance of not having been removed for months, probably years, and were covered with cobweb.

By Mr. BESLEY—The children could not look through the shutters; I could not see any space through which they could look; I do not think there were any fissures that could be seen through. I have tried myself from the outside and could see none; there was a policeman there who would not allow them

27

The Wainwrights.

Matthew Fox to come there. I am speaking of the windows looking into Vine Court from the flagged part of the warehouse; they are shown on the model. There are two windows looking into Vine Court from the warehouse, the others are from the floor above. The shutters were on the inside, and they had the appearance of having been kept shut for a long time.

J. Newman JOSEPH NEWMAN (detective officer H), examined—After the arrest of Henry Wainwright on 11th September I went to No. 215 Whitechapel Road. I got there about eight o'clock in the evening. I did not search till Inspector Fox came. I was present when he searched, and I assisted. I found nothing myself on that day. I observed that a board was loose, and Forster and I lifted it up. I went again on the Sunday morning about 12.30; I found nothing then; I saw Mr. Fox find the piece of rope. On the 16th I examined the loose earth, and found this wedding ring in the mould that came from the grave; I put a mark on it, and gave it to Mr. Fox the next day. The mark is on it now. On the 17th I put the mould that came from the grave through a second screen, and as I was screening it the keeper ring rolled down. I gave that also to Inspector Fox; I did not mark it, but I know this to be the one. I saw two jet buttons found by Mr. M'Donald on the 17th. On 9th October I was again on the premises, and again searched the mould from the grave, and found a human tooth. On Sunday, 10th October, I went again, and then found a kneecap, I mean the bone, and what I believe to be a piece of the scalp, with hair on it. Next day, the 11th, I found another tooth. I gave them all to M'Donald.

Cross-examined by Mr. BESLEY—I spent a good deal of time there. On the first day we had candles and lanterns. In the daytime it was perfectly light there from the skylight. Sometimes children came round the door and looked through the keyhole and watched us. There were fissures in the shutters, through which they looked when we were at work there. I was present when the earrings were found in the first floor back room, among the ashes, underneath the stove. I understand those ashes have been submitted to microscopic examination. The buttons were found in the ashes down on the floor; rubbish and vegetable refuse were mixed with the ashes. I call them ashes, as distinguished from the mould in the grave.

By the LORD CHIEF JUSTICE—There was a sort of rubbish heap where the ashes and other refuse things had been thrown together; that was lying on the raised floor.

28

Evidence for Prosecution.

J. C. M'Donald

JAMES CONSTANTINE M'DONALD, examined—I am chief inspector of the H division of police. On 16th and 17th September I went to the premises 215 Whitechapel Road, and searched the ashes that were in the grate there. I found in the ashes two jet buttons, about two yards from the grave. Newman put the ashes through a sand sieve screen, and what did not pass through the screen I turned off with a stick, and in turning it over I found these two buttons. I gave them to Inspector Fox. I noticed that the fasteners were in them, and they appeared as if they had been in the fire; they were cracked; the upper part is unbroken. I afterwards searched the upstairs room on the first floor, which is called the kitchen, and I there found two earrings underneath the grate on the hearth, among some ashes. I gave these to Inspector Fox. The ashes appeared to be ashes of wood burning. I found a quantity of small wire in them, as if the backs of brushes had been burnt there. There were a large number of brushes about the place. Some teeth and pieces of bone were given to me by Newman; I was present when they were found. I gave them to Mr. Bond. They were part of a kneecap, a piece of bone, and two teeth.

Cross-examined by Mr. BESLEY—I did not go with Newman on the first night. I went on the Sunday morning. I did not commence the sifting until 16th September. At that time the mould from the grave had been put into a separate and distinct heap, care had been taken to do that. I think the mould was sifted first, and after that the rubbish heap. The rubbish from the different parts of the house was not brought down and sifted also. That was examined casually, and afterwards more strictly. The sample was taken from the grate in which these earrings were found, and I gave it to Inspector Fox. The joists were cut on a slope, but at an angle; they dropped in and stood firmly. One or two of them were cut straighter than the others, and the others were cut a little on a slant. I can produce them if necessary. They were cut at each end. Each joist would require two sawings to get out the piece; I examined the boards that were over this part; they were not very clean. They were the same colour as the rest of the floor. I examined to see if there were any nail marks, and there were; and the nails were in the boards that were taken up from the flooring which rested on the joists.

Re-examined by the ATTORNEY-GENERAL—The boards had been nailed to the joists, in my opinion; I found four nails in the boards. The boards ran lengthways exactly across the paint room at the extreme end of the warehouse. The boards ran across in the direction from the front of the paint shop to the

29

The Wainwrights.

J. C. M'Donald back wall, lengthways of the warehouse. They were laid on the ground, and the boards ran from side to side in the room. The joists appeared to have been cut for the purpose of enabling the ground to be removed. The excavation in the ground could not have been made without removing the joists. It could not have been excavated with an ordinary shovel. It was only to the extent to which it had been excavated that the joists had been removed.

Edwin Allen EDWIN ALLEN, examined by Mr. BEASLEY—I married a daughter of John Lane, father of the deceased. On the 20th September last I was at Mr. Lane's house, Jessamine Cottage, Waltham Cross. I saw a stay-box (produced) there opened by Mrs. Lane. It contained a variety of buttons, and amongst them some jet buttons. I took possession of two, and brought them to London, and gave them to Mrs. Taylor. They were on a blue card, and I know that those produced are the same. They were on the card when in the stay-box.

The LORD CHIEF JUSTICE (examining them)—They are just like the others, as the jury will see.

Mr. BESLEY objected that the box had not been identified.

The LORD CHIEF JUSTICE—Mrs. Lane should have been called first. At present we do not know whose stay-box it was, and therefore, gentlemen of the jury, the buttons must be put aside for the present.

Examination continued—Mrs. Lane handed me a parcel of papers, and amongst them I found five envelopes. The one now put into my hand is one of them.

The LORD CHIEF JUSTICE—It would have been better to have called Mrs. Lane first.

The ATTORNEY-GENERAL—I may as well say at once I shall not be able to call Mrs. Lane. Her health will not permit it. We must prove what is wanted in some other way.

Examination continued—In one of the envelopes there was a letter, but I did not see it then; I only became aware of it afterwards. I handed them to Mrs. Taylor.

Ellen Wilmore ELLEN WILMORE, examined by Mr. POLAND—I am unmarried, and live at 36 Maryland Street, Stratford. I am a milliner and dressmaker. I knew Harriet Louisa Lane as a milliner. She was apprenticed with me in 1866 to a Mrs. Bray, Waltham Cross. She left Mrs. Bray on two occasions; on the first occasion she stayed about two years, and on the second the same. I do not remember her coming to live in London. I know the prisoner Henry Wainwright. I first knew him in 1872 by the

30

Evidence for Prosecution.

name of Percy King. I first met him at Temple Bar. Harriet **Ellen Wilmore**
Lane, whom I then knew as Mrs. King, was with him. I
believe she was at that time living near Bedford Square. I
knew her afterwards to be living in St. Peter Street, Mile End
Road. She had a child born there in August, 1872. She was
at that time living there as Mrs. King. I did not then know
who Percy King was, but I afterwards knew him as Mr. Wainwright, a brushmaker, of 84 Whitechapel Road.

Did you take charge of her first child?—I did, at Mr. Wainwright's request. When I met him at Temple Bar he told me to
take the baby and he would pay me £1 a week to keep the child,
and I had it in my charge, and I was to pay the doctor. I had
had the child three weeks at that time, and had received 12s.
first. It was a very delicate child.

By the LORD CHIEF JUSTICE—What reason was given why
you should take charge of the child?—There was no reason
whatever given.

Examination continued—The child was three months old
when I first took it. I had it three weeks before he spoke to me
about it. Henry Wainwright paid me then as Mr. King £1,
sometimes once a month, sometimes once in six weeks. I kept
the child until the following Christmas. A second child was
born on 3rd December, 1873, at 70 St. Peter Street, at Mrs.
Wells's, not at the same place as the first. I took the first child
to Mrs. King after the second one was born, as she wrote and
asked me to do so, and she had them both with her at Mrs.
Wells's, 70 St. Peter Street. She lived there, I think, till
May, 1874, but I don't quite remember. I used to visit her
there sometimes as Mrs. King. At that time I knew who Percy
King was. From 70 St. Peter Street she went to live at 3
Sidney Square, at Mrs. Foster's. She lived there, too, as Mrs.
King. I visited her there several times, generally on Sundays.
She had there the two children, and likely a monthly nurse.
Some time after I went there first she wrote me on 3rd August,
1874. I went to get the children, and I lived there for some
time. She wanted me to take the two children, but as I did
not see Wainwright to make any arrangement, I did not take
them. I slept and lived there from 3rd August to 11th September. The nurse left her before I went there, and we had a
little servant. I never saw Percy King there once. Only one
person visited her there—a gentleman named Edward Frieake.
I saw him only once for about half a moment. I knew his name
because Mrs. Foster opened the door of the sitting-room and
announced him to Mrs. King as Mr. Frieake. I passed out as
he came into the room.

The Wainwrights.

Can you say when this was? How many days before 11th
September?—I cannot remember how long before. It must have
been the beginning of September or the end of August; but I
cannot remember exactly.

Can you describe him at all?—He was not a tall man, with
rather a slight moustache, and he walked rather quick. He did
not stay long. It was in the evening when he came.

You have seen the two prisoners, one being the person you
know as Percy King or Henry Wainwright. Do you think that
either of them was the person?—No; I am not sure. I have
seen the other prisoner somewhere, but I cannot say where. It
may have been by passing him in the street.

You mean before you saw him at the Police Court?—Yes. I
have seen him before, but I don't know where. I cannot remember. It was arranged with Mrs. King while she was at Sidney
Square that I should take charge of the children, and that Mr.
King should pay me £5 a month.

Mr. Besley objected that unless this could be brought home
to Henry Wainwright it could not be evidence.

The Attorney-General—We shall show you that he did
afterwards actually pay the witness.

Examination continued—I took lodgings at No. 6 The Grove,
Stratford. Before 11th September, 1874, Mrs. King was in bad
circumstances. She had pawned some of her things several
times. Amongst other things, she used to wear a wedding ring
and keeper, and she was not wearing them when I went to
Sidney Square. They were in pledge. On 11th September I
took them out of pledge from Mr. Dickers, a pawnbroker in the
Commercial Road. She gave me the tickets, and I took them
and got them out of pawn. One was in for 10s., and the other
for 8s. or 9s. I forget which. I lent her the money to get them
out. I lent her £2 altogether. She had a lot of money, but
she had a lot of bills to pay, and not enough to get her wedding
ring out. I had received £5 in advance from Mr. King for
one month's keep of the two children. I took several things
out of pawn that day, to the amount of £3, but not all from
Dickers—linen and dresses, nearly everything she possessed. I
gave them to Mrs. King.

Look at those two rings (a wedding ring and keeper). Do
you recognise them?—Her rings were very much like these, but
I cannot swear these are them. I remember that the wedding
ring was larger than the keeper. These are the same. When
I gave her the two rings, she put them on, and went away with
them.

Before 11th September do you remember any disturbance
32

Evidence for Prosecution.

taking place in Sidney Square?—Yes; one night, four or five days from the beginning of September, I remember there was a very loud knocking at the door. It was late in the evening— about half-past nine or ten o'clock, I cannot say exactly, but I remember it was a very loud knocking at the door, and Mrs. Foster came up and asked me to go downstairs at once. In consequence of that I went downstairs to the front door, and when I got there I saw Mrs. King alone. She was intoxicated and excited. I got her in as quickly as I could, and she came in on the instant and remained indoors, and I was up with her all night.

Did you see any one else in the street at the time?—I did not. I looked, but I could see no one. Mrs. Foster came up the next morning to give her notice to leave in consequence of what had taken place overnight.

When was she to leave?—She was to have left on the Wed-nesday, 9th September, but she stayed on for two days longer, to the 11th. I assisted her to pack up her boxes. She gave me the keys first. When the boxes were all packed and the things were taken out of pawn, she left her lodgings at 3 Sidney Square on Friday, 11th September, 1874, at four o'clock in the after-noon. On the same day that I got the rings out of pawn she dressed herself in some of her best things.

Did she take anything with her?—Only a small parcel, which contained, I think, a nightdress only. She had also a new umbrella. She wore a grey dress, with a black bonnet; and a black cape trimmed with lace and velvet. Down the front of her dress were jet buttons, and no other trimming.

Do you know who put the buttons on the dress?—She put them on herself that morning. The buttons were bought in the Commercial Road. A few of them were left over, and I put them in this card stay-box (produced), which was on the table. I can swear to it. When the luggage was packed I put it into her big box—the box in Court. The buttons were on a card, a white card, I believe. They were large buttons, but I do not remember the pattern—about this size (two buttons produced). She always wore her hair done up at the back, with a large pad. She used a great number of hairpins, and her hair was frizzed over the pad. The pad was bought in the Hackney Road, but I do not know exactly the shop.

How did she fasten her hair?—With a band of black velvet. (The pad was here produced and handed to the witness.)

What do you say to that?—It is very much like the one she wore. It is the same colour.

Have you seen this velvet (produced)?—Yes. She usually

D   33

The Wainwrights.

Ellen Wilmore wore a band of velvet about the same width, but I do not know whether she wore it on that occasion.

[Mr. Poland said he proposed to ask the witness whether Harriet Lane made any communication to her when she left. The question was objected to.]

Examination continued—When she left her lodgings on that day, did she make some statement to you?—Yes, she did.

Did she take leave of her children?—Yes, most affectionately. She said "Good-bye" to me, and appeared to be in very good health and spirits.

The same evening did you leave the lodgings?—I did, at about half-past six or seven o'clock, when I went to No. 6 The Grove, Stratford. I took with me the two children and Mrs. King's luggage, which I was to keep until called for. There were several letters among her luggage. I did not see her on Saturday, Sunday, or Monday. I went to Harriet Lane's lodgings, but neither saw nor heard anything of her until Tuesday, the 15th. I then went to Henry Wainwright's premises, a brushmaker's shop, 84 Whitechapel Road. I had been there only once before, and then had not seen him. I sent a note in with a little boy to him, and in about ten minutes he met me a short distance from the house, at the corner of New Road. I said, "Where is Mrs. King," and he said he had sent her down to Brighton on Saturday morning. I was greatly astonished, and said, "Dear me! and she has not got any clothes?" "I gave her money to buy clothes," he said, and I replied, "Oh, did you? Can I send her any clothes?" He said I should probably hear from her in a day or two. I then requested the £2 which I had lent Mrs. King, £1 to take her rings out of pawn, some money for the laundress, and 7s. to pay for a dress that had been dyed. He gave me the £2, and bade me good-morning. I went away. I had baby with me. On the following Thursday, the 17th, hearing nothing, I could not rest any longer, and I wrote to Mrs. Taylor, Harriet Lane's sister, who was in the country. I saw her four days afterwards at my lodgings in Stratford Grove. We went together to 84 Whitechapel Road, and there in the shop we saw Henry Wainwright. I introduced Mrs. Taylor as Harriet Lane's sister, and he said, "Oh, is it? How like you look." She explained that she had come to inquire about her sister, where she was. He said she had gone to Brighton, he had not heard from her, and that he would get her address as soon as he possibly could.

By the Lord Chief Justice—Did he on either day say that he had seen her?—He did not; only that he had sent her to Brighton on Saturday morning.

34

Evidence for Prosecution.

Examination continued—A few days afterwards I was alone, Ellen Wilmore
and saw him again at the door of No. 84. I said, " I have not
heard from Mrs. King yet." He replied, " I have. She has gone
off with my friend Frieake." I did not know he had a friend
called Frieake. I think he said that this person was an auctioneer who had come into a large property. Nothing was said
as to what Mr. Frieake was or where he lived. I was too
astonished to say anything more. I afterwards received by post
a letter from the Charing Cross Hotel. I had not received a
previous one mentioned in it. It came in an envelope to my
address, No. 6 The Grove, Stratford. Wainwright never asked
my address, because he knew it; Mrs. King had told him I was
going there. I received this letter about three weeks after the
disappearance of Harriet Lane, that is, after 11th September.
I afterwards gave up the letter with the envelope to Mrs. Taylor,
and I don't know what has become of it. I took it to Mr. Wainwright's, at 84 Whitechapel Road, the next morning after
receiving it late at night. I said to him, " I have just received
this letter, sir," and I put it into his hand, and he read it. He
said, " I have one very much like it," and then he fetched a
letter out of his desk. I saw it in his hand, and the writing
was very much like in appearance to what I had had. I was
near enough to see the writing, but I did not take much notice.
He read a portion of it, which stated he had got the lady under
his protection, and said, " I dare you or any one else to interfere, as I intend to marry her." I don't remember all he read.
He gave me my letter back, and kept his own. When the letter
was first shown to him we were alone. I then took the letter
straight to Mrs. Taylor. I cannot say Wainwright read the
letter, but he appeared to. [Letter read, " Charing Cross Hotel.
—Dear Miss Wilmore, I am very much surprised at not receiving
a reply to my last letter, in which I gave you all particulars of
our arrangements. She is now quite content, and has solemnly
promised not to speak to King or any of his friends and family
again, as, if she did, I have told her we should have to part.
If her promise is kept, I intend to marry her in a few weeks.
I distinctly tell her that I will not allow her to see any of her
old acquaintances, as it will only cause unpleasantness. With
kind regards.—Yours truly, E. Frieake. We are just off to
Dover."]

Are you quite sure you received no letter before that?—I am
quite sure. I went straight to Mrs. Taylor and read it to her,
and at once we both went to Waltham to see the father and
mother. We returned together, and a few days afterwards I
received a telegram at my lodgings, 6 The Grove, in one of the

The Wainwrights.

Ellén Wilmore ordinary envelopes. I read it, and the next day Mrs. Taylor came to see it, and I read it to her. The next day, or the day following, Mrs. Taylor and I went to Henry Wainwright's, at 84 Whitechapel Road. I took the telegram with us. I showed him the telegram, and he read it. I said when I showed it to him, " I've received a telegram from Mr. Frieake from Dover." He did not say anything, but went to his desk and fetched a telegram like it, and read it to Mrs. Taylor and myself. I cannot say what were the exact words, or even the substance, but he read it to Mrs. Taylor, and I left her. I saw the telegram in his hand. He came out with us and asked us to have a glass of wine each, and we had it, and that was all that passed that day. Before I left my lodgings I had £5 in advance for a month, and when the month expired I went again. The first £5 was paid after the telegram. He then paid me another £5 for the next month in advance for the children. I asked if he had heard of Mrs. King, and he said he had not heard. He continued to pay the £5 in advance every month up to June, 1875. During all this while I was keeping the boxes of Mrs. King. I kept them up to January. Before giving them up the boxes were examined at my lodgings by Mrs. Taylor and Mr. Eeles, who passed as Fowler. There were several letters in them. She always left her letters in my charge. They were in another box. After the things had been examined they were all put back, and the boxes corded. I would not give them up till I received this letter from Percy King (letter produced)—" 21st January, 1875. I am quite willing that Mrs. King's boxes shall be given up to her father on your receiving a guarantee in writing exonerating you from all responsibility connected with them.—Percy King." " 28th January, 1875. Miss Wilmore, I hereby, with full instructions from Mr. Lane, of Jessamine Cottage, Waltham, Essex, exonerate you from any responsibility connected with the box and portmanteau and the property of Mrs. King, or Harriet Lane, and the articles contained in them as seen by Mrs. Taylor and yourself. Witness my mark, R. Fowler." I cannot swear this " Percy King " is his writing, but it is the writing he always wrote to me. I had spoken to him about giving up the boxes, and he said I had better give them up. I said, " Please send me a paper to do so," and he afterwards sent me an authority by Mr. Eeles. Mr. Fowler and a young man took the box, portmanteau, and bonnet box away to be given to the father. That was in January—about the 21st, as far as I can recollect.

How long did Wainwright continue further payments to you?
—He continued £5 a month payment up to June, and then he did not pay regularly. I do not think he had it. I saw him

36

Evidence for Prosecution.

several times about the money. Sometimes he gave me 5s.,
sometimes 3s., sometimes 2s., at different times. I always
asked whether he had heard of Mrs. King, and he said he had
seen her on several occasions, and at different places, which he
told me at the time, but I have forgotten them. He told me
also that other persons had seen her at different times—half a
dozen at least. I think he said one of his workmen, his porter
or his foreman, was the person who had seen her. I agreed to
take less money. He said he did not wish me to, and said he
would pay me some time. I said, "If you cannot afford to pay
me 25s. a week, I will take 20s." He said he did not wish
that. I said I would rather do that than part with the children.
He paid me small sums then at irregular times, and in small
amounts, before September of this year. He did not send them
to me; I went to see him.

Did you call and get any money?—I called, but I was not
able to get any. I was not able to get any the last six weeks
before 11th September last. I agreed to take a little weekly;
I did not say how much, and I did not make any agreement.
In September last I wrote to him while he was at Mr. Martin's.
I gave the letter to Mr. Martin's foreman, addressed "Henry
Wainwright, Esq." I received a reply on Friday, 10th September, at mid-day. I was then living at 36 Maryland Street,
Stratford. This does not look like his general writing, but I
have letters something like it. I believe it is his. [Letter read.
"I have told you I can do nothing for you till November, I
will then do as I have said; but if you give me all this annoyance by calling and leaving letters, I shall then do nothing for
you. You can make your choice. Your stupid threats are
quite absurd about it's being too late. I can see you at seven
o'clock if you like, at the back of the hospital.—Miss Wilmore,
Maryland Street, Stratford." Postmark, 10.45.] When we
met that night I do not recollect that he said anything about
my letter; he was most gentlemanly and most kind. In consequence of that letter I met him at the back of the London Hospital. The arrangement was seven o'clock, but he was not there
till nearly eight. I said, "I received your letter, and I think
it better that we arrange something at once." He gave me 5s.,
and said he would give me 5s. a week till November, and that he
would send me £2 or £3 by mid-day on the next day, Saturday,
without fail.

Next day you received no money?—No; I heard nothing the
next day, and the next I heard was on Monday evening at six
o'clock that he was in custody. Sergeant Cox came to me, and I
went to St. Saviour's dead-house, where I saw the body. I saw

The Wainwrights.

Ellen Wilmore a little of the hair, which was light auburn; that was the colour of Harriet Lane's.

From what you saw of the remains, did you form any positive opinion as to whose body it was?—I thought from the height and the size it was very like Harriet Lane's. In my own belief, I think it was her.

Did you notice her hands and feet?—Yes, they were like hers—very small.

Did you see a tooth?—She had a tooth decayed, and only one, in the upper jaw, next the eye tooth; but I cannot remember on which side it was. It showed when she laughed or talked.

By the LORD CHIEF JUSTICE—Can you not remember, when she looked at you and smiled, on which side of the face it was?—No, I cannot remember; I have tried, but I cannot. There were several teeth out of the jaw of the body I saw, but I did not notice any one in particular.

Examination continued—Had she any marks on her body?—She had a scar on her right knee—about 4 inches below the knee, on the right side. That was from a burn. I had seen it very often. I saw it the day before she left Sidney Square. One side was very white, and the other side was drawn, like burns generally are. It was about the size of a florin. These (produced) are her boots; I sent them home in her box to her father. She was in the habit of wearing earrings, and her ears were pierced.

Did you ever give up any letters of Mrs. King to Mr. Wainwright?—I gave him up a few. He asked me particularly for them about 23rd April last.

What did he say about them?—He only asked me if I would give them up to him, and I gave him a few. I think I asked whether I was to give everything up, her letters and all, and he said, "No, you had better let me have them," but I would not give him all. I gave him a few, but she had told me never to give them up. She wished me not; she was going to burn them, but she said, "You take charge of them; I don't want my father and mother to see them."

Cross-examined by Mr. BESLEY—Before I had any child to take care of I knew that Harriet Lane had left her father and come up to London. I used to go and see her.

Until 3rd August, 1874, you never lived under the same roof with Harriet Lane?—I did not.

In what year was it you first found her living in London?—The year that the first child was born, 1871. I found her living in lodgings. I left Waltham Abbey and lost sight of her for three months. I first saw her in London when I was living at

38

Evidence for Prosecution.

Chelsea; she was at the Green Dragon, in Bishopsgate Street. **Ellen Wilmore**
That was six or seven months before the birth of the first child,
and she then told me she was married, and I was under that
belief until just before the first child was born. She was then
passing by the name of Mrs. King.

You never saw Mr. King, otherwise Henry Wainwright, until
after the child was born, and had come to live with you?—I did
not. It was three months old when I first saw Henry Wainwright. When I had the first child I lived in Buckingham Road,
Pimlico. Harriet Lane did not pay me when I had the first
child; Mr. King paid me. He used to bring the money himself.
I always addressed him as Mr. King. The first child was with
me nearly up to 3rd December, 1873, rather more than twelve
months. I was not present when the second child was born,
but I saw Mrs. King at Christmas at Mrs. Wells's, 70 St. Peter
Street. I had a letter from her on 3rd August, when I went
to Sidney Square, Mrs. Foster's. The beginning of the arrangement about my having the children was by that letter, and I
went there instantly, and slept under the same roof with her till
7th September. I met Mr. King with her at the back of the
hospital about 4th August. She told me she would bring him
there, and then I, or Mrs. King, told him what the plans were,
and got his sanction. He asked me whether, if he furnished a
house, I would live with Mrs. King. I told him, " No, but that
I would take the children." He said, " Very well." That was
all that passed.

By Mr. Poland—On some occasion, between 3rd August and
11th September, a person came whom Mrs. King announced by
name?—Yes, Mr. Frieake. He was very young-looking, and
very nicely dressed and gentlemanly. He had a pale complexion
and a light moustache. I should call him rather fair. I do not
think he had light hair.

Cross-examination continued—You say that Mr. Wainwright,
when you were calling for the money, usually said either that
he had seen her himself, or that some one else had seen her?—
Yes.

Are you aware that you did not say before the magistrate
that Wainwright had ever said he had seen her himself?—No;
I don't know whether I did or not.

Have you not said to him on many occasions, after February,
1875, " I could almost swear I saw her "?—I said that I thought
I saw her in a cab. That was about six weeks after 11th
September. I was walking near the Bank with one of the
children, so I could not follow her. It was very cold weather,
just before Christmas, I think. I was always on the lookout

39

The Wainwrights.

Ellen Wilmore for her. I saw a hansom cab and a lady and gentleman in it, the colour of the lady's hair being an uncommon colour, like Harriet Lane's. I never saw Henry Wainwright at Sidney Square, but he called several times at St. Peter Street, and remained a short time.

You spoke of seeing Mrs. King on 11th September, 1874, with some money?—Yes.

Did you see who gave it to her?—No.

By the LORD CHIEF JUSTICE—Do you know how much it was? —I don't know. She gave me £5 out of it. I should think it must have been £15 nearly.

Cross-examination continued—Her wedding ring was larger than the keeper, which is generally the case.

Are the buttons the police have shown you buttons of the same kind?—Yes.

You spoke of Mrs. King's cape and dress being trimmed only with buttons. Were several dozens used?—Yes; quite two dozen.

You never dressed Mrs. King's hair?—No, but I watched her dress it from 4th August to 11th September, 1874. I had sent on the letter to Mr. Martin's, and I had written to him before. I had expressed a wish to keep the children, but had talked of applying to the relieving officer; that was the only threat I used. I thought he might spare something for the children. I think he was in difficulties, or he would have paid me. He fixed November as the time when he would pay me. When I suggested reducing the amount from 25s. to 20s. he did not wish it.

On the first occasion before the magistrate did you not say Harriet Lane had gone to Brighton, and not that he had sent her?—I might have said that.

Did you not say, "She has gone down to Brighton"?—I said, "How very strange; she has no clothes." I am not certain.

By the LORD CHIEF JUSTICE—Which did you say?—I might have said either.

Cross-examination continued—With your recollection, can you speak positively?—No. I think there was a slight projection of the upper lip. She had very beautiful teeth. They did project slightly, but not enough to disfigure the mouth. Her mouth was large, but a nice shape.

The doctors were correct in saying that the remains were quite unrecognisable?—They were.

Re-examined by the ATTORNEY-GENERAL—Were the teeth in

40

Evidence for Prosecution.

the upper jaw or the lower jaw which projected slightly?—In the upper jaw—very slightly.

Was the cab you spoke of driving rapidly or slowly?—At first very slowly, and afterwards quickly. The traffic stopped it. The telegram I received on 17th October I gave to Mrs. Taylor and Mr. Eeles. They have lost it.

By the LORD CHIEF JUSTICE—What was Mrs. King's manner towards her children? Did it lead you to think she was fond of them or not?—She was very fond of them, more especially of the younger one, very fond indeed.

From the time she disappeared until this time, has any one, indirectly or directly, made any inquiry about these children? —No one except the aunt. I have still got the children.

HENRY POLLARD, examined—I am one of the clerks in the office of the Solicitor to the Treasury. I served two notices to produce a letter, upon the prisoners in Newgate, the first on 23rd October, 1875, and the second on 23rd November, 1875. These (produced) are copies of the notices.

Mrs. ELIZABETH TAYLOR, examined by the ATTORNEY- GENERAL—I am the wife of William Taylor, coachman, residing at 7 Clarendon Mews, Hyde Park, daughter of John Lane, of Waltham, who is employed in the gunpowder works there, and sister of Harriet Louisa Lane. I have several other sisters, Mrs. Allen being one of them. Before my sister Harriet lived with Mrs. Foster she resided in different other places in London, passing always as Mrs. King. I knew she had two children. Before she went to Sidney Square to Mrs. Foster's she occasionally came to see me and my husband. I went to see her more than once when she was living at Mrs. Foster's. I found she was living there as Mrs. King with her children. The last time I went to see her when she was living in Sidney Square was in the second week in August. On 11th September, or about that time, I was in Weymouth with my husband. On my return I found a letter from Miss Wilmore, who, I knew, was a friend of my sister. In consequence of that letter I went with Miss Wilmore and saw Henry Wainwright at his place of business. I said to him I had come upon a very unpleasant affair concern- ing the missing of my sister. I also said, " I am her sister, and that you can see." He replied, " Oh, yes! No doubt of that." He said he did not know where my sister was; and that he gave her £15 the day before she left Sidney Square, and that he had also given her £10 to provide an outfit to go to Brighton. He remarked that he had seen her on that occasion

41

The Wainwrights.

Mrs. Taylor in his shop in Whitechapel, and he said, on the first occasion, that she was gone away with one Teddy Frieake, who had come in for a large fortune, and he thought she had gone with this Teddy Frieake to the Pavilion Theatre, that he waited in his shop until ten o'clock, but she did not return. Several weeks after this I received a letter from Mr. Wainwright.

By the LORD CHIEF JUSTICE—You knew him as Mr. King?—Yes, although when I came to talk to him in the shop I knew he was Mr. Wainwright.

Examination continued—I and Miss Wilmore subsequently, in consequence of a letter I received, visited Mr. Wainwright again. He said he knew nothing of my sister, but that his foreman had seen her in a cab. He read me a letter and a telegram. He kept the letter in his hand, and read it out. The letter, as far as I can recollect, was as follows:—" I have the lady now under my protection, and I dare you or any one else to annoy her in any way." He also read the telegram, which said, " We are now off to Paris, and mean to have a jolly spree." Wainwright said the telegram came from Dover, and, I think, from Teddy Frieake. The third time I saw him was in the latter part of October or beginning of November. I saw him at his place of business. He gave me a little brandy and water. I asked him about my sister, and he said she was all right and enjoying her luxuries, and that when they had their frolic out, he supposed they would return. I never saw him again, and never heard any tidings of my sister. It was I who got Mr. Eeles to make inquiry. He was a friend of mine. My sister, I think, was twenty-four. She was not so tall as I am, and was of very slight build. Her hands and feet were very small, and her fingers very long, and she had a nice quantity of very light hair, rather bright. She had a decayed tooth in the upper jaw on the right-hand side. It was next the eye tooth, and rather observable when she talked or smiled. She had a very nice set of teeth. She had a scar on her leg, just below the knee, about the size of a florin; she had had an accident—a burn. She was in the habit of wearing a wedding ring and a keeper. I went to St. Saviour's dead-house and saw the remains. The hair was very much like my sister's; so were the feet and hands. She used to wear a pad and hairpins over it to fasten it, a kind of frizzette. I have had a pad shown to me which is similar to that she wore. I have seen her with her children. She appeared to be very fond indeed of them. I was in frequent communication with her; she used to write to me. Mr. Allen, my brother-in-law, gave me five envelopes; one had a letter in it—this (produced) is it. I gave it to Detective Forster. It

42

Evidence for Prosecution.

is my sister's writing. Some time in October Miss Wilmore **Mrs. Taylor**
showed me a telegram. I went to her place, The Grove,
Stratford, with Mr. Eeles to fetch it. I gave it to Mr. Eeles,
and have not seen it since. I am quite confident I never had it
back from Mr. Eeles. Mr. Allen brought me two buttons on a
card, just as you get them from a draper. My husband gave
them to Inspector Fox in my presence.

Cross-examined by Mr. BESLEY—At the first interview I had
with Henry Wainwright I was accompanied by Miss Wilmore.
I said to him, " Can you tell me where my sister is?" He
said, " I cannot tell you where she is; I only wish I could."
He also said, " The day before your sister was missing I gave
her £15, and she said she was going to Brighton." He also
said he gave her £10 for an outfit before she went. It was
at that same interview that he spoke of having waited at the
shop till ten o'clock, expecting her to return from the Pavilion
Theatre, and that he had never seen her from that time. It
was at the second interview that he told me some one had seen
my sister in a cab, and at the third interview he said he should
not continue to do as he had done for the children, and when
the first child was old enough he would give it an education.
The children are both girls. On the same occasion Wainwright
said, " Should she return, I shall not take her back. Can you
blame me?" I said, " Certainly not, under the circumstances."
All the three interviews with Wainwright took place at 84
Whitechapel Road. When he referred to the letter, he held it
in his hand. I did not see in whose writing the letter was which
Wainwright produced. I am not certain whether I was the first
of my family to see the remains; my father and my husband
went with me.

Until you were examined as a witness, had your attention
been called to the length of the feet?—Yes. Both I and my
father, who saw the remains together, noticed that before we
gave any evidence, and the same with regard to the hands.

At the time you said all the parts were like, but your
attention was not then called to the decayed tooth?—Yes, it
was. I saw that several of the teeth were missing then. No
one opened the mouth to show us the teeth.

By the LORD CHIEF JUSTICE—Had you thought beforehand
of the particular points to which you would direct your attention
when you saw the remains?—Yes. I thought I should recognise her by her hair, for one thing; by the decayed tooth, and
by her hands and feet.

What were the peculiarities of the hands and feet?—The
feet and hands were very slight, and she had long fingers.

43

The Wainwrights.

Mrs. Taylor Did you find these things in the remains that you examined?
—Yes, I think I did, as near as I could see.

The mark of the burn did not occur to you at that first examination?—No, it did not at that time.

By Mr. Besley—As a matter of fact, had your sister two marks, one on each leg?—No, only one. I am quite positive she had not two.

With regard to the five envelopes you received from your brother-in-law, Mr. Allen, and gave to Detective Forster, did you notice the envelope from which you took the letter?—Yes, I took the letter out and put it back again in the same envelope. The whole of the five appear to be in the same handwriting.

Re-examined by the Attorney-General—This is the envelope directed to my sister. Although my sister was brought up as a dressmaker, she was at one time a governess. She had had some education; she was a very good scholar. When I said some teeth were absent, I meant absent from the jaw of the body shown me, not that my sister had lost any teeth. I remember my father, when before the magistrate, speaking about a scar, and it was not until after I had given my evidence. I did not recollect till it was drawn to my attention.

By the Lord Chief Justice—You have, I suppose, no knowledge of the handwriting on these envelopes?—No.

The Attorney-General—Perhaps it would be as well to prove the handwriting at once, as I am in a position to do so.

G. W. Rogers George William Rogers, examined—I am now in the service of Messrs. Hounsell Brothers, in the Minories. I was formerly employed by Mr. Henry Wainwright. I have seen him write, and I know his handwriting well. I also know the handwriting of Thomas Wainwright. (The several letters introduced into the case—letters marked B and I, and the envelopes which contained I—were here handed to the witness, and stated by him to be in the handwriting of the prisoner, Henry Wainwright; also all these envelopes and the signature to the letter marked G, dated 21st January, 1875—not the body of the letter; also envelope and letter marked F, addressed to Miss Wilmore, 26 Maryland Street, Stratford.) There is no date to this one of 15th or 16th February, 1874, but both letter and envelope are Henry Wainwright's writing. The letter marked E, headed " Charing Cross Hotel," to the best of my belief is in Thomas Wainwright's handwriting.

(Mr. Besley and Mr. Moody expressed their intention of not cross-examining with reference to the handwriting of the prisoners.)

44

Evidence for Prosecution.

examined by Mr. Bantry.—At the Miss Wilmore
ro fringed earrings were shown to me. The earrings
. King wore had a fringe on them, and were very like
rn to me. They were not gold.

Adjourned till to-morrow.

Third Day—Wednesday, 24th November, 1875.

W. Taylor WILLIAM TAYLOR, examined by Mr. POLAND—I am a coach-man, and live at 7 Clarendon Mews, Hyde Park Square. My wife is a daughter of Mr. John Lane. I knew her sister Harriet. She used to visit us as Mrs. King about once in three weeks or a fortnight, and she sometimes wrote. She had been in the habit of writing us at the Mews for very nearly four years. On 30th August, last year, I and my wife went out of town together. I saw Harriet Lane at my house three days before that. My wife was out of town. Harriet was then well, and I chatted with her. That was the last time I saw her. During the time we were out of town at my uncle's, near Yeovil, a letter came from her—that was early in September, the 4th or 5th. After our holidays we returned to town. On 15th September last I and my wife went to the dead-house at St. Saviour's Church, and saw the remains of a woman. In my opinion they were those of Harriet Lane. I recognised them by the small feet and the hands, and the colour of the hair. The last time she was at my house I noticed she complained of toothache, and she pointed to the right-hand side of the upper jaw as the place. She had a decayed tooth there, which was perceptible when she laughed or smiled.

By the LORD CHIEF JUSTICE—Did you ever observe it?—Yes.
Was it to the tooth that she pointed?—Yes.

Examination continued—Her two front upper teeth pro-jected a little. I remember two jet buttons being brought to my house by Mr. Allen, my brother-in-law. I gave them to Inspector Fox on a card in the same state as I received them. My wife was not present at the time.

Cross-examined by Mr. BESLEY—Before I saw the remains I was told there were no features by which I could recognise them. I knew I was going to see remains unrecognisable by features. I mentioned when before the magistrate that there was a decayed tooth, but I omitted all mention of the toothache. It did not occur to me at the time. The hair I saw was of the same colour, and I said when before the magistrate that by the decayed tooth and hair, and the small hands and feet, I had no doubt it was Harriet Lane.

46

Evidence for Prosecution.

Cross-examined by Mr. MOODY—While the envelope and the **W. Taylor** letter were in the possession of my wife I looked at them. My wife or I—I won't be certain which—took the letter out and read it. The next day we gave them to Detective Forster, and he also read the letter. We showed it to him because we thought it important. We did not show it to any one else. The other relatives did not observe it, and thought the papers were envelopes only. I thought it was an important letter. I saw my wife put it back into the envelope.

By the ATTORNEY-GENERAL—When Forster had looked at it, he put it back into the same envelope. They had heard of **Frieake**.

By the LORD CHIEF JUSTICE—What was the date of the post-mark?—5th September.

Mrs. SOPHIA ALLEN, examined—I am a sister of the deceased. **Mrs. Allen** I am the wife of Thomas Allen, and reside at Oldfield Road, Maidenhead. Harriet Louisa Lane was younger than I. She was the seventh daughter; I am the fifth. Harriet was a trifle taller than I. I have compared heights with her several times. standing back to back and measuring ourselves. She had peculiarly small hands and fingers. I remember an accident happening to her when she was about ten years old. There was a poker in the fire; while she was sitting on a little stool by the fire-grate the poker fell out, burning the right leg and leaving a scar. She cried very much. I fetched the oil for it to be dressed.

By the LORD CHIEF JUSTICE—Whereabouts was it on the leg?—To the best of my recollection, about 4 inches below the knee, on the outside of the leg. It had the appearance of a scar, and seemed to be drawn very much. I was about nineteen years old then.

Examination continued—The last time I recollect seeing the scar was about six years ago. It is three years come January since I left my father's house. My sister left about a year or eighteen months before me. She was well educated, and at one time she was a governess in a family. She afterwards became a dressmaker. On one occasion, about six years ago, I and my sister were photographed together at Shoreditch, in a standing posture. (Photograph produced and identified.) I was dressed in a blue silk and my sister in a black dress. She is the lady on the right hand. She had light hair of a golden tinge.

Cross-examined by Mr. BESLEY—My sister had not two

The Wainwrights.

Mrs Allen marks—one on each leg; she had only one. The mark was drawn very much.

At the Police Court did you not say it was about the size of a two-shilling piece, only a little drawn?—To the best of my recollection, I think I said so then, but now that I have come to refer back, it seems to me that it was very much drawn. Nothing until my sister disappeared, or until the inquest or police inquiry, occurred to call it to my mind. She said when we were together that, should anything happen to her, we should know her by the mark. I also have a mark on my forehead. I did not see the remains.

The LORD CHIEF JUSTICE—I saw the accident, and was present when the burn was dressed. The scar was in the same place as the burn, and I have no doubt it was the scar of the burn. To the best of my recollection it was about the size of a two-shilling piece.

John Lane JOHN LANE, examined by Mr. BEASLEY—I reside at Waltham Cross, and am gas manager to the Royal Gunpowder Mills at Waltham Abbey. I have had nine daughters born and christened, and two sons. I had a daughter named Harriet Louisa. She was born at Weymouth. I don't exactly recollect the year, but she would be now about twenty-four years of age. She was my youngest daughter, and she was brought up as a milliner and dressmaker at Waltham Cross. Whilst there she was in the habit of coming backwards and forwards to her home. She served her time there with Mrs. Bray, and she then went to London when about twenty-one. She used to frequently come and visit me and her mother during 1871, 1872, and 1873. She never stopped very long without coming to us.

Do you remember the last occasion on which she came to visit you?—I cannot recollect particularly about the time—that is, I cannot say to a day or two—but it was some time in August, 1874.

Did you know where she was living?—No; I never knew properly where she was living then, but I was informed she was living somewhere in Whitechapel.

Did you know what name she passed under?—I knew she was going by the name of Mrs. King.

Did you know she had at that time two children?—No, I did not know she had two. I knew she had one.

Was she said to be married?—It was supposed she was married, but I could not say that she was. She was on very friendly terms with us. No angry words ever came out of our

48

Evidence for Prosecution.

mouths towards her, or out of hers towards us, to my recollec- John Lane
tion. I have not seen her alive since that occasion in August,
1874. She appeared then to be in perfect good health. I
never saw Mr. King at all during that time. I first heard she
was missing in 1874—about the beginning of September, the
10th, 11th, or 12th. I set about making inquiries with my
daughters, and continued to do so, but without result. We could
not hear of anything to our satisfaction. I remember first
hearing the name of Frieake very soon after she was missing.
We did not at first try to find Mr. Frieake, but early last
February, I think, we tried to find him out, and we did not
see him.

By the LORD CHIEF JUSTICE—Was that before or after you
saw Henry Wainwright?—Before. I cannot say the day. I
know it was in very dark days and in very bad weather.

Examination continued—Where did you go to see Mr.
Frieake?—I went to the office of Mr. Frieake, in his auction
room, in Whitechapel Road, while he was selling there. Mr.
Eeles (or Mr. Fowler, as he is called) went with me. He was the
gentleman who took me there.

By the LORD CHIEF JUSTICE—You and Mr. Eeles went to
make the inquiry?—I had only seen Mr. Eeles once before that,
but my daughters and he had been making inquiries.

Examination continued—After having some conversation
with Frieake, we went direct (I and Mr. Eeles) to see Henry
Wainwright. I had never seen him before to my knowledge. I
think we found him in the front part of the house, just going
in, on the right-hand side of Whitechapel Road, just below the
church. It was a brushmaker's place of business. He was
pointed out to me as Mr. Wainwright by Mr. Eeles. He invited
us upstairs. I said, "I am Mr. Lane, and I have come to
know what has become of my daughter," because I wished to
know where she was. He seemed to make very light of it. I
don't mind his answer, but he said she was all right, she was
right enough. I asked him to let me know where she was,
for I wanted to know whether she was dead or alive, and if she
was dead, to let me know. He said she was all right, that she
had gone away with Mr. Frieake. To the best of my recollection,
I don't remember who he said Mr. Frieake was, but I am certain
he used that name. We then said we had seen Mr. Frieake, the
auctioneer, and that he denied all knowledge of knowing anything about my daughter. Then Wainwright said that Mr.
Frieake was not the man at all; it was a different man altogether
—a man with no moustache, or only just a little moustache.

E   49

The Wainwrights.

John Lane This was the only description he gave of him. He gave me no
address. I said I was determined to find out my daughter;
if not, I should take higher steps to find her.

Have you told us all you said?—I believe I have.

Was it at that time you showed him a letter? Was it you or
Mr. Eeles?—I never saw him but once, and I think it was I
who passed the letter into his hands myself. It was the letter
I got from Mr. Frieake. I think I should know it again. (Letter
produced.) I cannot read writing, but I believe this to be the
one I showed Wainwright. He took it in his hand and opened
it. I cannot say whether he read it or not. He kept it before
him, and seemed to read it. I said to him, "This is the letter
which came from Mr. Frieake, and he denies all knowledge of
my daughter."

By the LORD CHIEF JUSTICE—How long was he looking at it?
—It might have been a minute or two. I cannot say exactly,
but he unfolded and looked at it.

You cannot read yourself, but you have seen persons read
writing, and you can form a judgment as to whether, from the
way he took the letter and looked at it, he read it?—Well, I
supposed at the time he was reading it.

Examination continued—I think I have told all that I
said when I handed the letter. I said, besides, "If I cannot
find where my daughter is, it must come to an exposure."

Did Mr. Eeles say anything in your hearing about the letter?
—He said something, but I don't know what. I said, "If it
comes to an exposure, it will be worse for you than for me";
and he said, "If it comes to an exposure it must; I know it
will be worse for me." That is the only interview I had with
Henry Wainwright. In the following January I received my
daughter Harriet's boxes. On 14th September this year I was
taken to see the remains of a dead body. The body was not
shown to me till the 15th, by Inspector Fox and some other
gentlemen. It was in portions, cut up.

Did you form any judgment as to whose body it was?—The
moment I looked through the glass I seemed to feel that it was
my daughter's.

What did you recognise it by?—I recognised it by the hair,
the feet, the legs, and the hands. I was so satisfied nothing
would ever turn me the moment I saw her. The legs appeared
to me to be perfect. The feet and hands were quite perfect,
only very dark. I could not see any natural colour. The hair
was just the same as that of my daughter. She had small hands

Evidence for Prosecution.

and long fingers. I don't properly know her height, but, as John Lane nearly as I could judge, she was 5 feet high.

Was there anything else you recognised her by?—Nothing. I knew she had a scar upon her leg, but I had not seen it of late years. It has never been shown to me on the body, but I have made a statement of it. I know as a fact she had a scar on her leg. I could not remember for some time on which leg, but it proved to be on the right. It was some years since I saw it —six, seven, eight, nine, or ten years.

By the LORD CHIEF JUSTICE—Do you remember the accident happening?—I was not present at the time, but I was given to understand that it was done by a poker.

Cross-examined by Mr. BESLEY—Did you know of your daughter being a governess at all?—I understood she was a governess for some little time after she was out of her apprenticeship.

After she was out of her apprenticeship, did she not go to London to go into business with another young woman?—Yes.

How soon after she had gone to London did you know she was living at Whitechapel?—About two or three weeks.

You never had her address, and never went to any lodgings of hers?—Never in my life.

From the time she left home you believed she was provided for?—I did.

And you know nothing of any pawning of her clothing?—I was not aware of any.

You are unable to fix the date when she last came to Waltham? You spoke of August, 1874. Are you sure it was August?—I am sure it was in August—either the beginning or the middle.

Might it not have been at the end of July?—No, it was not. I am almost sure of that.

Long intervals often occurred between her coming to see you?—I can't say often, but it has occurred, sometimes six or seven weeks.

You have given an account of going with Mr. Eeles to Henry Wainwright. Let me ask you, is this what occurred— did Eeles say to Henry Wainwright, " Here is a letter that has come from Frieake, the auctioneer " ?—Yes.

By the LORD CHIEF JUSTICE—He mentioned the word " auctioneer " ?—He did.

Cross-examination continued—And did Wainwright immediately say, " The auctioneer is not the man " ?—He said he was not the man.

The Wainwrights.

John Lane   By the Lord Chief Justice—Did he say that before or after he looked at the letter?—I think it was after.

The learned counsel asked whether he said it immediately? —I am not quite certain whether it was before or after.

Cross-examination continued—Is it a fact that he held the letter for a moment or two, and that conversation was going on all the time?—I don't believe it was. He stopped for a time to look at the letter, and then the conversation went on.

Is this accurate then—"He had the letter for a moment or two. I cannot say whether the conversation was not going on while he held the letter"?—I am not certain.

Then what I have just read may be correct?

The Lord Chief Justice—I cannot allow that. We must be regular in every case. You must put questions and not read anything.

Cross-examination continued—Can you say whether the conversation was going on all the time Henry Wainwright held the letter?—I believe not.

Have you always said the same?—That is my belief.

Are you able to tell me, yes or no, whether you have always said the same?—To the best of my knowledge I have always said so.

Did you mention the word "exposure" first?—I mentioned it, but I cannot say at what part of the story. He said, "If it comes to an exposure it must." I said, "If it does, it will be heavier for you than for me." Mrs. Taylor was the tallest of my daughters, slightly taller than Harriet. I have two daughters shorter than Harriet. Harriet was not the shortest. I judge Mrs. Allen to be about the same height as Harriet.

When you were asked about the height, did you say that Harriet was outside five feet?—I judged her to be not more than five feet. I did not believe her to be more.

The Lord Chief Justice—That expression, "outside five feet," might have two meanings. It might mean five feet at the extreme, or it might mean over five feet.

Cross-examination continued—Before you saw the remains, had you been told the features were unrecognisable?—I heard so.

Had Mrs. Taylor seen them before you?—We saw them together.

Did you speak together upon the points upon which you relied for identity before you went to see the remains?—Not a word.

52

Evidence for Prosecution.

You went away thoroughly satisfied?—I did. Directly I went into the police office I mentioned the scar on the leg.

The LORD CHIEF JUSTICE—When did the fact of her having a scar on the leg occur to your mind?—When I was giving my first evidence.

Cross-examination continued—You had not seen the scar for many years?—I had not. I knew there was one. She was seven or eight years old at the time the accident happened.

Re-examined by the ATTORNEY-GENERAL—I gave my evidence first in the Police Court and saw the remains after. When before the magistrate I mentioned the scar. I have had nine daughters born and christened; three are dead. Two died young; one was a twin. Harriet was the youngest of my daughters.

ERNEST GEORGE EELES, examined by the ATTORNEY-GENERAL —I live at the office of the Charity Organisation Society at Wandsworth. I am an inquiry officer there. It is part of my duty to make inquiries about people. I have known Mr. and Mrs. Taylor for some years. I saw Harriet Lane once only. I knew she was the sister of Mrs. Taylor. I had known the Taylors about six or seven years. I first heard that Harriet Lane was missing in January of the present year. The Taylors came to see me, and, in consequence of a conversation I had with them, I, at their request, instituted inquiries. In prosecuting my inquiries I represented myself to be Mr. Fowler, because Harriet Lane knew me by the name of Eeles, and I thought possibly if she heard that a person named Eeles was making inquiries after her it might have the opposite effect to that desired. I went to Henry Wainwright at 215 Whitechapel Road, I think about 16th January of the present year. I saw him first outside the house. I came up rather behind him, put my hand against his shoulder, and said, "Mr. Wainwright, I think." He said, "Yes." I said, "I wish to speak privately for a minute." He said, "Step inside." I said to him, "Do you know a person named Mrs. King or Harriet Lane?" He said, "Yes" I then said, "You have known her about four years?" He said, "Yes." I said, "She has had two children by you?" He said, "Yes." I said, "Where is she now?" or "Do you know where she is?" I cannot remember the words exactly. He said, "I do not know." The surveyor for the Sun Fire Office was outside as he told me, and they were going across to measure the premises at No. 84. He said, "Are you in a hurry?" I said, "No." He said, "Will you

53

The Wainwrights.

E. G. Eeles step across?" I said, "Yes," and we went across. There was some measuring done at No. 84, and after it was over we returned to No. 215. I then asked him when he had last seen Harriet Lane. He said, "Some time ago now." I said, "Where do you think she is?" He said he thought she had gone away with a man named Teddy Frieake, who had lately come into about £2000; "there are five brothers who had had £11,000 left between them; no doubt they are enjoying themselves, and she will turn up again when the money is all spent." He said that Frieake was an auctioneer.

By the LORD CHIEF JUSTICE—Are you sure?—I am under the impression that he did. I know he said so on a subsequent occasion, if not then.

Examination continued—I gave him my name as Fowler, and my address at the post office, High Street, Wandsworth, if he should want to write to me. My impression is that I gave it to him as some sort of satisfaction at the time. Shortly after that interview I saw Mrs. Taylor, and she gave me the letter marked E, and a telegram. I have lost the telegram. I have made diligent search for it, and I cannot find it. I have no recollection of having given it to anybody. I then went to Mr. Frieake, of 11 Coleman Street. I saw his address on one of the handbills notifying that a sale was to take place at his auction room, Aldgate. I saw Mr. Frieake at Coleman Street, and showed him the letter that I had got from Mrs. Taylor. I am not quite positive whether I showed him the telegram or not. I had some conversation with him, and he showed me his letter book and some of his writing. After a little time we left the office and went together to Henry Wainwright at 215 Whitechapel Road.

On this second occasion did you see Wainwright?—Yes.

What did you say to him?—"Mr. Wainwright, I have found Mr. Frieake." He said, "Oh, this is not the Mr. Frieake. You have made a mistake." Frieake thereupon said, "What is this, Harry?" He replied, "Oh, it's a mistake altogether." This conversation took place just outside the house, on the opposite side of the road to No. 215. We crossed the road and went into a front room upstairs, in No. 215. Frieake about this time said to Wainwright, "You are getting me into a mess that I know nothing of, and you may do me a serious injury." In reply to that Wainwright said, "You are not the Teddy Frieake I mean. The Teddy Frieake I mean is a billiard player. I have seen him frequently at Purcell's, the Philharmonic, and the Nell Gwynne." Frieake then said, "Do you mean to say

54

Evidence for Prosecution.

you have ever known another Teddy Frieake and not inquired
who he was? I don't believe you will find another Teddy
Frieake with the name spelt the same as mine in the London
Directory. If you know anything about the affair, why don't
you tell them at once? I saw you with a fair-haired girl a short
time ago. Is that the one?" Wainwright said, "No; I can
produce her in five minutes." He said that Frieake was a young
man with no whiskers, and scarcely any moustache, not above a
dozen or a score of hairs. After that conversation I left. I left
just before Mr. Frieake, I think.

I saw Mrs. Taylor again, and afterwards Mr. Lane. I went
with Mr. Lane to Mr. Frieake's auction rooms. I and Mr. Lane
at that time had a conversation with Mr. Frieake. He gave
me this letter marked A (produced) in an envelope. I afterwards gave the letter and envelope to Mrs. Taylor. I think the
letter was not in the envelope; I did not get the letter back from
Mrs. Taylor. When I got the letter and envelope I and Mr.
Lane went to see Henry Wainwright at No. 215. He was not in
at first. We waited for him, and he came in after a short
interval. I said to him, "This is Mr. Lane, Harriet Lane's
father." He asked us to go upstairs, and we went up. Mr.
Lane said, "Where is my daughter?" He said, "I do not
know." Mr. Lane said, "If she is dead, tell me; and if alive,
let me know where she is." Wainwright said that he did not
know where she was, but he would do all he could to try and
find her. Mr. Lane said, "I am determined to find her; if
it comes to an exposure it must, but that will be worse for you
than for us." During the conversation Mr. Lane was pacing
backwards and forwards, wringing his hands in great agony of
mind. I showed this letter to Mr. Wainwright, told him I had
received it from Mr. Frieake, and asked him whether he could
give any explanation of it. He appeared to read it, and while
he had it in his hand I said, "Can you tell me what this part
alludes to?" pointing to that part, "If Harry and yourself
could see me to-morrow evening, we may be able to arrange
matters satisfactorily as the time is now very short." He said
he did not know what it meant. He appeared to read the letter,
and afterwards during the interview he gave it back to me. I
do not remember that he made any further remark upon it.
[Letter read. "Sunday night. My dear Mr. Frieake, I trust
you will pardon me writing to you, but I feel I ought to apologise
for my rude behaviour to you last evening, after the kindness
I have received from you. I had been worried and annoyed
during the day, which caused me to be very excited. I felt very

55

The Wainwrights.

E. G. Eeles sorry you left me so cross. I did not go out after, as you wished me not to. I have well considered the subject we spoke of, and think if Harry and yourself could see me to-morrow evening, we might be able to arrange matters satisfactorily, as the time is now very short. Please write by return, and let me know if you will call, or if I shall meet you anywhere. For the future I will promise to behave more ladylike. Should I not hear from you, I shall consider I am not forgiven. I remain, very truly yours,—L. KING."]

I have no means of fixing the date of my second interview with Henry Wainwright. I called upon him after that interview several times, and asked him about the missing woman. On one occasion he said that one of the workmen had seen her in a cab somewhere in the West End, but I forget the place he named. On another occasion he said that Miss Wilmore had seen her in a cab, and named the place, somewhere in the West End. He said on another occasion that she would turn up again some day, when the money was all gone. The last time I saw him I made inquiries about her. To the best of my recollection it was in the early part of July this year. I cannot find the telegram Mrs. Taylor gave me, but I read it. It was on the ordinary telegraph paper, I think. It was from E. Frieake, Dover, to Miss Wilmore, 6 The Grove, Stratford—I cannot recollect the date—"We are just off to Paris, and mean to have a jolly spree."

Mrs. Taylor   Mrs. TAYLOR, re-examined—Mr. Eeles gave me the letter which has been read, in an envelope; I have lost it. I have searched for it everywhere I could think of.

Cross-examined by Mr. BESLEY—I believe I gave it to Mr. Fowler.

E. G. Eeles   ERNEST GEORGE EELES, examination continued—I have searched for the letter, but I think I returned it to Mrs. Taylor.

Mrs. Taylor   Mrs. TAYLOR, re-examined—Mr. Eeles gave the letter back to me in an envelope; I did not give it back to him afterwards.

E. G. Eeles   ERNEST GEORGE EELES, examination continued—I had the envelope when I had the letter. I took the letter out of the envelope and gave him the letter, but not the envelope.

Mrs. Taylor   Mrs. TAYLOR, re-examined—I read the envelope which I have lost. This is the letter. (Produced.) I have got another

56

Evidence for Prosecution.

letter from Miss Wilmore; this is the letter I got from Eeles.
It is the envelope of this letter which I have lost, and looked
for and cannot find.

ERNEST GEORGE EELES, cross-examined by Mr. BESLEY—
Before I saw Henry Wainwright I cannot be positive where I
had an interview with Miss Wilmore. I made no memorandum
of my conversation with her. The name of Frieake was not
mentioned to me by her. I had his name from Mrs. Taylor.
I cannot say how she got the information. The first time I saw
Wainwright I had not had the letter from the Charing Cross
Hotel, and knew nothing about it. I pursued my inquiries
about the young man named Frieake with Miss Wilmore. Mrs.
Taylor called my attention to the name of Frieake being on an
auctioneer's bill, and that was how I came to go to Mr. Frieake.

Is it true that for some time you believed that both Edward
Frieake and Henry Wainwright were telling you untruths?—I
did for some time think they were deceiving me.

Did you say once to the prisoner you should go to his
private house in Tredegar Square and see his wife?—I don't
recollect saying so. I never said I should go and tell his wife
he had had two children. I am positive about that. I was
never in doubt about it, though at the moment I said, in answer
to the question, "I don't recollect."

The LORD CHIEF JUSTICE—A witness must have allowance
made for such a question being suddenly put to him.

Cross-examination continued—Did you afterwards believe
that both Edward Frieake and Wainwright were telling you the
truth?—No; I never believed that they were telling me the
truth, but I never saw Frieake afterwards.

By the LORD CHIEF JUSTICE—You believed all along that
they were deceiving you?—Yes.

Cross-examination continued—Did you learn from what was
said, or from the surveyor's measuring, that there was a dispute
with a fire office about the burning of Wainwright's premises?—
I heard there was, but I cannot say how. I did not say to
Wainwright, "I shall expect some money when you get the
money from the fire office."

Did you ever say that if the money were given to you, you
would give up making inquiries, and that you would guarantee
that no further inquiries should be made?—No, I did not.

Did you ever write in those terms, or anything like them?
—No, not in those terms at all.

Is there passing in your mind terms like these?—No.

57

The Wainwrights.

E. G. Eeles Did you write to Henry Wainwright?—I did, but I have not got his reply. I bought goods from him. The letters referred to the inquiries I was making about him.

Did he refuse in any way to give you money?—No, never; decidedly not.

When were the goods bought from him?—I cannot recollect. I have no receipt or invoice. I bought them, but they are not settled for yet.

By the LORD CHIEF JUSTICE—What was about the date?—About March or April.

And what was the amount?—About 17s. I bought one lot of goods, and no more.

Did you write to Mrs. Wainwright at Tredegar Square?—I did not. I addressed letters to Mr. Wainwright at Tredegar Square—not above two or three. After I had the goods I went as often to 215 Whitechapel Road as before.

By the ATTORNEY-GENERAL—What were the goods you bought?—Brushes and mats.

You have been asked whether you did not think both the prisoner and Edward Frieake were deceiving you. Up to what time did you believe it?—I believed they were deceiving me up to 14th September, when I first heard of this trouble.

By the LORD CHIEF JUSTICE—When did you first hear Frieake mentioned as "Teddy Frieake"—who first mentioned the name of "Teddy Frieake"?—Henry Wainwright mentioned that name to me first when I saw him on the first occasion after we came back from measuring the premises of No. 84; it was before I had seen Mr. Frieake at Coleman Street, and on the occasion of my first visit to Mr. Wainwright.

E. W. Frieake EDWARD WILLIAM FRIEAKE, examined—I am an auctioneer and public-house valuer, with offices at 11 Coleman Street, City, and auction rooms at 14 and 15 Aldgate. I have been in business about five years. I have known Henry Wainwright familiarly for twelve or fourteen years. I was on terms of intimacy with him for many years; he used to address me as "Teddy" or "Frieaky," and I used to address him as "Harry." I have lived at Bow for nearly sixteen years. Up to September last I was on friendly terms with him. In September last year I received by post this letter (produced) at my office in Coleman Street. I read it, of course, but I did not know the writer. I never knew a person named L. King to my knowledge. I was utterly astonished, and could not imagine what it referred to. As far as I recollect, it was received about the 29th, 30th, or

58

Evidence for Prosecution.

31st of August of last year; it was on a Monday morning. My **E. W. Frieake** father was at the office at the time. I took it home and showed it to my friends, after showing it to my father. For a time it was made rather a matter of joke in my family circle, and then it passed from my mind.

I recollect Eeles coming to my office as Mr. Fowler at the latter end of January or the beginning of February. He was alone. He made several, as I thought, impertinent inquiries, and showed a letter. This letter (E) is it to the best of my belief; I recollect Charing Cross Hotel on the top of it. It was signed "E. Frieake," leaving out the "W" and the "a." I always sign my name "Edward W. Frieake." I read it, and expressed my astonishment to Eeles. It was not written by me, and I know nothing about the matters referred to in it, or of a telegram which he also showed me. I produced my letter book, and said that he could look at any letters in it to see my writing. I then went with him to see Henry Wainwright at No. 215 Whitechapel Road. I asked to see Wainwright, and I said, "Harry, I want to see you privately." Eeles was behind me, and Wainwright, who met us, ushered us up into the first floor sitting-room. I then said, "This individual" (alluding to Fowler) "has been to my office and accused me of taking a girl away by the name of King, and has said that you are his informant to that effect." He said, "Oh, Teddy, old man, it is not you; it is another Teddy Frieake." I said, "Well, it is a very serious imputation to cast upon my character, and, should it get to the ears of the lady I am engaged to be married to, it will very likely ruin my happiness," or something to that effect. I said, "What sort of man is this Teddy Frieake, who has represented me"? He said, "Oh, he is only a young fellow about twenty-three or twenty-four, with a slight black moustache," and I think he said, "and a very little whisker, and has lately come into a lot of money." I then appealed to Fowler, and asked him whether he was satisfied that I was not the man alluded to. Before that I asked him where he had known this Teddy Frieake, and he said, "At the King's Head billiard rooms, Fenchurch Street, and the Philharmonic." I asked him whether he had ever seen me at either of those places, and he said, "No." I said, "Well, it is a strange thing that you should have known another Teddy Frieake and not have asked him whether he had relations living at Bow, as mine is not a Brown, Jones, or Robinson name." He said he had principally known him as Teddy. I said, "If I had met another Henry Wainwright, and been introduced to

59

The Wainwrights.

E. W. Frieake him, I should have asked him whether he had any relations in Whitechapel," and that, as mine was a very peculiar name, I was surprised that he had not made any inquiries about the said Teddy Frieake when he first met him. I turned round to Fowler and said, "As far as £10 or £20 would go, I would give it willingly to find out the person who has represented me, as it might be a very serious matter for me." I said, "Who is the fair girl I saw you with a few weeks before or since?" In fact, I had followed them into a public-house. Fowler then left, and I had some conversation with Wainwright alone. I said, "Harry, old man, if you know anything about this girl's where-abouts, why don't you ease their minds and let them know?" He said, "Teddy, old man, this is only a get-up to extort money from me; the girl is all right." I think that was all that passed.

When I heard of this matter I went to the police station, Borough, and gave my card, and saw Superintendent Garforth, to whom I gave information. The entries in my diary of this year (produced) are in my handwriting, all but one. From that I have very little doubt that I saw Henry Wainwright on 11th September, 1874. He asked me to send a cart down at six o'clock on that evening to No. 84 Whitechapel Road. It would be early in the morning as I passed up to town. He was going to give me a sale of surplus stock. I was in the habit of sending carts there. The cart left my office at 6.15 that evening; that is the time it is booked by the carman's bill, until a certain time when he charges me with it; he has charged me for two hours. He was not my carman. He occupied the ground floor of the premises which I occupy the first floor of. I do not know where he is now.

I never recollect seeing Thomas Wainwright in my life; I may have seen him; there is something familiar about his face, but I never recollect having any intercourse with him. I did not know that Henry had a brother Thomas. I have worn a beard and moustache ever since I was twenty-one or twenty-two. I have my portrait, taken years ago, in my pocket.

Cross-examined by Mr. BESLEY—We were young fellows together in the neighbourhood of Bow. That was the commence-ment of my knowledge of Wainwright. I have not been as intimate with him for the last two or three years as I used to be. I have not gone about with him lately, but I used to see his family several nights in the week. There had been no cold-ness between us, we were on perfectly good terms. The transaction of my selling goods for him was about July or August, at the time of his difficulties, when he was making

60

Evidence for Prosecution.

his composition. The goods were some of his surplus stock. E. W. Frieake
I think the goods were only partially lotted when his manager,
Rogers, came and finished them at my rooms. The goods were
not considerable in number. I believe the van only went twice
for them; I believe it went in the evening and in the morning.
The entry in my diary is Friday, September 11; I made that as
soon as I entered the office, and I have no doubt that I saw
Wainwright on the morning of the 11th, and received directions
to take the van there at six o'clock. This "evening, six
o'clock" is in my writing. I am certain that the order was
executed, because I have been paid for the cart. The goods
were in my possession some time before they were put up for
auction, and the fire occurred in November, some six weeks
after the sale. I did not act for Wainwright in any way after
the fire. I was asked to be a witness by the company, and also
by Wainwright. Fowler came to me in January, 1875. The
fire was in November, 1874, and my visit to Wainwright was
early in 1875. I was to be a witness for him in reference to
the action against him. I supplied him with an account for the
sale, and I have a claim against him, and he has one against
me. It is unsettled. He said that Frieake had come into a
lot of money, and as soon as it was spent the girl would return.
He also said, "You will hear nothing more about it." When
he said, "This is a get up to extort money from me," Fowler
had left.

Cross-examined by Mr. MOODY—I don't think I said before
the magistrate that the face of Thomas was familiar to me as
that of a person I had frequently seen in the neighbourhood
of Bow; I said it was a face I had seen at Bow, but could not
call to mind. After this was said about it being an attempt
to extort money, I took no further steps, although I said that
I was willing to spend money to investigate it. It entirely
passed from my memory, because, knowing Wainwright as I
did, I naturally believed him. I am speaking from memory
as to the date when I received the letter. I know it was a
Monday morning, but I have nothing to guide me but my
memory as to the particular Monday morning, except the
expression in the letter, "Sunday night." My young lady
called my attention to it, where I was on that Saturday evening.
That was an after-conversation between me and the lady I was
going to marry. Independent of that conversation, I feel certain
it was on a Monday morning, because when this came up I
referred to two or three things which still more fixed it. I
examined the paper, the envelope, and postmark. I carried it

61

The Wainwrights.

W. Frieake in my pocket some time, and I taxed my clerk as to whether he knew anything of it.

Re-examined by the ATTORNEY-GENERAL—The letters A.U. were on the envelope. I know from my diary that I got the order to send the van to Wainwright's place, No. 84, that day. It would get there in a quarter of an hour, have some goods put into it, and come back to my salerooms. The sale took place on 11th October, a month after. I don't remember how many goods there were. There were brushes and things of that sort. I gave the letter, which I did not understand, to Mr. Lane, and the envelope with it.

By the LORD CHIEF JUSTICE—When the first parties came to me I did not recollect the letter, not till I got home, and then I repeated the conversation between Fowler, Wainwright, and myself, and my lady called my attention to it, and my recollection was brought back to it.

A. Woodward ALFRED COOPER WOODWARD, examined—I am a clerk in the telegraph message branch of the General Post Office. I produce the telegraph message books of October last from the Admiralty Pier, Dover, and also from the Eastern District of London, the Stratford post office, and the Walham Green post office. The original telegraphic messages which are handed in by any person sending a telegram are sent to my branch, and after being kept for a month are sent to the mill to be reduced to pulp. These papers would be destroyed at the end of three months.

P. Crofts PETER CROFTS, examined—I am one of the telegraph clerks on the Admiralty Pier, Dover. I attended there daily in October, 1874. I find an entry in one of the books in my writing. It is the book in which the messages which are handed in are recorded. These messages would be telegraphed to London. Three telegraphic messages in the name of Frieake were sent in on 17th October.

Cross-examined by Mr. MOODY—The messages are in my writing. I make the entries at the close of the day. We copy them off at the close of the day from the original messages, not from any other document.

Re-examined by the ATTORNEY-GENERAL—The three messages are numbered consecutively 4029 to 4031 inclusive. Each telegram has a number impressed upon it. We do not number them at the time they are sent in; we number them up in the evening when we enter them up. There is no number on the message when it is sent in, but we number them in the evening

Evidence for Prosecution.

when we enter them up. If a man comes to the office and sends a telegram, it is put on a file face downwards after the message is sent, in the order in which it is sent in, and in the evening we take them off the file, numbering them at the same time. We look through to see that they are in their places as when they are handed in. The three messages in the name of Frieake are consecutive in my book. Frieake to London is one message, Frieake to London is another, and Frieake to Stratford is another. I should say that those messages were sent off between four and six o'clock.

ALICE BERRY, examined—I am a clerk in the Eastern District post office, and was so on 17th October, 1874. It was my duty if a telegraphic message came there to write it out and forward it. I find in my book on 17th October an entry, "Wainwright, Dover Pier." That is a telegram addressed to Wainwright from Dover Pier. I did not write it out—that was the duty of the instrument clerk, Catherine Folley—but I should put it in the envelope and send it out, and make an entry whence it comes, or to whom it is addressed, or the name of the office from which it is sent. Whitechapel Road is in our district, both 84 and 215, but not all parts of it.

Cross-examined by Mr. BESLEY—I know that of my own knowledge, and from the writing in the book. I have no numbers of Whitechapel Road in the books. No one has told me that 215 and 84 are in my district, but I know it because we send telegrams to Mr. Wainwright; this telegram to him is entered in the book. We have sent telegrams to him at 215 on other occasions; I believe 215 is my district, and I think No. 84 is, but I am not sure.

Re-examined by Mr. POLAND—If a telegram comes which is not in our district I think it would be sent on to another office.

PHILIP VINCENT, examined—I am a clerk in charge of the telegraph department at Walham Green, in the south-western district. I have seen the prisoner Thomas there. He resided at Rosamond's Cottage, but I never had occasion to go to his residence. I believe from telegrams received, and which he has sent from our office, that he lived at Parson's Green. I cannot say whether I have read the telegrams he sent in; I should read them if Little, the other clerk, was engaged at the instrument, and if I was engaged at the instrument Little would have to read them. Thomas Wainright has sent several

The Wainwrights.

Philip Vincent telegrams from the office. The last message I remember him sending was in December, 1874; that is the last entered in his name. I do not recollect any message which I read and sent; it is Little's business to make a memorandum in the proper book of messages sent out. He is not now in the service of the post office, but he was during all October, 1874. If I was at the instrument when a message came I should write it down, but his business was to write them in the abstract book. The messages are destroyed periodically. Parson's Green is in my district. I know Rosamond's Cottage there.

J. A. Little　　JOHN ALLEN LITTLE, examined—I am a pastry cook at the Queen's Hotel, Norwood. I was formerly telegraph clerk, and was employed at Walham Green two months. I left in November. I do not know Thomas Wainwright at all. It was my duty at the close of each day to enter in the abstract book the messages received for delivery in my district. All the entries on 17th October in this abstract book are in my writing. The last entry is "Wainwright, Dover Pier." That means for Wainwright, from Dover Pier. I have no recollection of that message. I enter the name of the person for whom the telegram is intended in my district, and the place from whence it comes, but not the name of the person who sends it. This entry shows me that on 17th October a message came for Wainwright from Dover Pier.

Cross-examined by Mr. MOODY—In entering the name of the sender we do not enter any initials.

E. M. Heard　　EDWIN MILLS HEARD, examined—I am in the service of the post office at Stratford Broadway. It is my duty to enter up the messages in the abstract book each day. I produce the abstract book in which I find an entry on 17th October, 1874—"Surname of the addressee, Wilmore; office of origin, Dover Pier." That shows that a message was sent on that day to Wilmore from Dover Pier, and that is all I know about it.

Mrs. Wells　　Mrs. SUSAN WELLS, examined by Mr. BESLEY—I am a widow, and live at 12 Valentine Road, South Hackney. In 1873 I lived at 14 St. Peter Street, Hackney Road, and let apartments there. About the last week in October, 1873, I let my apartments to Percy King, whom I identify as the elder prisoner. He brought Mrs. King with him. The apartment had been taken by another party for them previously. I knew the lady as Mrs. King. Mr. King did not stay there; he only visited occasion-

64

Evidence for Prosecution.

ally. He assisted in getting the luggage in that evening, and Mrs Wells
I asked him when he was going to return. He said, "I shall
not return this evening, Mrs. Wells. I leave this lady in your
care. Take care of her; she is to have all she requires."

Did he say who she was?—He said she was Mrs. King.

By the Lord Chief Justice—Do you recollect what he said
to you?—He hesitated a few minutes, and then he said she was
his brother's wife—his sister-in-law.

Examination continued—She remained till the last week in
April, 1874.

In September, 1873, did anything take place?—Yes, the
birth of a child, which was named Marian. Mr. King came
to see her in the first or second week of her confinement, and
saw her in her bedroom. No one was with him then, but some
one came with him after.

By the Lord Chief Justice—He came and saw her occasionally afterwards.

Examination continued—You say that some time after he
came and another man with him?—Yes, some time after Mrs.
King had got out of her confinement.

Did you see that man?—Yes, I saw the man. He came into
the house. It was afternoon when Mr. King brought the friend
with him. It was just after Mrs. King had got out of her room.
He remained a short time in my parlour while Mr. King went
upstairs, and then he was called up. He said, "Edward, I
want you," and the man went up. They remained up some
minutes, and then Edward came down, and waited till Mr. King
came downstairs, when they went away together. They were
in the house altogether about half an hour. I saw them both
go out together. The same person, "Edward," came again
very shortly after Mrs. King had left my house to go out, and
Mr. King and his friend brought her home in a cab. It was
between twelve and one o'clock at night that they came home.
I let her in. Mr. King sat in the cab, and his friend saw her
into the hall, where the gas was burning. Mr. King never got
out of the cab. I heard him laugh. Lights were burning in
her room and all over the house. I am sure Mr. King never
got out of the cab.

Have you seen the other man since?—Yes. I was taken to
the Southwark station house, and saw the other prisoner there,
and to the best of my belief he is the party who was brought to
my house by Mr. King as "Edward." I am not positive, but
to the best of my belief he is the party.

By the Lord Chief Justice—You have said that you could

The Wainwrights.

Mrs Wells not identify him?—Yes; I have said that I could not identify him, but I believe the other prisoner in the dock to be the party.

Examination continued—Had the man you saw whiskers or a beard?—No; he had a slight moustache, but now he looks so much older than when I saw him before that I could not say whether it was him.

I am speaking of the time you saw him with Mr. King. Had he then any whiskers or beard?—No, he did not seem to me to have any; he had a slight moustache.

Cross-examined by Mr. BESLEY—You are now near Christmas, 1875, and this was soon after Christmas, 1873?—Mrs. King left my house after Christmas, 1873.

All the time that Henry Wainwright was going to your house he never slept there, I believe?—No, never all the time.

Did you speak to the man in the cab?—I did not speak to the man in the cab or see him at all. I made an observation to Edward, "This is a very disorderly way." A gas light was burning in the lobby, a single burner, inside the fanlight.

Cross-examined by Mr. MOODY—Have you ever said when you were examined before the police magistrates anything at all about this person called Edward coming down a second time into your parlour and waiting there for Mr. King?—I believe I said there what I have said here.

You say it was after Mrs. King got out from her confinement that the two men came to see her. Was not the child born in December, 1873?—Yes.

I suppose she would get out then some time in February?—She went out on Christmas Day to be churched—three weeks and two days after her confinement.

It was soon after this then that the interview you speak of took place?—Yes.

And there was nothing to call the appearance of this person, "Edward," to your mind until you saw an account of this affair in the papers?—No.

The first time you saw him after was when you saw him sitting in the Police Court?—Yes, that was the first time.

Before the magistrate you were even doubtful whether "Edward" had a moustache or not?—I do not know that I said so; I said he looked very young.

Did you not make use of the expression, "If Edward had a moustache, it was a very slight one"?—I said that to-day.

Did you make use of that expression?—Yes.

So you are not quite certain whether he had or had not a moustache? I think you have said to-day that he did not seem

Evidence for Prosecution.

to have any beard or whiskers?—Yes. It was in the afternoon Mrs. Wells
that they came. I was not in the room with the man during
the whole of the time. I saw him go upstairs, because I said at
the time, "I think you are wanted. Mrs. King is calling."

You have said before the magistrate that during the whole
of that time the name of Mr. Frieake was never mentioned?—
Never.

Before you gave your evidence you heard that one of the
men had passed by the name of Teddy Frieake?—Yes.

Do you not think that circumstances might have induced
you to believe that the name Edward was used?—I am sure
that Mrs. King called him Edward.

Mrs. JEMIMA FOSTER, examined—I live at 3 Sidney Square, Mrs. Foster
Commercial Road, and have lived there since Christmas, 1873.
My daughter Lucy lives with me. I know Henry Wainwright;
he came to me as Mr. King somewhere about May, 1874. I had
"Apartments" in my window. He came in and said, "I see
you have apartments here to let; would you mind taking a lady,
her nurse, and two children?" After some conversation I agreed
to do so. I said I could not let them at less than £1 a week.
He agreed to that. I said, "I suppose it is Mrs. King?" I
cannot be positive that he said his name was King, but all his
transactions were in that name. He did not say whether the
lady was his wife or not, as I know of, but she always passed
as his wife. I fancy he said she was his wife. I am almost
sure he did. I asked what reference I could have; he said, "I
can give you a deposit if you wish it, and a reference." He
did not give me any reference; he paid me a deposit instead.
He said he should not come very often, that he was a traveller,
and his business called him very much away from home. He
came next morning and said, "Is Mrs. King come yet?" I
said, "No, she has not been here." He then left, and came
again about eleven o'clock with Mrs. King in a cab to look at
the apartments. The arrangement was then concluded, and
she came in the evening with the nurse and two children and
Mr. Rogers. They brought their luggage with them. The
nurse stayed about seven weeks. Mrs. King stayed till 11th
September. While she was there Henry Wainwright never came
to see her—never to come in. I saw him once at the door.
Rogers used to come very frequently, and most times he went
upstairs to Mrs. King. Miss Wilmore used to come to see her
very often, almost every Sunday, and about the end of August
she came to stay altogether. Whilst Mrs. King was with me

The Wainwrights.

Mrs. Foster I remember a gentleman coming to see her about twice or three times.

How was he announced?—Once I announced him as Mr. Frieake. I think that was the second time. On the first occasion Mrs. King was expecting him, and he went upstairs without being announced. I did not hear his name mentioned after he went upstairs.

By the LORD CHIEF JUSTICE—How did you first know about Mr. Frieake?—By Mrs. King saying a gentleman named Frieake was going to get her furniture for two rooms.

Did he give his name to you as Mr. Frieake?—Yes; on the second visit he told me his name was Frieake.

Examination continued—He asked whether Mrs. King was at home, and said it was Mr. Frieake. I first knew about Mr. Frieake, because Mrs. King said that there was a gentleman of the name of Frieake going to give her furniture for two rooms, and he gave his name as Frieake when he went upstairs; that was the second time. I think the first time he went up without giving his name. It was when I showed him upstairs that he gave the name of Frieake, and I opened the door and said, "Mr. Frieake." I did not know that he was the gentleman who was going to give her the furniture till he gave his name. I did not know it on the first occasion. It was the same gentleman that came on both occasions. She said that he was going to get her furniture, not to get rid of it, and she even said that he was coming to get her to choose what colour she would have. On one of the two occasions that he came he brought a bottle of champagne, and Mrs. King asked me for some champagne glasses, and I went out and borrowed some. I saw him bring in the bottle under his arm or in his hand in a paper; it was a champagne bottle. I saw it next day up in the room; I think it was a quart bottle. I got three glasses at the Princess Royal, nearly opposite, but only two were used. I saw nothing more of Mr. Frieake that day; he went out shortly afterwards. I think that was the second time he came.

On another occasion after that, I can't remember the date, about ten o'clock at night, there was a knocking at the door by one of my neighbours on account of a little disturbance in the street. I went out and found Mrs. King with Mr. King, as I thought it was, and another gentleman; I think it was the same gentleman that came before, Mr. Frieake. I only just saw them with a passing glance. I am certain it was the same gentleman that came with the champagne. I think Mrs. King was rather intoxicated; she seemed very much excited. I asked her to

68

come in with me, and she said I had no business to interfere with **Mrs. Foster** her and her husband, and, of course, I came in again directly. She appeared to be quarrelling with the gentlemen. They left her on the step of the door, and knocked, and rang, and went away, and she ran down the street after them. I went to the corner and said, "Do come in, Mrs. King." One of the gentlemen was standing on the corner of the kerb, and the other a little distance from him. At last Miss Wilmore went and got her in. Next day I gave her notice. I told her I should like her to leave that day week, which, I think, was on the Wednesday following. She asked me to let her stay two days longer, and I did so. That would be the 11th.

Champagne was brought on two occasions, once a pint bottle and once a quart bottle. Mr. Frieake brought it, not the same day—it was some days before, about a fortnight before Mrs. King left, I think, the first time he called. I am almost sure it was the last time he called that he brought the pint, and the other time he brought the quart. He went out for it after he came in. I am almost certain it was the small bottle that he brought last, now I come to think—the first was a large bottle. It was a week afterwards, I think, that he brought the second one.

Except on this one occasion Mrs. King was a well-conducted person; I never saw anything wrong in her. Twice before, I think, she came home very much excited, but nothing to speak of, a little the worse perhaps for a glass of anything. On other occasions she conducted herself quite as a lady, as we thought. Once, about a month before, she came home about nine or ten o'clock in the evening; she had been out the whole afternoon, and she was a little more talkative, and made herself a little more free with us, but that was all. She seemed very fond indeed of her children. They both slept in her bed when she had not got the nurse; before that one slept with the nurse. She left on Friday, 11th September, and she paid me all that was due to me. We parted on friendly terms; we shook hands, and I bade her good-bye, and watched her round the corner of the street. I never saw her again alive. She had with her a small paper parcel, which she carried on her finger with a piece of twine, and a new umbrella. I don't know what was in the parcel. Miss Wilmore left later on the same day with the children, about six or seven o'clock.

I saw Thomas Wainwright at the Borough Session-house. I was taken to see him. I had seen him before at Leman Street, but I could not recognise him then. When he was in the

The Wainwrights.

Mrs. Foster Borough I thought he was the same gentleman that brought the champagne; he had very little whiskers at that time. I did not notice whether he had any moustache. I only just let him in at the door as he passed through the passage, and I could hardly say.

Cross-examined by Mr. BESLEY—Your mind was not carried back to the taking of the lodgings in April, 1874, until it was stated that some remains were found, and that Henry Wainwright was in custody?—It was not. I saw Wainwright when he took the lodgings, and when the lady took possession. He came three times altogether—twice upon the day the apartments were taken, and once before.

As to this matter at the door, you went out to see who was knocking, as you did not wish any scandal with regard to your lodgings?—Yes.

And, I think, you said it lasted scarcely two minutes altogether?—Yes.

Was it half-past ten at night?—Quite that. It was some time in August or September. After I returned Miss Wilmore went out, and some time afterwards she brought Harriet Lane in.

By the LORD CHIEF JUSTICE—Did you know when you saw one gentleman of these two that he was the person who took the lodgings?—I did. I patted him on the shoulder, and said, "Mr. King, I will go and try to get her in," and she said, "How dare you interfere with me and my husband?"

By Mr. BESLEY—You never saw Mr. King who took the lodgings in April until that night—if you saw him that night? —I did not.

Cross-examined by Mr. MOODY—The person who passed as Mr. Frieake was the only gentleman that called on Mrs. King. I saw nothing more of him after 11th September, 1874. I don't know whether my daughter let him in once. I think I let him in most times; I have not said that Mrs. King let him in once. She was at the top of the stairs and asked him to come up, and that made me pronounce his name. There are only about a dozen steps from my passage. The stairs are right opposite the door, about 4 or 5 feet, and about ten or twelve steps up to the first floor. It was quite evening; I think it was gaslight. She said, "Come up," and he stepped up at once. That was the only occasion on which I had to announce him.

I heard of the discovery of the body on the Monday morning, I think—not till Mr. Forster came. I think I was taken to the Leman Street station, after Thomas Wainwright was taken

70

Evidence for Prosecution.

into custody. I did not know that I was taken to see the man Mrs. Foster
who had passed himself off as Mr. Frieake. I don't believe I
had heard that. I was shown some men together in the police
yard; I was told to have a good look, and I did have a good
look, and I could not recognise anybody there. It was not till
I saw Thomas Wainwright sitting in the dock at the Police
Court with the other prisoner that I began to have any recollection of him. I then said he was about the size and stature of
the man. I said he looked very much like the gentleman, and
I believed very possibly he was the man. I said there the man
had very light whiskers and a very light moustache, and I have
said to-day that he had rather light whiskers. That was my
impression at the time. The only time I speak to was his
coming on one occasion when Mrs. King was at the top of the
stairs, and said, "Step up, Mr. Frieake." I asked his name,
and announced him. On the night I went out and saw the
disturbance I saw two men moving, and I am positive one was
Mr. King, who I spoke to. I came back and saw nothing more.

JAMES HUMPHRIES, examined—I am a licensed victualler, and J. Humphries
keep the Old Red Lion, 339 Strand. I was proprietor of the
Princess Royal public-house, 1 and 2 Sidney Square, in August
and September. That is immediately opposite Mrs. Foster's.
I knew the prisoners. I have known Henry six or seven years,
and Thomas four or five years. Some time in the autumn of
last year I saw both the prisoners in my house together. The
last time I saw them was Saturday, 5th September. I saw
them only once before at the Princess Royal, about a week
previously. They were together on that occasion. I fix the
date by my day-book. I had to give the necessary notice for
the transfer of the licence, but I do not fix it by that date, but
by an entry I made in reference to lending some champagne
glasses. I remember the circumstances; it was on 5th September, and the two prisoners were at my house from four to six
or seven o'clock. They smoked two cigars, and had some brandy
and soda divided. My barman in my presence supplied them
with a pint bottle of champagne first, and then with a quart,
within an interval of half an hour or an hour. The pint bottle
was taken away, I do not remember who by, but it must have
been by one of them, because they were the only persons in
the private bar. I did not see it taken away by them, but I
infer that it must have been; I saw it on the counter waiting
to be taken. After the champagne was taken away Mrs. Foster
came to borrow some champagne glasses. There must have

71

The Wainwrights.

J. Humphries been two or three, because I made this memorandum to remind my storekeeper that our cabinets were short of champagne glasses. Within an hour I should imagine after. Mrs. Foster borrowed the glasses, Thomas Wainwright had a quart bottle of champagne, which he took away with him and did not return. Henry was not there when the second bottle was taken away. On the same night, between nine and ten o'clock, I saw both the prisoners and several other people outside Mrs. Foster's house, when a disturbance happened.

By the Lord Chief Justice—I am able to fix it as 5th September, because after handing over the champagne glasses I had to wait to see some one respecting the transfer of my licence, and I had to make my way west and to come back, and then it was 10.15, and it takes me half an hour to get from house to house.

Cross-examined by Mr. Besley—I was keeping one public-house at that time, but I have four, my own property. One is in Long Acre, one in the Strand, one in Sidney Square, and one in the Whitechapel Road. The licences are held by different people, one of whom is my brother. I conduct the business by means of managers, who are my servants, and I go about from one to the other, giving all my time and attention to them. I had had the Princess Royal about two years, and was going to transfer the licence to my brother's name, which was done on 28th September. I devoted my time principally to the Princess Alice. I was transferring Mr. Forster, my billiard-marker, to the position of manager. I had two barmen and two barmaids. The person who was to succeed to the licence was not there. The transfer of the licence does not mean the transfer of the public-house, but a transfer from one servant of mine to another servant of mine. It was about to go into the name of Robert Humphries, my brother, and until the licence was transferred Forster was manager. He is not here, nor are the barmen that I know of. I did not go before the magistrate on this charge, and I never gave an intimation to any one that I could give evidence. Inspector M'Donald called on me four or five times, I think. I cannot tell when he called first, but to the best of my knowledge it was a fortnight or three weeks previous to my having to go before the grand jury last session. I went to the Treasury a fortnight or three weeks before that. Mr. M'Donald had an appointment to go with me to the Treasury, which I did not keep, and another which I did. He took me there.

Cross-examined by Mr. Moody—I first heard of this matter by seeing it in the *Daily Telegraph*. It did not occur to me that I should go and give some information. I did not know at that

72

Evidence for Prosecution.

time that there was any question about Thomas Wainwright **J. Humphries** being Frieake. I read everything, and still I did not go to the police. Mrs. Foster had been examined at the Police Court at that time, and I had seen about the champagne glasses. I had seen Thomas Wainwright several times before August, 1874. I had seen him with his brother Henry in my public-house in Whitechapel Road, but not very frequently. That public-house is conducted by my son; it is one of the four between which I distribute my energies. I am there very frequently.

Re-examined by the ATTORNEY-GENERAL—The prisoners both went away with the pint bottle of champagne, and came back for a quart bottle, and did not return again. I cannot tell at what time Thomas went out with the quart bottle, but to the best of my memory it was about half an hour to an hour afterwards. I was just leaving my premises that night to go to the West End when the disturbance happened. I am positive as to the date.

[The following letter was here put in:—" Mrs. King, 3 Sidney Square, Mile-End Road.—Dear Pet,—E. F. is coming down at seven to-night. He will give you a call, with a message from me.—Yours, &c., P. K." The postmark on the envelope was September 5, 1874, London, N.E.]

Mrs. AMELIE STANLEY, examined by Mr. BEASLEY—I live at **Mrs. Stanley** Bow. I am the wife of George Edward Stanley, a master mariner. I am related to Mrs. Foster, of Sidney Square. Last August or beginning of September, 1874, I was on a visit one evening at Sidney Square. I knew there was a lady living there named King. I remember a gentleman calling when I was there, and I heard his name announced by Mrs. Foster as Mr. Frieake. He remained in the hall while Mrs. Foster went up to announce him. I was sitting opposite the parlour door, which was open. I saw him all the while he was there. He was standing there for two or three minutes. The gas was burning over his head. His hat was on. After being announced, he went upstairs, and I did not see him again.

Did you observe whether he had any beard or whiskers?—He had a moustache, but no whiskers.

You have been shown the prisoner Thomas Wainwright at the Police Court. What do you say as to him being the man announced as Frieake?—He is the man I saw, to the best of my knowledge.

Cross-examined by Mr. MOODY—When Mrs. Foster went upstairs, Miss Foster was left in the room with me. We were sitting on chairs. We were talking when the knock came. We

73

The Wainwrights.

were not doing needlework. Mrs. Foster went to the door, and then went up to announce him. I can't say whether she called him to come upstairs or came down and showed him up.

Your attention was not called to the circumstance again till you heard of this affair?—No. This was in August, 1874, and my attention was not called to it until 4th October, 1875.

You never saw the man before that night or afterwards until you saw him getting into the dock?—No.

You had had conversation with Mrs. Foster when you were taken to the Police Court, and you knew that the man who had been passing himself off as Frieake was one of the persons on his trial?—I did not know that.

You don't allege for a moment that you have ever seen Henry Wainwright?—No.

I think you said at the Police Court that, " to the best of my belief, the prisoner Thomas is the man. He had a moustache, a fair one, and no beard or whiskers." Did you say that?—I don't remember. I said he had a moustache and a clean-shaven face, to the best of my belief.

Did you not repeat the expression that he had a fair moustache? Have you no recollection whether you mentioned so important a particular as that?—To the best of my belief I did not.

Did you, in cross-examination at the Police Court, say that you had read the case in the papers, that the next time you saw him was in the dock, and that you knew the man was supposed to be Teddy Frieake?—I don't remember that.

You went down to the Treasury to have your evidence taken?—Yes.

And you had not up to that time seen the man who was in custody?—Yes, I had.

Were you down two days at the Police Court?—Yes.

You went down to the Court, saw the two men in the dock, then gave your statement to the Treasury?—Yes; but I was fetched to give my evidence.

Re-examined by the ATTORNEY-GENERAL—The man who was announced as Frieake had a medium moustache as to length; it was not dark.

JOHN BAYLIS, examined—I live at 149 Whitechapel Road. I am an oil and colour man, and, amongst other things, I deal in chloride of lime. I knew Henry Wainwright, carrying on business in the Whitechapel Road. On 10th September last year an order for chloride of lime was given to me. I do not know who gave it. It was either from Henry Wainwright or Rogers.

74

Evidence for Prosecution.

The quantity was half a hundredweight. It was packed in a John Baylis box, and I believe it was sent by one of my men to No. 84. It came to 7s. 6d. The box in which it was packed was sent down from Wainwright's. It was not paid for. I never sold any chloride of lime to Wainwright before. I do not know whether it was sent by one of my men or one of his.

Cross-examined by Mr. BESLEY—When we sell small quantities of chloride of lime for cash they are not entered at all, but I book it if it is not paid for. I do not profess to keep in mind all the numerous transactions in my shop. Mine is a ready-money business. My books have not got into arrears; that is an error. It is simply this rough entry-book; mine being a cash trade, very little is entered in it. It has not been posted for nearly two years. There may be a few entries in it besides mine. Sometimes my father comes to town and makes a few entries. Whenever I take an order, it is put upon a piece of paper, and I enter from that. I enter what is filed, but there is not always an order on the file, I am sorry to say. There was no order in this case, simply because I executed the order myself. I will not swear that there was no written order. My shopman also serves in the shop, and a second hand who acts as carman, and a youth. If either of them received an order, it would be their duty to put it on the file, and I should enter it in the day-book, but that order was executed by myself. I do not recollect whether it was given by Rogers or Mr. Wainwright. I do not think an interval has ever occurred between a transaction and my entering it. I do not think such a thing could happen while I am on the premises, but I am not infallible. I cannot tell what might happen, for I only know what does happen. I am speaking of a matter about which there has been an interval of twelve months.

Re-examined by the ATTORNEY-GENERAL—To the best of my belief, I made all the entries on the same day, 10th September They are all in my writing. It varies because sometimes the book is in this position and sometimes in that, and my hands are hard at work, and not always so steady at one time as at another.

Adjourned till to-morrow.

Fourth Day—Thursday, 25th November, 1875.

C. Titiens   CHARLES TITIENS, examined—I live at 84 Berners Street, Whitechapel, and am in the employment of Messrs. Ashford & Green, of Stratford. I was formerly a porter in the service of Henry Wainwright. I went into the service in July, I believe, and I was in the service three years last July. About the middle of September, 1874, I remember taking a case to Mr. Baylis. Henry Wainwright told me to take it there for some chloride of lime. I did so, and left it there. I do not know how long West was living at No. 215. I was in the habit of going to 215 White-chapel Road for the purpose of packing goods in the warehouse there. I noticed a smell at the back part of the premises about June. I noticed it for about a month before I left. I called Mr. Wainwright's attention to it, and told him there was a stench, and asked to have the ashes removed. I thought it came from there. He said he would. They were not removed. It was a kind of faint smell; I could not say exactly what it was. I bought two halfpennyworths of chloride of lime, and paid for it myself, and sprinkled it over the ashes in powder. The door leading into Vine Court had two bolts to it and one lock. It was always kept locked and bolted. I used to get in from the front entrance. On one occasion I saw it open when some fixtures were being removed. They went to Mr. Martin's, and they were taken out by that door. I believe that was about two months before I left.

Cross-examined by Mr. BESLEY—I did not notice the smell after putting down the second quantity of chloride of lime. I did not hear Henry Wainwright give directions for the rubbish and ashes to be removed. They had been accumulating for a long time. There was quite a cartload, if not more. It was all ashes. It was not removed when I left in July, 1875. The Rogers were living there at the time upstairs; they went out in April. I worked at No. 84, and I had to go to No. 215 as well. When the Rogers were living at No. 84 there were com-plaints of the smell of the drains at No. 215. I did not notice any smell at No. 84 myself. Rogers complained of the smell of the drains at No. 215 before he went to live there. Mr. West was living there at that time. That was before July, 1874. I am sure it was Rogers who complained, and West as well. I do

76

Evidence for Prosecution.

not know how long ago West was living at No. 215. I do not know whether complaint was made of the drains at the time West was there. I never heard of complaints made of the drains at No. 84. I had forgotten about the taking of the case to Mr. Baylis until Detective Forster came to me about 23rd September of this year. He asked me if I remembered it. That was how it arose. I was working at No. 215 usually all the time the place was opened.

I remember the things being brought from No. 84 and being loaded at No. 215 for the purpose of going to Mr. Frieake's salerooms. I believe only two lots were sent there. I remember a van coming one evening about 6.30, and it came the following morning to take the rest of the things. I was there with Rogers in the evening when the van came. I do not remember Vostius being there. I did not notice how long it took putting the goods out into the van. We shut up from about 7.30 to 8 o'clock. Very likely that evening we may have been later than usual. Eight o'clock was my usual time for leaving work. When it became dark the gas was lighted at No. 215. It was dark by eight o'clock in September. We had not the gas lighted when the goods were being loaded in the van. We had finished by daylight. We worked by gaslight when it was needed, but on this evening we had finished before we had occasion to light the gas. I and Vostius generally packed the goods at No. 215. That was the ordinary place for packing the goods. Saturdays were not very busy days. From July to November, 1874, Mr. Wainwright generally made it a practice to clear up on Saturday. He always paid us our wages on Saturday. What I mean by clearing up is getting the place ready for Monday morning's packing. I used to leave before Rogers.

Re-examined by Mr. POLAND—I was employed at No. 84, and used to go to No. 215 to do any packing that there might be. If there was no packing to do, the premises would be shut up. Sometimes they shut up earlier at No. 215. The goods were made up at No. 84, and what were required for orders were sent over to No. 215 to be packed. No. 84 was the retail shop. When we had finished our packing at No. 215 the doors would be closed until we went there to pack again ; they would not be open all day long. There were some days at the latter part, just before I left, when No. 215 was not opened at all. The two big doors of the warehouse were kept closed. The van that came on the evening that I speak of came to No. 215. I did not notice it at No. 84. The goods were put into the van at No. 215 ; I do not remember how long the van was there. I believe the premises were shut up before 7.30 or 8 o'clock. I

77

The Wainwrights.

C. Titiens have no clear memory about it. After the fire at No. 84, the business ceased there, and the goods that were not consumed were taken to No. 215. The lotting of the goods sent for sale was before the fire.

G. W. Rogers GEORGE WILLIAM ROGERS, examined by Mr. POLAND—I live at 11 Teddington Terrace, Tredegar Road, Bow. I was formerly in the service of Henry Wainwright. I entered it on 11th August, 1873, and remained till April, 1875. During that time he had premises at 84 and 215 Whitechapel Road. Up to July, 1874, Mr. West lived at No. 215. From that time until November, 1875, they were not used as a residence. Shortly before the fire I went to live there with my wife, and continued to live there till April of this year. Before going there I had been living at No. 84 with my wife, from July till the beginning of November. I knew Mrs. King. I first saw her at 8 St. Peter Street, at Mrs. Wells'. Henry Wainwright asked me to take a letter with some money in it in February, 1874, I believe. He said, "Will you take a letter for me to Mrs. King? Say it is from Mr. King, and that there is £5 in it, and obtain a receipt."

Did he say who Mrs. King was?—No. He gave me the letter with the address written on it to "Mrs. King." I took it to the lodgings and saw Mrs. King, and gave it to her.

Did she write a receipt?—No; Miss Wilmore wrote the receipt, and next morning I gave it to Wainwright.

By the LORD CHIEF JUSTICE—I suppose Mrs. King signed it?—No, I think not.

Examination continued—Was it a stamped receipt?—Yes; and I found the stamp. That was the first time I had seen Miss Wilmore.

Did you go afterwards to the same lodgings?—I think on two occasions afterwards, with letters or messages from Henry Wainwright. I usually left them in the tea hour. He did not say what the letters were.

Do you remember Mrs. King leaving these lodgings?—I do. I went by Wainwright's directions the day she left. He told me to get a cab and go and take Mrs. King and two children to 3 Sidney Square. He gave me 10s. to pay expenses. That was in the evening—early in May, I think.

Did Miss Wilmore go with you in the cab?—No, she did not go with us. I went as directed, got a cab, and took Mrs. King and the two children, and we picked up the nurse at the corner of a street in Bethnal Green Road. We then went to 3 Sidney Square, where I helped to get the luggage upstairs,

78

Evidence for Prosecution.

and then left. I saw Henry Wainwright next morning, and told him what I had done. After that I used to go to Sidney Square. I went four or five times with money and letters from Wainwright. I saw Mrs. King there, and took on one occasion £5, and on another £2, and gave them to her. I did not get receipts for these.

On the occasion of giving her the £2, did she say anything?—Yes; she threw it on the table and said, "That is no use to me, as I have to pay my rent."

By the Lord Chief Justice—Did she appear to be dissatisfied?—Yes.

You cannot, for the purpose of evidence, tell us what she said, but if you made any statement to Wainwright about it, you can repeat what you said to him?—I told him she was dissatisfied, and he said, "Oh, all right; never mind."

Tell us what you told him she had said to you?—She told me it was not enough to pay her rent.

I don't want what she told you, but what you told him?—I said to Mr. Henry Wainwright she was dissatisfied with the amount, as she had to pay her rent, and he replied, "Oh, all right," or "I will see to it," or some short answer of that kind.

Did you go to her again?—Once more.

Did you take any money then?—No.

Examination continued—On the occasion that you went without taking any money, did you go with a message?—I did, to say that he would send to her shortly. I don't think he said anything else. Oh, yes; he said when he got his business settled with Mr. Sawyer he would send to her shortly. Mr. Sawyer had been in partnership with him, and there had been disputes. I think it was some time in July. It must have been the commencement of July that I took the £2.

On one occasion when you went there, did Mrs. King show you a telegram?—Yes. She handed it to me, but I left it there. I afterwards saw Henry Wainwright and told him, " Mrs. King has received a telegram stating that I and you have gone out of town. You know that is false."

By the Lord Chief Justice—Did you tell him from whom she said the telegram had come?—She said it had come from Mr. Wainwright, and I said to him, "You know that is false. You know I have not been out of town."

Did he deny the fact of having sent the telegram?—No. He said, "Oh, never mind," or something short, and I did not trouble myself further about it. This was about the middle of

79

The Wainwrights.

G. W. Rogers July. I think that was the last occasion I went to Sidney
Square.

Examination continued—Have you seen Mrs. King at 84
Whitechapel Road?—Yes. I saw her there at least a dozen
times while I was in Wainwright's employment. She used to
come into the shop, and I have seen her and Wainwright together
there frequently.

Do you remember hearing some conversation between Mrs.
King and Wainwright on the last occasion?—Yes. She saw
him in the front of the shop. I was sitting in the counting-
house, and saw them apparently very quarrelsome. I did not
hear what passed, but I judged from their gesticulation. That
was the last time I saw her.

By the LORD CHIEF JUSTICE—Can you fix the date of that?—
I cannot. It was some time in August.

Examination continued—I remember on one occasion Mrs.
King being ill at No. 84; that was at the commencement of
August, 1874. I saw her for a moment. My wife told me of
her being ill; I only knew it from my wife. No one lived at
the premises, No. 215, from July to November, 1874. During
that period the premises were locked up, and the keys kept at
No. 84, behind the counting-house door, and the counting-house
was not locked up at night. There was a broom rack on wheels
with a door to it, and the key of that door was always kept by
Henry Wainwright. It was a sliding broom rack which formed
a passage to the dwelling-house when the shop was shut up.
It was a partition with a door in it, and that locked up the
counting-house and the shop. Henry Wainwright always took
home that key with him. When I came in the morning I could
not get to No. 215 to do any work there, and I have sometimes
said to him jokingly, " I shall fine you if you are not earlier ";
that was when I wanted the place open. I remember in September last his speaking to me about some chloride of lime; I think
it was on the 10th. He asked me to inquire of Mr. Baylis the
price of chloride of lime, that he had got an order from Southend
for half a hundredweight. I went and inquired at Mr. Baylis,
which is only a few hundred yards from No. 84, and took him
the price. I forget the quotation, but he said it would do. I
don't think I ordered it. Henry Wainwright only dealt in
chloride of lime for the police contract when he had it, which
was some time afterwards. The police contract was for small
stores. We only obtained that contract in the early part of
this year. At that time he did not deal in chloride of lime.

80

Evidence for Prosecution.

He was the manager there, and I was the chief man; I did not G. W. Rogers
know of any customer at Southend.

On the day after the shop shut up, I saw a box on the
premises. I saw it arrive from Baylis's. That was the same
day I had inquired the price. After the shop was closed, which
was at eight o'clock, it was brought in a hand truck and placed
in the passage by Baylis's man. I saw that done. I could tell
by the smell that it contained chloride of lime; it was so
pungent. My wife saw it, and spoke to me about it. It
remained there during the night, and next morning before the
shop was opened I saw it lying in the passage. I did not see
it removed, and do not know who removed it, or where it went;
I missed it while I was upstairs at breakfast; that would be
about 8.30 or 9 o'clock; when I came down it was gone. Henry
Wainwright came to business sometimes at 8.15, 8.30, 8.45.

There were complaints of the drains at No. 84 while I was
living there. No chloride of lime was used for them to my
knowledge while I was there. The premises at No. 215 at that
time were only used specially for large orders. Sometimes
nobody went into the premises for days, only for opening and
shutting them; they were opened and shut every day, and kept
open till the time of closing at No. 84. The shutters were
taken down, so that there would be light for any packing that
was wanted, but the place was thoroughly closed. The doors
would not be open; we had the keys at No. 84. At the time
I and my wife were living at No. 215, I noticed a smell at the
end of the shop. I could not say when I first perceived it; I
should say shortly after Christmas. I put it down to the
accumulation of ashes and vegetable refuse. We had no dust-
hole there. I spoke about it to Henry Wainwright. I told him
the smell was very bad, and the ashes had accumulated. He
said, "When Ladbrooks' men pass get them to clear it out."
Ladbrooks are brushmakers; they used to burn all the refuse
in their furnace. They were cleared out on one occasion. I
smelt the unpleasant smell again as they accumulated. I only
spoke about the smell on one occasion to my knowledge.

At the latter end of July, 1874, Henry Wainwright showed
me a revolver in the counting-house at No. 84. He took it from
his desk; it was in a green baize bag; it had five or six
chambers—I could not say which—and it was about 9 or 10
inches long, including the barrel. He asked me to pawn it.
He said, "I am short this week. I bought it of Sawyer; I gave
£6 for it. Get £2 10s. on it." He did not tell me where to
pawn it. It had no case to it. I said these sort of things usually

G   81

The Wainwrights.

G. W. Rogers had a case of fittings, and I did not believe they would take it in. He said, "Yes, they will." I then left No. 84 and took the pistol with me in the green baize bag to a pawnbroker in Mile-End Road. I am not sure which pawnbroker it was, as there are two close together. I offered it in pledge, but was only offered 15s., so I took it back to No. 84, and told Henry Wainwright so. He put it in his desk, and I have not seen it since.

Cross-examined by Mr. BESLEY—When the shutters at No. 215 were taken down it left a large amount of glass, so that you could see into the warehouse, the whole 110 feet to the end, and owing to the three glass doors at the end of the warehouse it was very easy to see. In the performance of my duties I was going about London getting orders for goods, and the principal part of my time was spent away from No. 84. I put the prices into the police contract in November, 1874, previous to which I inquired at a great number of wholesale places the prices of different articles, and a letter was written to inquire the price of chloride of lime. I fancy that the order for the chloride of lime was written on special order paper by one of the clerks. It should have been in the ordinary routine of business, but I did not give it myself. Any statement of mine that it was a special order paper was because that was the proper course. I did not say it as a fact; we are all liable to mistakes. I said at the Police Court that it should have been done. I think my expression was, "I think the order was written on special order paper by one of our clerks."

Did you ever until this hour mention the word "10th" in reference to the order spoken to as being given on 10th September, 1874?—I think so.

Did you ever swear until to-day that you saw Baylis's man bring the package into the passage of No. 84?—I think I may swear I did. I do swear I did.

At the Police Court did you say, "I don't know what became of it, for I did not see it in the morning"?—I believe I did.

Did you ever swear until to-day that you saw the package in the passage before you went up to breakfast, and that when you came down it was gone?—I think not. I was discharged by Mr. Sawyer in April, 1874, and kept by Mr. Wainwright. I entered his service about 12th July, 1874. I was not in his service between April and July, 1874. When difficulties in business arose through Mr. Behrend's claim, I did not negotiate with Mr. Behrend to take over 215 Whitechapel Road. Some_ thing was mentioned about my becoming proprietor and he to

Evidence for Prosecution.

supply the capital. It was done to benefit Mr. Wainwright **G. W. Rogers** until the fire action was settled.

Were you engaged as a "travelling agent in advance" for a dramatic company?—I have been on two occasions.

The first was in 1869?—I think it was. We went through Yorkshire, and were a good deal about the north.

Were you then in the service of Miss Edith Sandford?—No; I was in the employ of Mr. Charles Wood, and Miss Edith Sandford was the principal member of the company.

Was your wife, Susannah Clementina, formerly Susannah Clementina Dolby, with you?—No.

You were married to her on 26th June, 1859, in the Parish Church at St. George's, Bloomsbury, I think?—Yes. At least it is eighteen years ago; I do not know the date.

Have you seen your wife recently?—I have not. I heard something about her six months ago.

Do you know whether she is now alive?—I do not.

Did you rejoin the dramatic company in May, 1873?—Yes, at Leicester.

And did the witness, Mrs. Jane Rogers, also join you there? —She did.

Were you going under the name of King then?—I was. That was my mother's name.

When were you married to Jane Rogers?—In April, 1872.

Re-examined by the ATTORNEY-GENERAL—How old were you when you were married to Susannah Clementina Dolby?— Fifteen years of age.

How old was she?—The same age as myself.

Were you married with or without the consent of your parents?—Without the consent of either.

And you did not live happily together?—Certainly not.

You ultimately were married to Jane Rogers, your present wife, on 14th April, 1872?—Yes.

Before you married her, did you ask legal advice?—I did.

As agent for the dramatic company, you went in advance to the various towns where they were going to perform in order to make arrangements for them?—Yes.

Was Miss Davis, your wife, one of the company?—Certainly not.

When you were travelling agent you took the name of King?—Yes, on Mr. Wood's, my employer's, advice. He was the manager of the company.

Did Henry Wainwright know that you travelled as King?— No; I told him I had travelled with Mr. Wood. As agent in

The Wainwrights.

G. W. Rogers advance I was known as King; as Mr. Wood's secretary, by my own name. In fact, the two names were used to fill up the playbill. When I joined Wainwright I referred him to the manager of the dramatic company for a reference if he required it.

You were asked whether you ever said before that Baylis's man brought a box of chloride of lime. When you were before the magistrate, did you say it was delivered after the shop was closed, and also this, " I was living at No. 84. It was brought in a hand-cart, and I took it in. I know it came from Baylis. I don't know what became of it"?—I believe I did.

The LORD CHIEF JUSTICE—I don't attach much importance to the actual accordance between what a witness says when he comes forward at a trial and what he says at a police office—or, rather, what he is reported to say. I know how difficult it is, even writing as fast as I do—and I believe, with the exception of shorthand writers, I write as fast as any one—to take down the exact words of a witness when that is attempted at the police office, or by the coroner or coroner's clerk. As long as you get the substance, you ought not to attach too great importance to variation. A witness gives a long sentence; the clerk in taking it down is struck by this or that particular word, and that goes down; but the whole of the context—which often makes all the difference—is not taken down. I quite agree that if there be a substantial difference it should be seriously taken into account; but as to slight irregularities, it does not make so much difference.

The ATTORNEY-GENERAL—I am obliged to your lordship. I think I was a little out of order.

Re-examination resumed—Did you say anything before the coroner about the chloride of lime being brought to No. 84?—To the best of my belief, I said it was brought in late one evening by Baylis's man. When No. 84 was open the shutters of No. 215 were down. It was kept open as long as No. 84 was open. When the shutters of No. 215 were put up, the shutters of No. 84 were put up. We could see from one end of the warehouse to the other in the daytime. There was a paint room at the end of the warehouse, where brushes were kept. It was partitioned off, and a door led to it from the rest of the warehouse. The only light in that room was a gas burner. There was no glass light in the paint room. The partition of the paint room was partly taken away while I was there. The police contract was made on the last Friday in November last year. I recollect when I began to make inquiries about the price of the articles

Evidence for Prosecution.

that it was about a fortnight or three weeks before the com- G. W. Rogers
mencement of November. My wife was confined early on the
morning of 12th September. She spoke to me about the chloride
of lime; that was before her confinement—on the 10th.

    Mrs. JANE ROGERS, examined—I am the wife of the last Mrs. Rogers
witness. We lived from July to November, 1874, in the upper
part of 84 Whitechapel Road. While I was there a young
woman, whom I knew as Mrs. King, came to the house to visit
Henry Wainwright. I have seen her there on several occasions
with him at the end of the shop and in the counting-house,
which was at the end of the shop. I have seen her in the shop;
I cannot say whether she has remained there. I have seen her
sitting in the room with him as I have passed through the shop,
but I have not heard what they said when they were together.
One evening I heard loud talking, but I did not hear what was
said; it appeared to me as if they were quarrelling. The particular evening I am speaking of was about the beginning of
September. I heard the talking for some minutes. I saw her
go out that night, through the fanlight of the door, and Henry
Wainwright followed immediately after.

    I remember on another occasion hearing a noise or disturb-
ance at No. 84. It was in August, as far as I can recollect; I
cannot say the exact date. I heard loud voices in the shop, and
the words, "Don't! don't!" in a woman's voice in a loud tone,
and then Henry Wainwright called my husband. The voice was
in the shop. My husband went downstairs. It was after the
shop was closed, after eight o'clock. Immediately afterwards
the shop door shut, I heard it slam, and Henry Wainwright
went out, I believe. Soon after that the bell rang, and I went
downstairs and opened the door. Henry Wainwright came in.
I said, "Mr. Wainwright, there is a woman lying on the shop
floor." He said, "Oh, is there? She has only fainted; will
you give me a little vinegar, please." I returned upstairs
and brought some vinegar down, and saw the woman lying on
the floor. She appeared to be insensible; she did not speak.
Henry Wainwright took the vinegar and said, "Thank you, I
can manage now," and I returned upstairs. I heard them go
out about a quarter of an hour after. That is all that occurred.

    . I remember a smell at No. 84 which attracted my attention on
10th September. What makes me remember that is that I was
in a delicate state of health, and it was the last time I went out
previous to my baby being born on 12th September. The smell
appeared to proceed from a square case which I saw in
the passage on 10th September. My little girl fell

The Wainwrights.

Mrs. Rogers down on the 11th, and I was upset, and my baby was born the next day. I smelt what appeared to me to be chloride of lime, both on going out and coming in. I was taken ill on 11th. Chloride of lime always makes me feel sick, and that smell made me feel sick. I spoke to my husband about it.

I have seen the prisoner Thomas at the shop in Whitechapel Road with his brother a great many times; he wore a moustache, but he did not have any whiskers at all. His moustache was rather slight, but not large, and he had no beard.

Cross-examined by Mr. Douglas Straight—Prior to September, 1874, there had been no complaint of smells at No. 84. The rooms we occupied were over the shop. I was sitting there when I heard this talking in the kitchen. I believe my husband was with me—it lasted some few minutes. I did not go right to the bottom of the stairs; I went part of the way down, and then came back again. I had seen Mrs. King many times at No. 84—it may have been twenty times; in the daytime as well as in the evening. I remember the earrings worn by Mrs. King because they had a fringe round them. I had closely observed them, and admired them very much.

Did you, when shown the earrings at the Police Court on 6th October, identify them as those worn by Mrs. King?—No; I said they were like them, because they had a fringe round them.

Then all you swore was that they were like the earrings worn by Mrs. King?—Yes.

Did you know that Mrs. King's earrings were gold?—They appeared to be.

Did you not see that the earrings shown to you in Court were brass?—I do not know that they were brass.

But you now know the fact that Mrs. Izzard has sworn that those earrings were hers?—Yes.

Now, be careful, Mrs. Rogers. Did you on 6th October, or on any other occasion when before the magistrates, give a word of evidence regarding the transaction you have now spoken to when you fetched the vinegar?—I did not.

When before the magistrates did you mention that on one evening you heard a woman call out, " Oh, don't "—that Wainwright called down your husband; that you went down afterwards, and saw a woman lying on the floor in the shop?—No, I did not.

You did not say one word about the vinegar?—No.

To whom did you first make that statement?—To Mr. Pollard.

When?—Some time last week; but I cannot say the day.

Did you make it at the Treasury?—Yes.

Evidence for Prosecution.

I think in your deposition you stated it had gone out of your mind till you recalled it by this matter?—Yes.

When did this matter first occur to you?—It was some time after I had given my evidence. I was in the kitchen with my husband and servant when I heard the words, " Don't! don't! " uttered, and a few minutes afterwards Henry Wainwright called my husband down.

By the LORD CHIEF JUSTICE—Did your husband hear the words, " Don't! don't! " the same as you?—I don't know whether he did or not. To the best of my belief, that occurred about the middle of August.

Have you not said either the end of August or the beginning of September?—I think about the end of August I was in a delicate state of health, expecting my second child.

Re-examined by the ATTORNEY-GENERAL—You say you knew the woman who came as Mrs. King. Just look at that photograph. (Photograph handed to witness, in which the deceased and her sister were taken standing together.) Do you recognise in either of those ladies any you have seen before?—Yes, the one in the dark dress is Mrs. King.

By the LORD CHIEF JUSTICE—Is it a good likeness of her?— Yes, I think it is a very good one. After being before the magistrate I talked to my husband and different people about the case and about the woman being found. It was the talk of the neighbourhood.

Re-examination continued—I believe you admired the earrings worn by Mrs. King, and that led you to examine them?— Yes, the earrings I admired had fringes, and so had those shown me in the Police Court. I was attracted to them because they looked so nice.

Did you know Miss Wilmore?—Yes.

Do you remember her coming to the shop at No. 84?—Yes, she came to No. 84 and to No. 215 also.

GEORGE WILLIAM ROGERS, recalled, by the LORD CHIEF JUSTICE—Do you recollect upon any occasion when Mrs. King was at No. 84 you were called down from the room where you were with your wife upstairs by Henry Wainwright?—I do.

Did you hear, before you were called down by Wainwright, any calling on the part of a woman?—Nothing particularly.

You say you remember his calling you down?—I do.

Did you then see Mrs. King?—Yes.

Where was she then?—Just by the partition door.

What did Henry Wainwright say to·you when you went

The Wainwrights.

G. W Rogers down?—He handed me a letter to take to 40 Tredegar Square, and Mrs. King snatched at the letter and tore it open. I then left the premises.

Where did you go to?—I was going to Tredegar Square.

Then you did not go?—No; I did not, though I went out with the intention of going to 40 Tredegar Square.

You say she snatched the letter out of your hand?—She tore it in my hand, but I still held the letter.

When you went out did you still keep the letter in your hand and take it to 40 Tredegar Square, or what did you do with it?—I read it.

Having read it, what did you do with it?—I thought it was a piece of nonsense, and I did not deliver it.

How long were you out?—About half an hour.

Did you say anything to Wainwright when you came in?—Nothing more than that I did not take it. It was a letter from himself to Mrs. Wainwright, and he gave it to me to take to Tredegar Square himself.

The LORD CHIEF JUSTICE—This is entirely new evidence, and if you desire to cross-examine upon it you shall.

Mr. BESLEY—I prefer to leave the fact to the jury, that this has not been mentioned till this moment.

The LORD CHIEF JUSTICE—The fact of the wife having given evidence is quite enough to call for inquiry how far the husband was aware of the facts as to which his wife spoke. (*To Witness*) —What did you do with the letter afterwards?—I brought it home and threw it down in the fireplace.

The ATTORNEY-GENERAL—May I ask him whether it was in Wainwright's handwriting?

The LORD CHIEF JUSTICE—The difficulty I feel is that all this has been got out by the prosecution, and the other side has had no notice; so I don't think I can let the matter go further.

J. M. Steele JOHN MATTHEW STEELE, examined—I am foreman to William Dicker, a pawnbroker in the Commercial Road. I produce two pawn tickets; one of them is in my handwriting, and is for a wedding ring for 10s. on May, 1874, in the name of Ann King, 3 Sidney Square. The name of King was given to me. I don't know that she gave the name of Ann. I put "Ann," as it was pawned by a woman; we put "John" and "Ann" for man and woman. We affix a ticket to the ring and give a duplicate. I also produce a pawn ticket for a keeper ring for 8s. That ticket is in the writing of George Overall, who is present. I cannot from memory tell when these rings were

88

Evidence for Prosecution.

taken out of pawn. When things are taken out the tickets are taken from them and put on a file on which the days are kept separate. The duplicate tickets are pinned together and filed, and they are kept for three years. A tab or memorandum is put between each day on the file. I got these tickets from the day's file of 11th September, 1874. I made a memorandum on the ticket when I took it off that that was the date.

GEORGE OVERALL, examined—I am now an assistant to Mr. Rowley, a pawnbroker of 44 Ledbury Road, Bayswater. I was formerly in the service of Mr. Dicker, when Steele was foreman. This ticket for the keeper ring is in my writing; it was pawned in the name of Ann King, 3 Sidney Square, for 8s. on 22nd May, 1874. I wrote out the ticket myself. I don't remember whether I advanced the money. The ticket has the foreman's initials on it.

HERRIBIN MASON LEETS, examined—I was in the employment of Mr. Dicker twelve months ago. I see some writing of mine on these two tickets for the wedding ring and keeper. I gave those things out of pawn some time in September last year. 19s. 1½d. was paid altogether. There was 13½d. interest. I do not remember who took them out; they were taken out together. The tickets are then filed the same day. Each day's tickets are kept separate. We do not endorse the date on them when the things are taken out. The figures "11-9" on the back are not in my writing.

JAMES KAY, examined—I live at 7 Barchester Street, Poplar, and am a blacksmith in the employment of Mr. Wiseman, coachbuilder, of 216 Whitechapel Road. I have been in his service upwards of sixteen years. My brother William is also in his employ. We were both working there in September last year. I remember in that month doing some work on a van of Mr. Martin's. At the back part of our premises there is an open-fronted shed in the yard, the back of which goes against the back part of 215 Whitechapel Road. There are gates to the yard leading into Vine Court. This was an extraordinarily heavy job for us. Young Master Wiseman, my employer's son, was assisting us. I made an entry of my work in a book. This (produced) is it. I have an entry here in my own handwriting about this job, and on referring to that I am able to say on what day I was doing this job. It looks to me like 11th September. I made the entry on the evening of the same day as the

The Wainwrights.

James Kay job was finished. We were at work from about eleven o'clock in the morning till between seven and eight o'clock in the evening. We finished it in the one day. I referred to the book for the purposes of this case on 20th September last. It had been hanging up behind the door ever since it was done with last year, and I found it there on 20th September.

While we were working at the van, between five and seven o'clock, about six o'clock, as near as I can recollect, there were three loud reports of pistol shots. I was under the shed at the forge at the time, and I had got a heater very nearly ready to bring out. The report seemed to come over my head, from the direction of Wainwright's premises. There were about six seconds between the shots, as near as I can say. They were very rapid, one after the other. My brother ran and opened the gates and went into Vine Court; young Mr. Wiseman followed him. They went in the direction of Mr. Pinnell's gates. I called them back again, because I had got a heater hot, and was just going to heat one of the tires together. They came back directly, and shut the gates. I did not leave the yard; we went on with our work, and did not take any further notice. In September this year I heard of this case.

Cross-examined by Mr. BESLEY—You say it was between five and seven in the evening, and only get at the date by the book? —Yes.

By the LORD CHIEF JUSTICE—Does your employer keep a book in which the work is entered?—Yes; he copies it from this book—in a week or a fortnight afterwards, perhaps longer sometimes.

Cross-examination continued—You have said before you would not like to swear the date was not the 17th. I may take it now that after your attention has been called to the book you have doubts?—I do not see that there can be very much doubt. There are two strokes. I had often before this time heard Mr. Pinnell fire shots in his yard. Before I was questioned as to the affair I had heard that the surgeons had found bullets in the remains. Before that a gentleman connected with a London newspaper came without introducing himself and interviewed myself and my brother. The newspaper gentleman did not ask me or my brother if we had heard shots. I remember now he asked me if I recollected hearing any shots fired, but I was busy with work, and did not stop to talk to him.

By the LORD CHIEF JUSTICE—How did you know he was a gentleman connected with a newspaper?—Because he called again on Saturday, and then he told me who he was.

90

Evidence for Prosecution.

Cross-examination continued—I was not there when he **James Kay** asked my brother William the first time. On the Saturday when he came my brother was present, and the "governor," the elder Mr. Wiseman. It was my brother who first recollected about the shots. Before that we had talked the matter over with young Mr. Wiseman, and afterwards the newspaper gentleman came half a dozen times.

The LORD CHIEF JUSTICE (interposing) said that the questions put by the learned counsel were distinctly irregular. If he wished to contradict the witnesses by the depositions, those depositions must be put in.

To the LORD CHIEF JUSTICE—I told Sergeant Forster that my brother recollected it first.

Cross-examination continued—I had described the rapidity of the shots as three reports all in six seconds.

You have always said you could not fix the time nearer than between five and seven o'clock?—Yes; I made the remark that it was just our tea-time, and my brother agreed. We have no regular tea-time. I did not go by that, but by the fact that we had to finish our job before dark.

Did you talk that over with William?—No.

I ask you again to tell me whether, since your first conversation with the newspaper gentlemen, you talked the matter over several times with your brother and young Mr. Wiseman? —We might have talked of it about three times.

There is another little matter I want to ask you about— that of running up to Pinnell's gate and looking through the keyhole and about the iron being hot. Did you talk of that? —No.

Re-examined by the ATTORNEY-GENERAL—These shots were fired in quick succession?—Yes. I am sure I heard three.

Had you heard shots in rapid succession like those from Mr. Pinnell's before?—Never. I have heard single shots only.

By the LORD CHIEF JUSTICE—At what intervals?—Sometimes one in a day, and one the next day, but never more than one.

By the ATTORNEY-GENERAL—Do you remember, without your books, that you were that day working on this large van?— Yes.

Do you recollect that you had to finish it that day?—Yes, I recollect that we had to finish it that night.

WILLIAM KAY, examined by Mr. BESLEY—I am a wheeler **William Kay** by trade, and am a brother of the previous witness. I work for Mr. Wiseman, and have done so for twelve years. I remember

91

The Wainwrights.

William Kay last year a job being done to a very large van of Mr. Martin's.

Was there anything remarkable about the job?—The only remarkable thing was that it was a heavy job.

Whilst at work did anything attract your attention?—Yes, three reports of firearms.

How were they fired?—Do you mean how rapid?

Yes?—About six seconds, as near as I can recollect now.

By the LORD CHIEF JUSTICE—Six seconds between them?—No, sir; all three of them; they were in very quick succession.

Examination continued—They appeared to be fired just outside our gates. Standing in our yard and looking at the gates, the shots seemed at the left-hand corner.

Would that be by Wainwright's premises?—Yes.

From the loudness of the reports, did it seem as if the shots must have been fired very near?—Very near indeed. It seemed an ordinary report from a pistol, but I don't know the difference in sound between a gun and a pistol. It was between five and seven, as near as I can remember. On hearing the reports I ran and opened the gates leading into Vine Court, but I did not see any one. Young Mr. Wiseman followed me out. After looking about and seeing no one, I went to Pinnell's gate, and looked through the keyhole to see if I could see any one there.

By the LORD CHIEF JUSTICE—I saw no one there.

Examination continued—I knew that Pinnell had a pistol—a single-barrelled one, an ordinary old pistol. My brother called us back, and we went to work again. This must have been after August, 1874, because we had a man working there up to the last Saturday in August, and it was in consequence of his leaving that I went to help my brother. I could not say what time it was in September.

Cross-examined by Mr. BESLEY—There was a great deal of excitement outside Mr. Wiseman's premises after Henry Wainwright was in custody; people were coming about there. On one occasion a gentleman connected with the newspapers asked me and my brother whether we recollected about the shots, and I said no. I recollected it the next day. I talked it over with my brother on the Saturday, and Detective Forster came on the Monday. After he came my brother and I very seldom had anything to say about it; we had something else to do. We never talked the whole matter over; as we thought of anything, we reminded one another of it, that is all. I was not in Court at the inquest when my brother was examined. At the Police

Evidence for Prosecution.

Court I said the time was six seconds. I did not talk about the six seconds with my brother. I could not fix the time of day nearer than between five and seven, because it was the tea-time, and tea-time varies. I did not talk that over with my brother. We were considering what job we had done. That was what we went by; we could tell how long the job was done before dark, and that was how we got at the time. I said that by the time the job was done it was nearer eight than seven o'clock. I am not sure that the van went home that night. I have no recollection of its stopping there two or three days; my impression is that it went home either that night or the next morning. When I was at the inquest I recollected about looking through the keyhole of Mr. Pinnell's door. I am not aware that I forgot to say anything about it; I believe I mentioned it. I daresay I partly read my brother's evidence at the inquest. I did not read the evidence of every witness, but I dare say I read my own. I believe it was me that mentioned about looking through the keyhole, not my brother. I had not talked with him about it. I don't know that he knew anything about it.

Re-examined by the ATTORNEY-GENERAL—I went out, and young Mr. Wiseman followed me. My brother stayed in the yard. I did not see him out there. I don't recollect the van coming to be oiled (looking at a book)—I went round there to do it.

JAMES WISEMAN, examined—My father carries on business at 216 and 217 Whitechapel Road; I assist in his business. I remember some time last year assisting the Kays in a job; I don't remember what it was. I assist them pretty often. I think I was blowing the bellows at the forge under the shed. Whilst there I heard three reports so (tapping the witness-box slowly three times), about that as near as I could judge, coming in succession one after the other. It was in the evening, somewhere between five and seven o'clock, I should think. On hearing the reports Will Kay went out into Vine Court, and I went with him. We could not see anything, and we went back in a minute or two. I could not say what month it was in. I had never heard three reports one after the other like that about there—never but one, that was from the back part of Mr. Pinnell's premises. I know that he sometimes fired a pistol. I have seen his pistol; it has a single barrel.

Cross-examined by Mr. BESLEY—One of the Kays asked me if I remembered three pistol shots, and I at first said no, and then I remembered them. I don't remember which of the Kays it was.

93

The Wainwrights.

J. Wiseman I talked it over with them not more than once or twice, I think. I did not remember it for the minute. I am quite sure that I remember it now.

Mrs. Trew   Mrs. MARY JANE TREW, examined—I am the wife of James Trew and the daughter of Mr. Wiseman. I live at home with my father, and did so in September last year. I was in the habit of keeping his books. James Kay had a little memorandum book, from which I used to enter up my father's books; I mostly copied it. We only keep one book; this is it (produced). I copied it into that. The top entry on the right-hand side is my writing. I copied this from the memorandum book. I have no independent recollection of when Mr. Martin's van was repaired; this entry is all I know about it. I have put it down here as the 9th. I believed it was the 9th when I saw the book. I must have thought so at the time I copied it. Perhaps I made the entry two or three days after the work was done; it might have been a week; I can't remember. I don't know when it may have been done. I do not know anything but what I gather from this book. When I saw this book lately I thought it was very much like a 9.

Cross-examined by Mr. BESLEY—I am accustomed to copy the writing of this workman; he has been a long time in my father's employment; I have done all the copying.

J. H. Pinnell   JOHN HOOD PINNELL, examined by Mr. POLAND—I am an oilman, and am in business at 214 Whitechapel Road. I have a small single-barrelled pistol, only a toy; it is not a revolver (produced). I frequently fired it in my back yard for amusement. I used small bullets or cartridges. I generally kept it hanging up in my shop. I have known Henry Wainwright for many years as a neighbour. I remember on Friday, 10th September, of this year, Henry Wainwright coming to my shop about 11 or 11.30 in the morning and buying some cord. I sold him 8 yards; the price was 2d. He paid me for it and took it away. Nothing more was said about it. This was on the Friday before the discovery was made. The rope I sold was similar to that produced, but I cannot swear to it.

Cross-examined by Mr. DOUGLAS STRAIGHT—How long have you had the pistol?—Four or five years.

Have you been in the habit of practising with it from time to time?—During the whole of that period.

Have you got anything in the shape of a target in the place where you used to practise?—No; I just put it in my pocket to fire for amusement.

94

Evidence for Prosecution.

Is there any portion of the yard to which you were in the J. H. Pinnell habit of directing your shots?—I fired at anything I took it into my head to fire at.

By the LORD CHIEF JUSTICE—Was it with the view of practising to make yourself a shot, or at little birds hopping about, or had you any particular mark to fire at?—I had no particular mark.

Cross-examination continued—Did you practise at night with it?—No.

Did you ever stay in the yard and fire, perhaps, half a dozen shots?—I dare say I might.

By the LORD CHIEF JUSTICE—Where do you keep your cartridges?—In my pocket. [The witness showed how the cartridges were fitted to the pistol.]

You have to take the used-up cartridge out and then put in another?—Yes. It does not throw itself out.

CHARLES SAWYER, examined—I am a wholesale brushmaker C. Sawyer at 63 and 65 Southwark Bridge Road. I was formerly in partnership with Henry Wainwright, and we carried on business together from November, 1873, to January, 1874, as brushmakers, at 84 and 215 Whitechapel Road. I did not reside on either of the premises. The partnership was dissolved on 8th January, 1874.

When your partnership was dissolved, did you act as receiver?—Yes, under the order of the Court of Chancery I took possession of the keys of both 84 and 215. I examined the property on the premises. There was a private office at No. 84, on the first floor. I and my partner had the use of that. I examined the desk and other things in the office. In one of the drawers I found a packet of bullets in a small tin box or brown paper parcel. I think they were conical pin-fire cartridges, bullet and cartridge together. I did not keep them, but passed them to Wainwright. I drew his attention to them when I found them, and he said they were his. I gave them to him, and I have not seen them since. I never sold a revolver to Wainwright. I have a revolver of my own. I should say the bullets Wainwright took away were a size larger than mine. I have my revolver here.

SAMUEL HESSAN BEHREND, examined—I am a solicitor. I S. H. Behrend know the prisoner, Henry Wainwright. In September, 1874, he was first introduced to me. Some money was lent by one of my clients, through me, to him. I took as security a mortgage on the premises, 215 and 84 Whitechapel Road, and also some life assurance policies. Some time in 1875, about the middle of

The Wainwrights.

S. H. Behrend May or June, I wrote to him about the repayment of the money. I issued a writ of ejectment, but at his request I never served it. As soon as I saw the advertisement of the appointment of a trustee in July, I at once took possession of No. 215, and put in a man named Francois, a tenant of mine.

Did you afterwards put a woman called Emma Izzard in possession?—Yes, on 18th July, and when I got possession I gave instructions that a bill should be placed in the shop windows. I also instructed Francois to paint and fix boards outside, announcing that the lease of these premises was to be sold by me.

A. Francois ALBERT FRANCOIS, examined—I am a house decorator, of 31 Greyhound Lane, Fulham. In July of this year I got possession from Mr. Behrend, the mortgagee, of 215 Whitechapel Road. I had no key. I fixed up two boards in the shape of a V, on which was—" The lease of these premises to be sold. Inquire within, or at Mr. Behrend's, 30 Bucklersbury." I did not remain in possession very long. I gave possession and the key to Mr. Behrend.

Mrs. Izzard Mrs. EMMA IZZARD, examined—I am the wife of John Izzard, a carman in the service of Mr. Walker. On 27th August we were sent by Mr. Behrend to 215 Whitechapel Road. We remained there six weeks all but two days, and occupied the rooms in the front part facing Whitechapel Road. We used the kitchen, which is on the first floor back. There were parts of old brushes there which we used to burn. While we lived there Henry Wainwright came pretty nearly every morning for his letters, and I used to give them to him. That continued up to the time we left. I had some old metal earrings, and before I left I threw them into the kitchen fireplace, but I took the rings out of them and wore them. I bought them for common ones, and when I threw them away they were almost black. I left an old umbrella and an old slipper there. I was shown the earrings before the magistrates. I do not know whether Henry Wainwright had a key of the premises; I always let him in. One day he tried the door with a key, but there was no lock on, only a padlock and bolt. I do not know that he had a key of the back door.

Cross-examined by Mr. BESLEY—When any one wanted to make us hear, the proper course was to come to the back door. Inspector Fox has my earrings now. I had had them between two and three years. I do not know whether they were remarkable, but I never saw any like them. A policeman came on

96

Evidence for Prosecution.

Saturday night and told me that .they were sworn to as Mrs. **Mrs. Izzard** King's earrings, and I said that I had thrown them away.

Re-examined by Mr. POLAND—I went to Stones End police station. I bought the earrings at a stall in the street, at **Paddington.**

WALTER ARCHER, examined—I am now an invoice clerk with **W. Archer** Messrs. Venables & Son, of Whitechapel. I have known Thomas Wainwright eighteen months. I entered into his service in January of this year as an assistant. He opened the business of an ironmonger at the Hen and Chickens; the house had been closed before. I was the only person in his service at that time. A stock of goods was brought into the premises. I remained with him for four or five months, until the latter end of June. During that time I have occasionally seen Henry Wainwright there, perhaps five times; I never saw them there together. Goods passed from one to the other. I remember an execution being put in, a man being put in possession about the middle of May. There was a sale after that, in June. The sale was under the control of Mr. George Lewis, who is an accountant in the Borough. Herrick's man was in possession (the auctioneer). The door was fastened by a padlock outside, to which there were two keys. After the sale a new padlock was put on, I believe by Mr. Lewis's instructions, and he had the key of it, which he kept at his place; I do not believe there was more than one key to that padlock. After the sale the business at the Hen and Chickens was discontinued, and all the things were cleared away, and I left. I went into Mr. Lewis's employ temporarily. From the time of the sale I remained there almost a fortnight. At that time the key of the padlock was in Mr. Lewis's place. Thomas Wainwright came to Mr. Lewis's a few days after I had been there, and asked me for the key of the Borough (meaning the Hen and Chickens). Mr. Lewis was out, but I gave it him. He asked me if I would have a glass of stout, and afterwards, with Thomas Wainwright, I met Mr. Lewis. I went into the office while Mr. Lewis and Mr. Wainwright had some conversation which I did not hear. I told Mr. Lewis I had given the key to Thomas Wainwright. On the following Friday I saw Thomas Wainwright again, but nothing passed about the key. I noticed a change in his appearance. He had some hair missing from his face; I do not exactly remember whether it was his moustache or any hair shaved off here. In his ordinary appearance he wore a slight moustache, not particularly light nor yet particularly

H 97

The Wainwrights.

W. Archer dark. I do not remember whether he wore whiskers or beard; he used to shave, and the difference in his hair was parting it down the middle. This is the key of the padlock, to the best of my belief, that I gave to Thomas Wainwright.

Cross-examined by Mr. Moody—At the time he parted his hair differently he used to have the services of a barber. I noticed the change in his hair at Southwark Police Court, and the other change I noticed on or about 2nd July. The sale took place on 28th June. Herrick was an officer of the Sheriff of Surrey. I continued on the premises until the property was sold, until 28th June; as soon as it was sold I went into Mr. Lewis's office from a week to a fortnight. On a Tuesday before 2nd July Thomas Wainwright came to my master's office and asked me for the key. The new padlock was bought shortly after the 18th—before the sale, not after it. No person was left on the premises. I went into Mr. Lewis's office after the sale, and the key was hanging up over the mantelpiece. I never saw it from the time I gave it to Wainwright till it was put into my hands at the Police Court. I had business on the premises after the sale. Mr. Lewis was coming over the bridge, and, to the best of my knowledge, Wainwright had a conversation with him.

I should say that 9d. was about the price of the padlock; it was a very common one. The property being seized under a judgment, Mr. Lewis had no right at all on the premises, so I gave the key to my former employer, Mr. Wainwright.

Re-examined by the Attorney-General—The first change I noticed in Thomas Wainwright's appearance was about his face. I do not recollect whether he had whiskers or beard. One of the two had gone. He was bare where he had had hair. I don't think his moustache was gone. I noticed that there was a difference about the appearance of his face. When I saw him at the Police Court his moustache was gone, and his hair was parted down the middle, with a little curl on each side. I do not recollect whether he wore whiskers at the Police Court; I do not think he did. He had a moustache when I saw him in July. Either his beard or whiskers had gone; it might have been his moustache; I did not take stock of his appearance.

By the Lord Chief Justice—The sale being over, Mr. Lewis had no right to the premises, and was not entitled to the key. Mr. Lewis bought a new padlock, so that Mr. Wainwright should not get in when there were goods in the house before the sale. After that there was no necessity to keep him out.

Evidence for Prosecution.

GEORGE LEWIS, examined—I am an accountant at 14 Southwark Bridge Road. I have known Thomas Wainwright nearly
six years. In November, 1874, he asked me if I would discount
a bill of his brother's. He did not tell me what the money was
wanted for. I said, "You are not friendly with your brother."
He said, "Yes, I am; I have made it up with him." I said,
"Get me the bill, and I will look at it and let you know."
I was aware some years ago that he was not friendly with his
brother. He brought me the bill the following morning; this
is it; it is dated 20th November, at two months, drawn by
Thomas Wainwright, accepted by Henry Wainwright,
for £30, payable at the London City Bank, Whitechapel. I communicated with his brother, who wrote
me a letter, and I discounted the bill. Thomas wore
no whiskers at that time, but he had a small fair moustache.
I afterwards discounted this second bill for him for £62, at
four months. It is drawn by Thomas Wainwright, and accepted
by Henry. Those bills were both dishonoured. They were not
renewed, and I have to lay an attachment against the money
which was in the Sun Fire Office coming to Henry. The arrangement was made between me and Thomas Wainwright, because he
was to receive £300 from his brother when that money came.
I laid the attachment against the two bills, making £92. I
made that arrangement with Thomas in consequence of his
telling me he was to get £300 of it. He said, "When my
brother gets his money I shall receive £200, and if you attach
it you will get your money." He was in no business then,
but he told me he was about to take the Hen and Chickens. I
do not know what he had been doing previously; I had not
seen him for three years. He did ultimately take the Hen and
Chickens, and stocked it very nicely with ironmongery goods.
I lent him not only this £92, but £19 besides, unfortunately
for me. I took a bill of sale on the goods of him. I had sued
him on the £30 bill, and threatened to put in an execution. He
said, "Don't do that; I will give you a bill of sale on my
goods." That was on the £92, and £17 or £18 besides. Mr.
Herrick took possession under the execution, and I told him
to levy.

On the same day as the sale, the man refused to remain in
possession unless a fresh padlock was put on, as seven or eight
lots were left, and I got a fresh padlock for the door. That
was on 18th June. The lots were to be cleared the same day,
but some gentleman could not clear his lots. After all the lots
had been taken out and delivered I locked the place up safely,

The Wainwrights.

G. Lewis brought the key away with me, and hung it up in my office under the clock. There was only one key there. I did not know that Archer had given the key up.

When I returned from the city to my office, I found my papers all turned about, and I said, "Who has been here?" Archer told me that Mr. Wainwright had taken the key from the nail. I know that he had removed the key from the place.

The signature to these bills is in Thomas Wainwright's writing; I know his writing. I produce a letter in Thomas Wainwright's writing, dated 21st November, 1874. I do not know Henry Wainwright's writing. This receipt for some boxes, dated 29th May, 1875, is in Thomas Wainwright's writing; he wrote it in my presence. There is a stamped receipt on it. This paper of 26th July is also his writing, but I did not see him write that. This paper dated "Wednesday" is also in his writing, but I did not see him write it. This paper, dated 22nd May, 1875, he wrote in my presence, giving me possession of the premises. I did not see him write this paper of 10th May, 1875, but he sent it to my office; it is in his writing. I am almost certain that this letter marked E is in Thomas Wainwright's writing. There is no question at all about the others.

Cross-examined by Mr. Moody—Only three of these documents were written in my presence, and I am more clear about the others being his writing than I am about letter E. The lease of the Hen and Chickens is not to Thomas Wainwright only, but to him and a person named Moore, and another person; it is a joint lease. I had no instructions giving me any title to the premises themselves. There was no writ authorising the Sheriff to take possession. The lease has not been executed at all; he went away and left the premises. Everything to which I had a title on the premises was removed before the key was obtained. Thomas himself advised me to put an attachment on the money coming from the Sun Fire Office, and he went with me to see it done, in order that I might get repayment of the £92 owing on the two bills of exchange, and the £18 of which I have never received a shilling, as the goods only realised £7. I charged the usual interest. I charged him 50 per cent. for the money. That was my rate of charge. I was asked before the magistrate, and I did not give the same particulars about the attachment as I have to-day. Thomas had whiskers when he was in the dock before the magistrate, but he had not worn them previously. I saw no difference in him barring the whiskers. I will not be positive whether I have mentioned

100

Evidence · for · Prosecution.

before to-day "a small moustache, fair in colour." Moore G. Lewis was a partner at one time, but he went away in difficulties.

J. M. STEELE, recalled—This is my file, on which the tickets J. M. Steele of each day are kept distinct by a tab. There is a fresh tab at the end of each day. These are five months' tickets. I find here the tab for 10th and 11th September, 1874. These two tickets (produced) were taken from the part for 11th September, 1874. In my daily balance book, in which I entered the number of tickets delivered on that day, I find here in my own writing that the number delivered on that day was thirty-six; there are thirty-four on the file now, two have been taken off

Adjourned till to-morrow.

Fifth Day—Friday, 26th November, 1875.

W. Graydon

WILLIAM GRAYDON, examined—I am manager for Messrs. Rowlandson, upholsterers, 83 Whitechapel Road. I have known Henry Wainwright for seventeen or eighteen years. On 10th September last he came to the shop and bought 2 yards of thick leather cloth, common black American cloth, the commonest we have. The price was 1s. 4d., or 8d. a yard. He did not say what he wanted it for. I have been shown some American cloth by Inspector Fox, which is exactly similar in quantity and colour.

H. Young

HENRY YOUNG, examined—I am assistant to my father, a livery stable keeper in the Whitechapel Road. I have known the two prisoners for ten or fifteen years. I know Mr. Martin's shop and place of business. On the morning of 11th September I saw the prisoners in the New Road outside Martin's shop, between ten and eleven o'clock.

By the LORD CHIEF JUSTICE—How do you know it was the 11th?—Because that was the day of the arrest of Henry Wainwright.

Examination continued—The two prisoners were talking together, and just as I came up Henry left his brother Thomas and said, "Good morning." I spoke to Thomas and said, "You're not looking very well." There was something very different in his appearance, and I asked him if he had shaved off his moustache. He replied, "Yes," put his hand up to his mouth, said "Good morning," and left. I had always known him to have a slight moustache, a little whiskers, and no beard.

I remember on 9th April last removing some fixtures for Henry Wainwright, at his foreman, Rogers', request, from 215 Whitechapel Road. There was a good one-horse vanload of fixtures. I removed them to Collier's Yard, Gloucester Street, Commercial Road. It was a place that Henry Wainwright had had in his occupation some time, and it was in his occupation then. It was his store place when he had the police contract. When I removed the fixtures I took my van to the big door of the warehouse in Vine Court, and Rogers and Titiens took out the things. In taking them out there was an interval, and I went inside the warehouse by the big door. I perceived a heap

102

Evidence for Prosecution.

of ashes on the right-hand side as I went in, and some few minutes afterwards I noticed there was a very strong smell. I can hardly describe the smell; it was very unpleasant indeed. I mentioned it to Titiens, and said that the drains were out of order. We both observed it.

Cross-examined by Mr. BESLEY—I knew soon afterwards that Henry Wainwright was in custody, and I knew of some of the details of Stokes's evidence. It was a good time after the arrest of Henry Wainwright before I made any statement; it might have been in November. I talked it over first with my father, and I believe he communicated with Inspector M'Donald. A few days after that Inspector M'Donald came to see me, and after a week had elapsed, or a little more, from the time of the conversation with my father, I saw some one connected with the Treasury. I did not come to the Central Criminal Court with all the witnesses to go before the grand jury. During the last nine months I have been on business to Collier's Yard, Gloucester Street, a great many times. There are sheds round the yard, and the middle is uncovered. Altogether the premises might be about half an acre in extent. The sheds were the ordinary sheds, with doors that could be locked, and stores were kept in them. When I was at the stores on the occasion referred to in April last, I was there about an hour and a half I should think.

Cross-examined by Mr. MOODY—I had known Thomas Wainwright for many years, and had seen him since July. I don't know that I could fix the time of seeing him except by another witness.

By the LORD CHIEF JUSTICE—How could another witness prove that?—The prisoner was riding about with us all day long, and another witness can prove that.

Cross-examination continued—May not the interview you speak to on the 11th have occurred on the 10th?—No, it was on the 11th.

There was nothing at the time very special to call your attention to their being together?—No, I had seen them together before.

When did you first mention that fact?—I mentioned it the same evening. I spoke to several tradesmen of Whitechapel who were talking about the arrest.

By the LORD CHIEF JUSTICE—You say it was the subject of conversation the same evening?—It was.

Re-examined by the ATTORNEY-GENERAL—There was a great deal of talk in the neighbourhood at the time, and I spoke about it to my father. Inspector M'Donald then came to my father's

103

The Wainwrights.

H. Young house. I do not live there, and I was sent for, and it was then I made my statement.

Do you remember whether it was this month or last?—I think it was in November.

Do you remember that you were asked to come to this Court last session?—Yes, but not to go before the grand jury. I came to this Court as a witness.

The LORD CHIEF JUSTICE—I have been reconsidering my decision not to allow any questions to be put as to the contents of the letter which the prisoner, Henry Wainwright, directed Rogers to take to Tredegar Square, and I think I ought, in justice to the prosecution and to the prisoner, to allow the question to be put to Rogers. Therefore I will allow you to recall him.

Mr. BESLEY said that in the exercise of his discretion at the time, as the existence and contents of the destroyed document depended on the witness who had to give the secondary evidence, he had declined to put any questions.

The LORD CHIEF JUSTICE—Of course, it is open to you to tell the jury to disbelieve everything the witness has said.

The ATTORNEY-GENERAL—I am bound to say that the witness's statement had never been communicated to me or to my learned friends.

The LORD CHIEF JUSTICE—Still, I think that the witness, having seen the scene which he described, and the woman King having torn the letter in his hand, and he having received the letter and read it, it would be best to have its contents.

G. W. Rogers GEORGE WILLIAM ROGERS, recalled, examined by the ATTORNEY-GENERAL—You told us that on one occasion Henry Wainwright called you downstairs, and that he gave you a letter? —Yes.

And you say that Harriet Lane snatched at it in your hand, and that you afterwards went outside and read it?—Yes.

Was that letter afterwards destroyed?—Yes.

By the LORD CHIEF JUSTICE—You destroyed it yourself?—I threw it into the fireplace.

Examination continued—Go slowly now, and tell us, to the best of your recollection, what the contents of the letter were. Tell us, first, was that letter in Henry Wainwright's handwriting?—It was. I cannot recollect all of it, but it was—" I cannot survive the disgrace, and you will never see me any more," or something to that effect. That is as much as I can recollect of it.

104

Evidence for Prosecution.

By the Lord Chief Justice—Was there any particular cir- G. W. Rogers cumstance referred to as causing the "disgrace"?—No, he referred to nothing particular in that letter.

Examination continued—It was in an envelope?—Yes. It was addressed to "Mrs. Wainwright, 40 Tredegar Square."

How did it commence?—I don't think it commenced in any terms, but began, "I cannot survive the disgrace."

By the Lord Chief Justice—There was nothing to show, as far as you can recollect, what that "disgrace" was?—Nothing **whatever**.

Examination continued—How soon after you read the letter did you see the prisoner Henry Wainwright?—I think in about half an hour. I got outside and went for a walk, and when I came back I met him outside the door and told him I had not taken the letter. I did not tell him why, and I cannot remember what he said.

By the Lord Chief Justice—Did you see him coming out?—I met him just outside the door.

Mr. Besley—I have no questions to ask on that.

George William Forster (detective sergeant H), examined— G. W. Forster I took the prisoner Thomas into custody on 1st October in the Fulham Road, near Parson's Green. I told him I was going to apprehend him on a warrant for deserting his wife and children.

What did he say?—He asked me to show him the warrant, and I told him I had not got the warrant with me, but I had seen it. I took him to Leman Street police station, and on the following night he was taken to Clerkenwell Police Court. That charge was dismissed. On the previous day, the 1st, the adjourned inquest had been held, and on the following day I took him again upon the present charge. I was in the waiting room at Clerkenwell Police Court waiting with the prisoner to have the charge heard before the magistrate, and he said to me, "I suppose there will be another charge preferred against me in reference to the spade and axe?" I said, "I expect so." He said, "I was not coming forward voluntarily to give evidence against my brother, but to save myself I had better speak the truth." He then was going to make a statement, and I said, "Stop a moment. What you are going to say I will take down in writing, so that there may be no mistake; it may be used in evidence against you." He then made a statement, which I took down in the book now before me. He said, "I bought a spade and wood chopper on Friday, 10th September, for my brother at Mr. Pettigrew's, 181 Whitechapel Road, for which I paid 3s., and charged him 5s., he having stated that he wanted

105

The Wainwrights.

G. W. Forster them for his house at Chingford." I showed him what I had written. He was looking at me while I wrote. I asked him whether it was correct, and he said "Yes." I then said, "I have seen Mr. Pettigrew, and shown him the axe and spade, and he states that you bought them, or similar ones, of him." He said, "That is quite right. We went round the corner, and Mr. Pettigrew had a glass of brandy, and I had a glass of stout." That is all that passed. After the charge was dismissed there he was taken over to the Southwark police station, and thence to the Court.

I received five envelopes from Mrs. Taylor. One of them contained the letter marked I. This is the envelope that contained it (produced). I took out the note and read it. When I had read it I put it back into the same envelope I had taken it from, marked it, put it into my pocket book, and gave it to Mr. Poland at the Police Court. I remember the letter very well. The envelope had the postmark of 5th September upon it, and the letter began "Dear Pet." The other envelopes were also produced at the Court.

Cross-examined by Mr. Moody—I have stated that I took Thomas Wainwright into custody on the day of the first hearing of the charge against Henry, but I find that it was a mistake; my meaning was the first day I was at the Police Court was on the Monday after 13th September. I knew the warrant was out against Thomas, but I did not arrest him until the 20th. I cannot tell the day on which the warrant was actually issued. He spoke to me about the spade and the chopper prior to going before Mr. Hannay, but I did not mention anything to him about the charge until after he was discharged. Mr. Pettigrew, who has been in business many years in the Whitechapel Road, told me that he knew both prisoners well. I did not know Thomas Wainwright, but I have seen him once before. I had his address given to me by Mr. Mason, the warrant officer. I had not known it before.

J. C. M'Donald JAMES CONSTANTINE M'DONALD, recalled, re-examined—I was at the Southwark police station when the prisoner Thomas was there. He said, "Shall I be taken across to the Court this afternoon?" I said, "Yes; and you will be charged with being an accessory after the fact to the murder of Harriet Louisa Lane. We have found out that you purchased the spade and axe, and that will be proved." He replied, "I will tell you all about it." I replied, "If you wish to say anything, you had better put it in writing." I furnished him with pen and ink and paper, and he wrote the statement produced.

106

Evidence for Prosecution.

Did he say anything at the time?—Yes; he said his brother J. C. M'Donald was a very good fellow, and he only did what one brother would do for another. He signed the paper in my presence.

[The statement of Thomas Wainwright was put in. It was dated " 2nd October, 1875," signed by Thomas Wainwright, and headed "Statement of Facts." It was as follows:—" I beg to state that on Friday, 10th September, at 12.30, I was with some friends at the Black Lion, Bishopsgate Street. From there I called on my brother Henry at Mr. Martin's. He then asked me if I would go and buy for him a garden spade and a chopper for chopping wood. I then went to Mr. Pettigrew's, an ironmonger in Whitechapel Road, and purchased the articles, for which I paid 3s., and charged my brother 5s. I was with Mr. Pettigrew, I dare say, half or three-quarters of an hour. We went and had a drink together, for which, I think, I paid. I then took the parcel, which was in a sheet of brown paper, to my brother at 78 New Road. I then left him. I met Mr. Martin, and went into Clayten's, in Whitechapel, and had some sherry. That was about 2.30. From there I went to Gold's and had my dinner; from there to the Black Lion, Bishopsgate Street, and from there to 1 Racquet Court, Fleet Street, about 4.30, and from there to the Surrey Gardens, and remained with at least a dozen friends until 10.45 p.m.—(Sgd.) Thomas G. Wainwright."]

I saw some keys taken from Thomas at the station, which I produce. I tried one of them on the padlock taken from the door of the Hen and Chickens, and produced by Fox, and found that it would lock that padlock. It does not appear to me to be the proper key. I have seen the other key that was taken from **Henry.**

THOMAS HENN, examined—I am a butcher at Parson's Green. Thomas Henn I knew Thomas Wainwright, who was living at Parson's Green for about twelve months at the Rosamond. He lived there up to the time he was taken into custody. He passed my shop in the morning. I did not supply him with meat. I supplied a person named Raper in the house with meat.

By the LORD CHIEF JUSTICE—Was Raper a person lodging in the house?—Raper was the owner of the house, and Wainwright was a lodger. I knew Thomas Wainwright lived there, because some goods came to the house for him, and I told the man where it was. I have seen him at the house. It is a cottage. I have seen Thomas go to the house and come away from it, but I have never seen him in it.

The Wainwrights.

The Lord Chief Justice—This is very unsatisfactory evidence. Where is the man who was in his service in the Borough?

W. Archer

Walter Archer, recalled, re-examined—I was in Thomas Wainwright's service from January to June, 1875. During the first part of the time, in February and March, he was living at 33 Fentiman Road, Clapham, and the latter part of the time at the Rosamond, Parson's Green, Fulham. I cannot say whether he was on a visit to the Rosamond. Mrs. Raper from there used to visit him at the Hen and Chickens.

F. Pettigrew

Frederick Pettigrew, examined by Mr. Beasley—I am an ironmonger, carrying on business at 81 Whitechapel Road. I knew Henry and Thomas Wainwright. I remember selling a spade and an axe to Thomas Wainwright on 10th September, between twelve and one o'clock in the day. I charged him 3s. for the two, because he was in the trade. The retail price was 5s. It would be impossible for me to say if the spade and axe produced are the same, because I supply other ironmongers with the same sort of articles.

Can you say positively that these articles passed through your hands?—Yes; from the marks upon them I know they have passed through my hands.

Cross-examined by Mr. Moody—I have known Thomas for eight or nine years.

When you were applied to about it, you could not remember the day he came?—That is quite true.

You say you are in the habit of supplying other ironmongers in Whitechapel?—Yes; I send goods to some of them. The mark on the axe is "H. H." and 1s. 9d. The "H. H." means the cost price, and 1s. 9d. means the selling price. The marks were put on by myself, and would be known by any person to whom I supplied goods. The spade is marked in a similar way.

You had not seen him for some few months before this occurrence?—I had not.

And when you did see him, you noticed no change in his appearance?—No. I had some refreshment with him.

By the Lord Chief Justice—You said in your examination-in-chief that this spade and axe were sold on 10th September. What means have you for fixing the date?—I said about 10th September. I am not certain as to the date. I cannot tell why I fixed it for the 10th.

The Lord Chief Justice—Probably from hearing of this matter from the papers.

Evidence for Prosecution.

FRANCIS JOHNSTON, examined by the ATTORNEY-GENERAL—I F. Johnston am a builder and decorator, residing at the Mount, Whitechapel Road. I know Henry Wainwright. Some time in 1874 I got instructions from him to repair his premises at 215 Whitechapel Road. I stippled a window in the warehouse, looking through which from the kitchen one could see into the warehouse. By "stippled" I mean obscured so that it could not be seen through. This window is in the wall nearest the Whitechapel Road. There was a pane of broken glass in it. When it was stippled one could not see from the kitchen window, nor from the skylight into the warehouse, nor *vice versa*. This and other work occupied from the Monday, the 2nd, to Saturday, the 21st November. The house was vacant during that period. We were doing general repairs in the warehouse.

By the LORD CHIEF JUSTICE—Rogers went into the house as soon as I had finished the repairs.

Examination continued—I remember a meeting of Henry Wainwright's creditors, of whom I was one. It took place in July of the present year. A committee of inspection was appointed. I was a member. After the committee was appointed, I saw on a Friday evening in the beginning of August some fixtures being taken away from No. 215, from the back part at Vine Court. I was talking to Mr. Wilcox. The fixtures were being removed by some of Mr. Martin's men. I spoke to them, and after another truck-load had been taken I saw Henry Wainwright passing. I did not speak to him. This was between eight and nine in the evening of a Friday, and it was in the early part of August. I am still on the committee of investigation.

Cross-examined by Mr. BESLEY—I know the difference between liquidation by arrangement on the petition of the debtor and the adjudication of bankruptcy by an adverse creditor. The July meeting was not the first meeting under the petition for liquidation by arrangement.

Is it not a fact that before the second meeting for receiving a proposal from the debtor he was in custody on this charge, and afterwards the proceedings were turned into bankruptcy?—I think it was so.

By the LORD CHIEF JUSTICE—Last year there was a liquidation by arrangement. This year there were proceedings in bankruptcy. I was on the former occasion a creditor also.

Cross-examination continued—Do you not know that these fixtures removed in August were sold to Mr. Martin by the

The Wainwrights.

F. Johnston sanction of the trustee?—I heard afterwards that a portion of them had been so sold.

The repairs you spoke of were necessary to make the house habitable for Rogers?—Yes. Rogers saw me doing the repairs. A pane of glass was broken in the window, and a new one replaced it, and all were stippled the same colour.

By the LORD CHIEF JUSTICE—Henry Wainwright told me he intended to let the house, and that therefore the window required to be stippled and the glass repaired, so that the view of the tenant might be shut out from the warehouse.

Re-examined by the ATTORNEY-GENERAL—He told me that he thought of letting it when he gave me instructions to repair the house and to have the window stippled. I said that I thought it was a very good suggestion that they should not see from the dwelling-house into the warehouse. I was a creditor under the liquidation of 1874. There was a dissolution of partnership between Henry Wainwright and Sawyer. The liquidation was by arrangement. The creditors were before Mr. Sawyer came into the firm in about November; the bankruptcy was in 1875. There was only an arrangement with creditors in 1874. The creditors of Henry Wainwright were paid 12s. in the pound—6s. and, I think, two 3s. It is in bankruptcy now.

C. L'Enfant CHARLES GROJEAN RENNIE L'ENFANT, examined by the ATTORNEY-GENERAL—I am a clerk in the Bankruptcy Court, and produce the books of the Court detailing the proceedings there with reference to the affairs of Henry Wainwright. There was a proceeding for the liquidation of Wainwright's affairs in 1874, and a meeting on 15th March, 1874, at which a resolution was come to, to accept 12s. in the pound, 6s. in seven days, 3s. within a period of three months, and 3s. within a period of six months from that time. In 1875, 30th June, there were proceedings in bankruptcy on the petition of one of the creditors. Wainwright was then declared bankrupt, and the proceedings in that bankruptcy are still pending.

Cross-examined by Mr. BESLEY—The person petitioning in bankruptcy was one of the creditors under the liquidation proceedings, on account of the non-payment of the third instalment of 3s. That does not appear in the official records. The declaration of bankruptcy was on 30th June, 1875, the first meeting of creditors in July, and the second meeting was in November, 1875. Nothing was done between the first and second meeting. The prisoner was arrested in the interval.

110

Evidence for Prosecution.

CHARLES CHABOT, examined—I am an expert in handwriting, and live in Red Lion Square. I have examined the letter E and the documents placed in my hands, together with one headed " Statement of facts," written and signed by Thomas Wainwright. The papers I have before me are the " Statement of facts," marked 1; a letter, from Thomas Wainwright to Mrs. E. Lewis, marked 2; another letter, signed Thomas Wainwright, dated Wednesday evening, 29th May, 1875, marked 3; a letter, signed Thomas George Wainwright, which is dated 26th July, 1875, and not addressed to any person; and a letter, dated 21st November, 1874, to Mr. George Lewis, signed T. Wainwright. Those documents are all in the same handwriting. I have no doubt whatever that the person who wrote the letter E wrote the others. Letter E is not a disguised handwriting. It is the *bona fide* handwriting of the person who penned it.

Mr. MOODY—I have never disputed letter E or the statement; but I must object to Mr. Chabot as an expert being asked to form his opinion on another person's opinion. I submit that he cannot take letters said by Lewis to be, he believed, in Thomas Wainwright's handwriting, but which he did not see him write, as any foundation for his comparisons.

The ATTORNEY-GENERAL said several of the documents had been proved by Lewis to be in the handwriting of Thomas Wainwright.

Mr. MOODY—Mr. Chabot may say that from his knowledge of handwriting and his experience this second document was penned by the hand which wrote the first, but it is still a matter of reasoning and of opinion.

The LORD CHIEF JUSTICE—I have no doubt that this evidence is admissible, but, on the other hand, in a case of this kind, it is unwise to press the evidence of Mr. Chabot beyond the point on which it is founded on undoubted documents.

The ATTORNEY-GENERAL—He has got letter marked 1 and 2, which are undoubted, and is not that enough? (*To Witness*)— You have got a paper marked No. 1, and headed " Statement of facts "—the statement made by Thomas Wainwright after his arrest, being his own explanation of the purchase of the shovel and chopper?—I have.

And you have a letter, dated 29th May, 1875, marked No. 2?—I have.

Will you give your opinion as to the letter (the one signed " E. Frieake," and dated from Dover) as compared with the " Statement of facts " and the letter dated 29th May, 1875?— Am I to exclude the other letters? It is by comparison with

The Wainwrights.

C. Chabot them that the most important facts arise. I now have all the documents here. I may have seen this paper (another) at the Police Court. It is dated 10th May; it is in Thomas Wainwright's writing; I can see that. I do not wish to refer to it, but there are some points in it which are useful. In letter E here are the words " I am," and the " I " is connected with the " a " in a very distinct manner; and in the concluding word of the letter marked 4 the words " I am " are as nearly as possible identical with the words "I am " in letter E. The word " Wednesday " in the memorandum has all the characteristics of the word " Wednesday " in letter E; there is a break in the middle of the word, and the " d " in the middle of the word is made in the same way, and the " y " is made in the same way. There is a little difference in the " W." The manner in which the " t's " are crossed is conspicuous, but the whole word is conspicuous in agreement. The letter " r " of the word " Frieake " in the signature to letter E is like the letter " r " in the word " trunks " in the memorandum of 29th May; it is also like the " r " in the word " remain " in the twenty-second line of the statement marked 1. The " d's " in the word " friends " in letter E is extremely characteristic, and the formation of the " d's " in the word " goods " in memorandum 2 and in this document are equally characteristic. The " s " is, as it were, looped on to the " d." The formation of the final letter " y " is very characteristic in the writing of Thomas Wainwright, and it is very conspicuous in the letter E. There are two instances in letter E where the words " rashly " and " kindly " follow each other, that only occurs once in the letter E in the word " solemnly," and in line eight in the word " any," in line ten in the word " marry," and on page four, line two, in the word " distinctively." The same remark applies to the " y " in the word " sherry," and in the statement of facts in lines fourteen and seventeen the word, too, is characteristic.

By the LORD CHIEF JUSTICE—Besides the characteristic letters to which you have referred, does not the general character of the two hands strike you?—Yes, undoubtedly.

Have you any doubt as to their being the same?—I am perfectly satisfied in this instance of the general character being the same, but I do not rely wholly on the general character.

What is your opinion of the handwriting?—It is a very good handwriting of a very common stamp. But I did not take those letters and form an opinion at once, for I found there were strong characteristics of the handwriting, so much so as to leave no doubt whatever in my mind.

112

Evidence for Prosecution.

[On this positive expression on the part of the witness, the Lord Chief Justice submitted to the prosecution that they had carried the matter of comparison of handwriting quite far enough.]

Cross-examined by Mr. Moody—You have said that the writing is entirely undisguised, and that it would not require such skill as yours to detect the similarity in the writing?—It is undisguised, and is an honestly written letter so far as the handwriting is concerned.

The Attorney-General—There is a letter of the 16th of February from Henry Wainwright, which was found in Harriet Lane's box. Although I referred to it in my opening, I do not think it has been read yet. It is one of the letters which was spoken to as having been given to him by Mr. Lane.

The Lord Chief Justice—There is no doubt as to the handwriting.

Mr. Besley—I don't say it is not a genuine letter, but there is no proved connection between the envelope and the letter. It came from Mrs. Lane, who is not a witness, and it might not be the letter that was sent in the envelope.

The Lord Chief Justice—I can only admit it as a letter of Henry Wainwright's, and not as the letter that came out of the envelope in which it now is.

[The letter, which was read by the Clerk of the Court, was signed " P. King." It ran as follows : —

" I have told you I object to you writing to me at present. I will meet you on Saturday at four o'clock at the same place as last Saturday."

The envelope was dated 16th February, 1874, and was addressed to Mrs. King, Mrs. Wells, 70 St. Peter's Street, Hackney Road. The initials " E. W." were on the envelope.]

[Another letter (marked " B ") was also read, as follows :—

" Dear Madam,—Since I wrote to you yesterday I have heard news of them. I will see Miss Wilmore, and let her know about it. In haste, yours, P. King."]

Henry William French, examined by Mr. Beasley—I am a locksmith, living in Kent Street, in the Borough. I have examined a padlock and two keys (produced). The key produced by Inspector Fox is the proper key of the lock. The other key produced by Inspector M'Donald is not the proper key, although it will open the lock. It was made for a different-sized lock.

Cross-examined by Mr. Moody—I have not opened the lock for examination. I speak from the fact of one of the keys not

The Wainwrights.

H. W. French fitting so well as the other. It is a common lock; both keys will open it, but one is not large enough.

The LORD CHIEF JUSTICE—This key was found upon Thomas Wainwright, and by accident it will open the lock, but that is no reason for saying that he knew that it would open the padlock. There is nothing in this.

F. G. Larkin FREDERICK GEORGE LARKIN, examined by the ATTORNEY-GENERAL—I am a surgeon, practising at 44 Trinity Square. I was called to see the remains of a human body before half-past five on the afternoon of 11th September. I was shown two parcels containing the remains of a female human body. I then made a short examination, and on the Monday gave some evidence. Some portions of the body were mummified.

By the LORD CHIEF JUSTICE—Really, I don't understand what you mean?—Dried.

Examination continued—Some parts were moist and decomposed, in a state known as adipocere. The parts had been separated very unscientifically. The body had been divided into ten parts—head and neck one part, two hands, two arms, one trunk, two thighs, and two legs and feet connected.

Did you notice on the first occasion that a portion of the pelvis was absent from the trunk?—Yes; there were fragments of the pelvis attached to the thighs, and a portion of the kneecap to the right thigh, another part of the kneecap was connected with the left leg. Upon the hair was dried blood. The body had been recently divided.

Did you form any opinion at first as to how long the body had been dead?—At the time, only that it had been a long time dead.

Did you subsequently examine the remains?—Yes, on Monday morning, the 13th, before I gave my evidence, simply to identify the parts. I found that the parts taken together made up a body. Afterwards, on the 14th, I made another partial examination of the body with Mr. Smith. We then removed the viscera, and I observed a cut in the throat. I removed all the viscera, except the brain, which, being in a soft, watery condition, I left for subsequent examination. I put each viscus into a separate jar, which had been thoroughly cleaned out with distilled water, for any possible subsequent examination. Those jars were sealed up and locked in the vestry. I kept the key. Mr. Bond and I together made an examination on the 16th. The age of the woman whose body we were examining appeared to be about twenty-five years.

114

Evidence for Prosecution.

How did you form that opinion?—I was led to this conclusion F. G. Larkin by the condition of the wisdom teeth, all of which, with the exception of one, were cut, and that one was evidently being cut at the time. Her make was slender; her height about 5 feet. The hands and the feet were small proportionately to the rest of the body. I mean they were small for the body. To ascertain the height we put the parts as nearly into position as possible, and repeatedly measured them. The cutting up had been done very roughly and very recently. I have seen the chopper produced. The body might have been cut up with such an instrument. A knife might have been used for cutting some parts. There was a very great deal of dirt on the body, mixed with chloride of lime. The effect of chloride of lime thrown upon a body would tend to preserve the external parts more especially. It is a disinfectant. It retards the decomposition of those parts with which it comes in contact. Its principal agency is to deodorise.

What is the effect of quicklime?

By the LORD CHIEF JUSTICE—Did you find any quicklime?— No.

The ATTORNEY-GENERAL—I perhaps ought not to have asked the question, but I was anxious to have the effect of lime proper. (*To Witness*)—Did you examine the skull?—We found a fracture of the skull just behind and nearly level with the top of the right ear. It was an old fracture. We found some bullets in the head. On inspecting the interior of the skull we found one bullet in the cerebellum.

Did that correspond with the fracture?—We could trace the course of the fracture to where we found the bullet. We found two bullets, and discovered the second before we found the corresponding fracture. We found the second bullet lying on the base of the skull, on a part known as the sphenoid bone. By tracing the direction of that bullet outwards we found another fracture in the skull just in front and nearly level with the top of the same ear, just above that prominence of bone which every one can feel, called the zygomatic arch. One of the bullets had certainly entered during life. That was the one behind the ear. The extravasation of blood led us to that conclusion. It was underneath the scalp, and for a considerable distance around the wound, and also slightly within the skull in the direction in which the bullet had gone, having a diameter of at least 2 inches. There was slight extravasation underneath the scalp, in the direction in which the second bullet had gone. That led to the conclusion that the bullet had entered the head

115

The Wainwrights.

F. G. Larkin during life, while the circulation was active. Similar, but much slighter, appearances of extravasation attended the entry of the second bullet.

By the LORD CHIEF JUSTICE—My inference is that the penetration of the second bullet was when life was fast ebbing. Either would have produced death, but not necessarily instantaneously.

Is that so?—There is a remarkable case in which a bullet was lodged in the brain, and did not immediately destroy life.

It must eventually have caused death?—Oh, yes, if it lodged there sufficient time for an abscess to be formed.

And it might have done so instantaneously?—It might.

Examination continued—Did you find a third bullet?—Yes, later on. Having discovered the bullets, we turned our attention to her cut throat. It was a cut from right to left, beginning just beyond the medial line on the right side of the middle of the neck across to a point above opposite the angle of the lower jaw on the left side. It had severed all the structures from the windpipe down to the vertebræ. It extended about 2 inches to the left, upwards and backwards, below and opposite the angle of the lower jaw—it must have severed the carotid artery. That cut must have been made immediately before or immediately after death. The extravasation of blood in and about the part led me to that conclusion.

Did the extravasation of blood imply that the circulation was still going on?—Had it been done at a time very remote from death, the blood would not have been circulating. It was a wound quite sufficient to cause death in a minute or two. It was an old cut at the time I saw it. I removed the hair pad off the head, took it home, and examined it, and found a third bullet in it sticking very closely to it. There were also in the pad an immense quantity of hairpins. I also took home a piece of velvet ribbon. The hairpins in the pad were bent, broken, and rusty. They were innumerable all over the pad, and sufficient to have arrested the progress of a bullet. The pad itself would help to do it. The velvet was in a rotten state, more particularly the part saturated with blood. We gave the bullets to Inspector Fox. The one I found in the pad was of a different shape from the others. The other two were out of shape, which would result from the way they entered the skull.

- The one found in the pad is also flattened?—More so than either of the others.

When you were with Mr. Bond did you make an examination to endeavour to ascertain whether the woman had borne a

116

Evidence for Prosecution.

child?—We did make a little examination, and then I made F. G. Larkin further examination.

I believe you examined the hair?—Not minutely, as far as I am concerned. I took some of the hair away with me, examined it, ultimately washed it, and gave it to Inspector Forster. Washing it made it reasonably lighter.

Did you notice anything peculiar in one of the teeth when you were examining with Mr. Bond?—I did. There was one—and only one as far as I saw—decayed down level with the jaw. It was the next behind the eye tooth on the right side.

By the LORD CHIEF JUSTICE—From the position which the tooth occupied in the mouth, do you think it would have been visible when she was laughing or smiling?—It might; in fact, I will undertake to say it would.

Examination continued—Did you notice anything else with respect to the teeth?—There were some missing. With the exception of that decayed one, they were a good set of teeth. The only other point I noticed about the teeth was that the remaining incisor tooth at the top indicated that it might have been slightly prominent during life.

Did you notice anything about the ears?—I could only see the remains of one ear, but I could see that it had been pierced for an earring. I think I have now described the various matters to which my attention was directed, which I examined with Mr. Bond. The examination with Mr. Bond was on the 16th.

You say you made a further examination for the purpose of seeing whether the woman had borne a child?—Yes, I did; and that examination gave me a strong idea that the uterus was that of a person who had been a mother.

Suppose the body had not been in a state of decomposition, could you have ascertained the fact with certainty or not?—I should speak nearly as positively as I do now. This is only my opinion, however.

Your attention was not at first, I believe, directed to the fact that it was alleged that there was a scar on the leg?—No, not at first. My attention was first directed to that when I heard Mr. Lane's statement in the Police Court.

When you first saw the body, was it in such a condition that if a scar existed you could have observed it?—It was perfectly impossible for any one to find it unless they made diligent search for it, on account of the state of decomposition.

After Mr. Lane had given his evidence on 21st September, did you and Mr. Bond make an examination for the purpose of

117

The Wainwrights.

F. G. Larkin ascertaining whether there was or was not a scar?—We did. We made the examination in the presence of the surgeon, Mr. Aubyn, who was there on behalf of Henry Wainwright. We examined the left leg first, and then the right leg, and we found a scar on the right leg about 4 inches below the middle of knee. It was very much puckered, an elongated scar running diagonally from upwards down the outside of the leg. It was about the size of a shilling, but the puckering was much bigger, that is the way the skin was drawn. It was such a scar as very possibly would be produced by a red-hot poker falling on the part.

Have you seen a pair of boots produced by Inspector Fox?—I have.

What do you say about them?—I have compared one of them with the corresponding foot, and in my opinion it would fit. I went to the warehouse, 215 Whitechapel Road, and on the flags I saw the remains of stains which might have been produced by chopping up the body, but I cannot say what those stains were.

I think you said there were some teeth missing?—I did. One I picked up myself in the original parcel of the remains, and the others that were missing Mr. Bond had given me.

By the Lord Chief Justice—How many were missing?—Both upper incisors—I think the left eye tooth on the upper jaw, and one or both of the lower incisors. However, they were found and replaced, and only two, the left lower incisor and the right upper incisor were then missing, and they have never been found.

Do you know how the teeth came out of the jaw?—That is very easily accounted for. It is a well-known fact that when the gum recedes from the jaw, and the jaw becomes dry, the teeth are very apt to fall out.

It would not require any violence?—No. The natural progress of decay is quite sufficient to account for their falling out.

Examination continued—Could you form any idea as to how long the woman had been dead?—Only a rough idea. I should say from nine or twelve months.

By the Lord Chief Justice—If I understand you right, chloride of lime, when it came in contact with the body, would have the effect of retarding decomposition?—Yes, I don't think, however, it would affect the internal parts. I don't say it might not, though, to a certain extent.

Cross-examined by Mr. Besley—You say, speaking roughly,

118

Evidence for Prosecution.

you suppose death to have occurred from nine to twelve months. F. G. Larkin
But is it not impossible from the state of decomposition of a
body to judge how long a person has been dead?—I would not
swear.

Is it not scientifically impossible?—It is, to give the exact
date.

What do you mean by extravasation?—An oozing of the
blood.

May there not be extravasation of venous as well as of
arterial blood?—Oh, yes.

Is it not a fact that in some subjects the blood of a dead
person will not coagulate? Some of it will coagulate, and some
will not?—I don't know that I quite understand you.

As I understand the matter, venous blood will extravasate,
but it will not coagulate?—It is so in some subjects.

You are aware there are well authenticated instances of
blood extravasating and coagulating four days, and two days,
after death?—No; I do not know of four days or two days, but I
have not directed my studies to that. The head was decomposed
in proportion to the rest of the body; not more. It was in an
advanced stage of decomposition.

Were not some of the parts of the remains more greasy, or
in the state which you have described as adipocere, but more
in the state you have described as mummified?—I think there
was more of the body mummified.

Is the stage before that, known as adipocere, that in which
the body swells and gases are evolved?—It may be so; I have
not gone much into that.

You don't know that a body, when first becoming decomposed, swells and gives out gases which may be burnt?—I have
heard of that.

Does the stage vary according to the person when the evolu-
tion of gases ceases, and the state known as adipocere commences? Is not the stage well defined between the two?—I don't
think the stage is well defined.

· Your experience has not been so great as to have such a
case as this within your knowledge?—I never had one before.
I have never examined a body in that stage of decomposition.

You did not make at your several examinations an exhaustive
report?—I made an exhaustive report.

How many examinations did you make?—About four, I
think.

At how many examinations had Mr. Bond been present
before the scar was found?—One or two, I think. I did not see

The Wainwrights.

F. G. Larkin Mr. Bond cut out the scar on the leg, nor did I see Mr. Aubyn cut out anything from the other leg, but I heard him say that he should. He called my attention to what he said might be a scar on the other leg.

Were there altogether as many as twelve examinations?—If the slight examinations of the remains or part of the remains were taken into account, it would be as many as that. The remains were very dirty.

In appearance were the remains a dark brown?—They were dark.

Was there any flesh on the face?—A slight portion on the right side.

All the soft parts were decomposed?—Yes; the eyes were much changed, and shrunken back into the socket.

It was quite impossible, then, for any one to recognise the features?—Certainly, unless it was the cheekbones. I should have thought the chloride of lime would tend to bleach the parts, but I have made no experiment to know.

Was the scalp entire?—No; it was not all there; a great deal of the back of it was there, but not all of it, especially where the wound was; it was drawn back.

Are you able to say that the scalp at the places of the two orifices was capable of being dissected?—Certainly not, especially in the case of the front one, The fracture behind the ear was not a round hole, but the front was perforated. Some of the bone was carried away.

Was the brain in such a state that you could follow the direction of the bullet?—Only by following the direction of the dura-mater, the covering of the brain.

The brain was in such a pulpy state that you did not like to remove it?—It was.

Then how do you form your opinion as to the course of the bullet?—By a mark on the inner part of the skull.

Are not the causes of death from gunshot wounds either from shock or hæmorrhage?—I have not sufficiently studied the matter, but that would be the common-sense view.

Don't you know that there are cases of men living six days after receiving a bullet in the brain?—I think it is possible. I have heard of such cases.

And is it not possible for a person to cry out after receiving a bullet in the brain?—Yes.

And is it not a fact that a man who has shot himself through the brain has cried out, and placed himself in a particular attitude?

120

Evidence for Prosecution.

The LORD CHIEF JUSTICE—Do you mean in a studied attitude? F. G. Larkin

Mr. BESLEY—Yes, I read that in "Taylor."

The WITNESS—I cannot say.

Cross-examination continued—Could you say, in the case of two shots being fired within three seconds, whether death resulted from the first or the second?—No. In this case I can only give it as my opinion that it would have been impossible if the first wound behind the ear had been inflicted shortly after death, or closely after death, for the bullet to have got so far under the scalp as it did. In the state in which the remains were I could not point to the exact spot in the scalp where the bullet had got to the skull. There is nothing by which I could say whether the bullet in the pad was from the first, second, or third shot. I am not quite clear as to the extent of the cut into the vertebræ. It might have been done with an ordinary knife.

What makes you say that you are inclined to the opinion that this was the body of a person who had borne a child?—Why I am inclined to the opinion that the body was that of a person who had borne a child is because the measurements of the uterus were greater than those acknowledged to be the measurements of a virgin uterus. Virgin uteri of adult women are very much the same in measurement, also in weight and general size, provided they are healthy. The external measurement of a virgin uterus, including the substance, the extreme length would be about $2\frac{1}{4}$ inches to $2\frac{3}{4}$ inches, and the breadth about an inch and a third, while this uterus that I examined was, as near as possible, 3 inches, and its breadth about $2\frac{1}{2}$ inches. Another reason for my opinion is the thinness of the walls. I should say, taken conjointly, the front wall and the back wall of a virgin uterus would measure about an inch, half an inch one side and half an inch the other. There is no cavity; the surfaces lie flat. After child-bearing the walls become thinner, and, as near as I could say, the measurement of the walls of this uterus were five-eighths of an inch. I think it is not a fact that the walls get thicker after child-bearing, I certainly shall not admit it. I cannot explain why they should get thinner. I adhere to my opinion; perhaps it is not worth much. Another ground for my opinion is, that I have compared this uterus with the several uteri in the museum of Guy's Hospital, both those of the virgin and those of persons who have borne children, and it is certainly inconsistent to think it is that of a virgin, because it is so unlike all what I see there of virgin uteri. Another reason is, the condition of the walls

121

The Wainwrights.

F. G. Larkin of the abdomen. In the state of decomposition it was possible for me to form an inference. I do not give positive testimony to any of it. At the lower part of the abdomen I observed what appeared to be a scarred-like surface, a whitish colour, and lower down the decomposition had progressed very rapidly in between what appeared to be little cicatrices, little scars, and as the surface of the abdomen would be there a little irregular, uneven, I can quite understand that the decomposition would in between those scarred places have gone on more rapidly; that is only inference. I gather from all this that after a woman had borne a child, of course the abdomen being very much stretched during pregnancy (especially the latter months of pregnancy), when the child is born, of course, it leaves the abdomen in a flabby condition, and these scars are the result of that, the contraction of the abdomen to a certain extent. This appearance is just as consistent with a person who has suffered in their lifetime from fever or dropsy, but I take it in conjunction with what I have observed elsewhere. If I had had the best opportunity of noticing what are called cicatrices, I should not have formed any different opinion. I met two or three gentlemen with the uteri at Guy's Hospital, once before I was cross-examined at the Southwark Police Court. I did not find any hair on other parts of the body besides the head to recognise it. I have not made any experiments as to the effect of chloride of lime respecting its colour.

Would it be a natural inference to suppose that you would find a furrowed finger if a woman had been wearing a wedding ring for three or four years?—Yes. These particular fingers were not in such a state that you could trace the furrow of a wedding ring. I made a careful examination for that purpose, but I could not see anything—it might possibly be traced in a fresh subject. The condition of the hand was similar to the rest in its greasy state.

Did you measure the foot?—I measured the foot, and found it 8½ inches in length. That was not too large a foot for a person 5 feet 1 inch in height. I cannot say it was a smaller foot than I would expect to find in a woman of such a height. The uterus weighed, as nearly as possible, 12 drachms, and one source says a virgin uterus weighs 8 drachms.

You measured the body?—I took the actual measurement of the body from head to feet, and made it 5 feet. Through death many months previously and decomposition the length might be in excess of that during life. I can understand that the decayed tooth could have been seen if she laughed, and must

Evidence for Prosecution.

have been seen in smiling. I should not describe the whole of the upper set of teeth as projecting very much; there was nothing extraordinary about the teeth except that the central incisors were slightly prominent.

Re-examined by the ATTORNEY-GENERAL—It would be perfectly impossible for the woman to have inflicted the wounds found on her body herself.

By the LORD CHIEF JUSTICE—Suppose the bullet that first entered the brain allowed life to continue for some time, can you form a judgment as to what its effect upon the sensibility of a person would be? Do you think a person would be in possession of his faculties when he got such a bullet as that in the brain, so that he would be able to cut his own throat afterwards? —I cannot say.

THOMAS BOND, examined by Mr. POLAND—I live at 50 Parliament Street, Westminster, and am a Fellow of the Royal College of Surgeons, assistant surgeon to the Westminster Hospital, and Lecturer on Forensic Medicine at the Hospital. On 16th September last I saw the remains of this body at the deadhouse. Mr. Larkin was present. The body was that of a female of short stature, about 5 feet in height, of slender make, limbs, and body. I thought she was from twenty to twenty-five years of age, and that the body had been dead many months. The hands were slender, and covered with a greasy substance. The skin underneath was dry and sunken. The feet were in the same condition. As to the wedding ring, I think if there had been a very deep furrow during life I should have found it. The hand was a very slight one, the fingers very thin.

By the LORD CHIEF JUSTICE—Would a ring worn upon the finger make more or less of a furrow according as the hand was full or thin?—It is obvious it would make a deeper furrow on a fat hand than on a thin one.

If the ring were discontinued some time, would the furrow still remain?—I cannot say.

Examination continued—The boots (produced) could have been worn by the deceased person. I found four teeth absent on my first examination. Those in the head were all sound, with the exception of one, when I examined them. That one was the first bicuspid of the upper jaw, which was decayed almost to the bone. I have seen that tooth decayed in persons when they laughed. There was no means of telling whether the mouth was small, as the features were quite gone. In the upper jaw the left wisdom tooth was still uncut. I exposed it by cutting away the mucous membrane. I noticed that the one remaining upper

123

The Wainwrights.

T. Bond incisor was prominent when my attention had been called to it by Mr. Aubyn.

The marks upon the body where it was cut appeared to be comparatively fresh, but the throat had been cut for a long time. It commenced at the thyroid cartilage. It was cut from the larynx to the angle of the lower jaw from right to left. Part of the windpipe and the arteries were severed. I cannot say when this was done, but I believe it was during life, or soon after death, at a long period anterior to my seeing it. Considerable force must have been used. I examined the head. I heard Mr. Larkin describe the fracture behind the right ear, and I agree with him that it was an old fracture. I found the bullet in the head, and was able to trace its course from the fracture behind the ear. It had lodged in the cerebellum, and must have gone there during life. I am sure of it from the blood extravasated under the skull, and also under the dura-mater, which is the lining of the skull. Blood was extravasated under the scalp for a circumference of about 3 inches, and to the depth of 1-16 of an inch into the substance of the scalp. I found a second bullet in the base of the skull lying on the sphenoid bone. I traced it outwards to an orifice by the right ear. I formed the opinion that it had entered during life or immediately after death. There was extravasation of blood under the scalp, but not to so great an extent as where the first bullet had entered. It was quite impossible after receiving those shots that a person could have cut her own throat, and it was perfectly impossible that a person's throat being so cut she could have fired the shots afterwards.

I am of opinion that this woman had borne children, but I believe it to be impossible to give a positive opinion by an inspection of the uterus. No scar could be seen at the first examination, but in consequence of Mr. Lane's statement at the Police Court, I made an examination. I scraped off the greasy matter first from the left leg, and there was no scar. I then scraped the right leg, and I found there a scar, on the outer side of the leg, about 2 inches below the head of the fibula, or 3 inches below the joint of the knee. It was a very distinct scar, about the size of a shilling. It was elongated from above downwards and slightly backwards, thick and fibrous. The skin was puckered a good deal in front of it, and the skin at the back part of it was white. It was perfectly consistent with the appearance of a burn from a red-hot poker. Till I scraped, I could not see this scar. I cut it out.

Is it capable of being produced?—I have it in my pocket.

Evidence for Prosecution.

[The object was preserved in a white bottle filled with spirits, T. Bond which was handed in the first instance to the bench.]

The LORD CHIEF JUSTICE—It requires daylight to see it. [The gas in the Court had been lit.]

The WITNESS—Undoubtedly, my lord.

Examination continued—You had the bullets, I believe, which were found in the skull?—I had. (The bullets were produced.) They are conical, and appear to have hit something. The first which I found weighed 66 grains. The second which I found weighed 78 grains. The third, which Mr. Larkin found, weighed 82 grains.

Would not the bullet in the course of coming into contact with bone be apt to lose lead?—I know from experience that a bullet loses lead by coming into contact with bone.

You saw the yard at the premises, 215 Whitechapel Road?—Yes.

Did you notice before you went there any appearance of chloride of lime on the remains?—Yes, I did, and earth also.

You then went to the premises?—I went into the premises at No. 215 and examined the earth, and found a quantity of chloride of lime mixed with the earth, and I saw some lumps of it which had been picked out by Inspector Fox. I did not find any hairs in the grave, but I saw some on the shovel. I took some of them, and I compared them under a microscope with some of the hairs on the body, and they corresponded in colour and substance and in the marking of the medullary substance. I also compared them with some shown me by Inspector Fox, and they corresponded in the same way. I saw a chopper at the station. It looked dirty, and smelt very like the remains. I agree that the chopper might have been used for roughly cutting up the body.

Did you see any marks on the stones in the yard?—Yes; I saw marks on the stones that might have been produced by chopping, pieces of the stone being broken, and I saw a faint, smeary outline on the stones.

By the LORD CHIEF JUSTICE—Did the marks on the broken stone appear to you to be greasy?—Undoubtedly they were; and one corner piece of a step was clearly chopped off.

Cross-examined by Mr. BESLEY—In the process of decomposition gases are evolved very soon after death, I believe to such an extent that flame can be kindled with them, sometimes in a much shorter period than a month or six weeks, sometimes in two or three days. I am of opinion that the remains were those of a woman who had borne a child, because the cavity of the uterus was large in proportion to the thinness of the walls; that was my reason then for that opinion. There were

125

The Wainwrights.

T. Bond no indications to lead me to a contrary opinion. I have since had another reason for thinking she had had a child. I have had the uterus soaked, and it has swelled to at least three times the size that it was when I first examined it, and now the walls have become very much thicker, and the whole organ heavier and larger than the healthy uterus of a virgin. The inference I draw from that is that the uterus was then about its proper size; when I first examined it it was exceedingly shrunken and dry. I differ from Mr. Larkin that the bearing of children thins the walls; I think it thickens them. The soaking process commenced after my first examination, after the first evidence at the Police Court, and after I was examined at the inquest, within a day or two. Mr. Larkin soaked it; I did not. He told me it was soaked in spirit and water. I saw it in the spirit and water. I believe it has been kept there ever since. I did not measure the walls before the soaking process; they were very thin, a little thinner than thick brown paper. I have measured the whole uterus since the soaking process, not the thickness of the walls. My measurement of the whole uterus was just over 3 inches long, and the width about $2\frac{1}{2}$ inches, and the thickness over an inch.

The wisdom teeth sometimes come late in life, sometimes over thirty years of age. I think it is impossible to fix the age of the person whose remains these were within ten years. I don't know that the decayed tooth is the one with least enamel and most subject to decay. I had an impression the other way, that the wisdom teeth were the first to decay, the last to come, and the first to go; such has been the case with me.

Chloride of lime takes away some colours. I don't know that it will take away colour from hair. I would not say it would not, but I don't think it would. It would take it from unstable colours. It undoubtedly retards decomposition.

I was present when Mr. Aubyn took a piece from the other leg; I looked at it as he held it; I saw him cut it out. I examined it as he cut it out and as he held it in his hand. I am quite prepared to say that it had not a scar. I measured the height very exactly several times; I did not make her quite 5 feet; I made her 4 feet 11 inches and one-eighth. I think the fact of death having occurred so long back as nine months would not lengthen the height; it would shorten it; but I don't think to any great extent; it might to the extent of an inch. I was of the same opinion at the Police Court. I made four examinations altogether. The cut in the throat was done with great force. I am most undoubtedly of opinion that it was done by

126

Evidence for Prosecution.

some other hand than that of the individual whose remains I **T. Bond**
saw. I cannot pledge myself to what period of time after death
that injury was inflicted.

By the Lord Chief Justice—I say that the deceased could
not have fired the two bullets into the brain, and after that cut
the throat, or *vice versa*, she could not have cut her own throat,
and then have fired the bullets into the brain. The force with
which the cut was done is one reason why I say she could not
have done it herself, and another reason is the direction; it was
not a direction in which a suicidal wound is caused; it has
scarcely ever been found except in the case of a left-handed
person. A person would not cut up in this way (describing);
they would cut downwards with the right hand. The cut was
carried deeply in under the jaw; it must have been commenced
in the medial line. What I say is that, from the position of the
cut, it could not have been done by the person herself unless
she was left-handed. I have a very strong opinion that it could
not have been inflicted recently because of the retraction of the
tissues and the great dryness of the tissues quite down to the
bone.

Cross-examination continued—I could not say positively at
what date it was done. I say positively that to me it appeared
not a recent cut; it was quite different from the other cuts I
saw. As to a positive opinion, it is not for me to give it. When
the muscles and ligaments are relaxed shortly after death I
believe persons measure more after death than in life. I have
never actually found the measurement longer myself. I have
not had occasion to do so; but I think it would be the reverse
after the drying of the tissues. I think the inter-vertebral
ligaments would shrink and the ligaments retract. I am not
able to give a definite opinion as to that from experiments, but
I can tell as a fact that all these tissues do contract. I know
as a fact that immediately after death they relax, and they
retract when dryness takes place. I have not had occasion to
examine remains in such an advanced stage of decomposition
for the purpose of measuring height. I have dissected bodies
much longer decomposed, but I did not know them in life or
measure them in life.

Re-examined by the Attorney-General—I had some difficulty in putting the parts together so as to measure accurately.
I was guided by the exact anatomical position of the parts. It
is not an easy thing to get them exactly placed in position. I did
it to the best of my ability. In the condition of the body that
I examined the ligaments were contracted, and the inter-vertebral

127

The Wainwrights.

T. Bond cartilages must have contracted from the extreme dryness; in fact, I cut out the vertebræ, so I know as a fact that they were contracted and dried; I think it might make the difference of an inch. The wisdom teeth usually appear from twenty to twenty-five, and even earlier sometimes.

As to the cut in the throat, I cannot say whether it was inflicted during life, or immediately after death. There was nothing to lead me to tell which. There was nothing to lead me to say that it was not inflicted during life. There was blood around the cut, but I can't say that the blood came from the cut. It might have come from the gunshot wounds. If I had seen blood in the cut I should have said that it must have been done during life, or otherwise before the circulation had ceased. The cut extended just to the left ear, and the ear around that particular part was exceedingly much clotted with blood directly at the end of the cut, but I cannot tell whether it came from the cut or the other wounds. The blood from the wounded head might have flowed over. If I could have traced the blood to the cut and nothing else, then I should have been certain that it must have been inflicted during life, or before the circulation had ceased. I saw no blood in the cut; the cut commenced on the right-hand side, in the cartilage, and it went deeper and deeper until it got very deep, quite under the angle of the lower jaw. In my opinion it was a cut upwards, because the only way to make it downwards would be quite to make a slanting cut down under the jaw and then draw it down, which would be a very unlikely thing to do. In my opinion it went from the centre of the throat up, under the left angle of the lower jaw, going deeper as it went on towards the left ear; the head was severed from the trunk lower down, underneath the cut; the cut had nothing to do with the severance from the trunk. There was greater extravasation below the scalp where the first bullet had entered and below the dura-mater than the other. I think the pistol shot wound would produce death instantly. If it did, that would account for the less quantity of extravasation from the other wound.

By the LORD CHIEF JUSTICE—The heart would probably stop within a minute when death was caused by the shot. I have said that it is difficult by the inspection of the uterus after death to form an opinion whether a woman has borne a child or not; but I should expect after child-bearing to find the walls of the uterus thickened. That would give me some material upon which to form a judgment. Thickened walls are compatible

128

Evidence for Prosecution.

with child-bearing, but they are also compatible with inflamma- T. Bond
tion of the uterus or other diseases of the uterus, therefore it
would not be a safe inference. I should expect to find general
enlargement and thickening of the walls of the uterus. I think
no reliable judgment is to be formed as to whether a woman has
had more than one child. I think that is impossible, because
I do not believe it makes the slightest difference to the uterus
whether she has borne one child or two or three. Since the
parts have been soaked they have become much thicker than they
were; but I do not say much thicker than in a virgin
uterus. The walls of the uterus of a woman who has borne
children are not much thicker than a virgin uterus; but they
are thicker. In my judgment it was impossible to form a confident opinion as to whether this woman had had one child or
more.

JAMES SQUIRES, examined—I am a gunmaker at Newcastle J. Squires
Road, Whitechapel. The three bullets which were shown to me
by Inspector Fox are either the central fire, No. 320, or the
rim fire, 297. They would fit either of the revolvers produced,
and not a pin fire revolver. I have here a rim fire revolver and
a central fire; the 297 would fit one and the 320 the other.
All the bullets fit both pistols, they are all one-sized bullets.
I cannot tell which they belong to; they might be fired from
either; all the three bullets fit the same revolver. You could not
fire these bullets from either revolver, because one is a central
fire and the other a rim fire. I cannot tell to which they belong.
They are conical-shaped bullets. This little bullet of Mr.
Pinnell's would not fit this pistol. Mr. Sawyer's bullet is the
same size; it is called a pin fire; it does not compare with the
three.

MATTHEW FOX, recalled, re-examined—I have measured Mrs. Matthew Fox
Allen. She is 5 feet ½ inch without her boots.

GEORGE WILLIAM ROGERS, recalled, re-examined—I cannot G. W. Rogers
swear that this is Thomas Wainwright's signature in the
signature-book, but it is something after the character of it.
I cannot say to the best of my belief that it is his; the character
is different. I have looked from page 33 to the other corner,
and there are two handwritings. This " H. Wainwright & Co."
is in Henry Wainwright's writing as the referee.

Court adjourned till to-morrow.

W. L. Moet   WILLIAM LOUIS MOET, examined by the ATTORNEY-GENERAL—
I was formerly a clerk in the City and County Bank, at 33
Abchurch Lane. That bank is now in liquidation. Thomas
Wainwright kept an account there. I have his signature in our
signature-book. In it all the customers who open an account
sign their names. I saw that signature written by some one
who said his name was Thomas Wainwright. I cannot identify
the prisoner as the man who wrote it.

By the LORD CHIEF JUSTICE—Do you remember the person
of the individual who wrote it?—No.

Mr. MOODY objected to the evidence as the writer of the
signature was not identified.

The ATTORNEY-GENERAL—At present I am only proving a
fact. I can only go by steps. I am going to ask how much was
written by the man who represented himself as Thomas Wainwright; but perhaps I can shorten the matter.

The LORD CHIEF JUSTICE—The fact of a person signing a
name is nothing unless he is identified.

The ATTORNEY-GENERAL—I am aware of that. Let Rogers
stand up. (To Rogers)—Do you know that writing?—I could
not swear it is Thomas Wainwright's writing.

Examination continued—There are two handwritings in the
entry. The signature of the referee, "H. Wainwright," is
Henry Wainwright's writing.

T. Bond   THOMAS BOND, recalled, re-examined—Since yesterday I have
measured the neck of the uterus and find it to be an inch in
thickness. I measured the fundus and found it to be one-eighth
of an inch in thickness; that is Mr. Larkin's measurement.
The part he measured was very flaccid, and if not held up, but
pressed down by its own weight, it was much more; and may
I say as to the scar, if it is taken out and put in water it will
measure more; it is now contracted. [The witness was directed
to do so.]

Evidence for the Prosecution closed.

Address to Jury.

Opening Speech for Henry Wainwright.

Mr. Besley Mr. BESLEY addressed the jury on behalf of the prisoner Henry Wainwright. He referred at the outset to the undue excitement in the minds of the public occasioned by the. many reports and articles that had already appeared in the papers in respect to this case; and contended that all this excitement was prejudicial to the prisoner. It was also injurious to a prisoner, that he was not informed before the trial of every detail of such evidence as that of surgeons that would be brought against him. These things, together with the production of evidence in the witness-box, of which even the prosecution knew no word beforehand, made the defence of a prisoner a task of stupendous difficulty. It was often spoken of as a chain of evidence, and the jury must be satisfied that the whole chain was in the perfect state in which the Attorney-General had alleged it to be. No evidence had been given to show that the prisoner took Harriet Lane from home when she left her father's in 1871, nor had it been proved when or how she became acquainted with Henry Wainwright. They were first met with together at Temple Bar in August, 1872, when an arrangement was made for Miss Wilmore to take the child; and in that matter the prisoner did what he had done all through, viz., acknowledged his children and paid for them far more than the law would have compelled him to pay if he was disposed to act towards Harriet Lane in an unworthy manner. After he took the lodgings for her at Mrs. Wells's, he had never spent a night under the same roof with her, and to say that he had a motive for getting rid of her was pure speculation.

Referring to the Frieake incident, the learned counsel said— the Frieake incident is divided into two parts; one will be devoted to dealing with that part which refers to Frieake up to the letter of 31st August, 1874, and the other to the period subsequently, when Miss Wilmore and the other persons come to make inquiries as to Harriet Lane. With reference to the evidence who Edward Frieake was before September, 1874, you were to have had the facts laid before you by the Attorney-General supplemented, because that which was given before the magistrates was untrustworthy. A servant of Mrs. Foster was to have been referred to as proving having fetched some champagne glasses; but in any case it was to have been clearly established that Thomas Wainwright was Edward Frieake. Now, it is part of Henry Wainwright's case that there was a person other than the gentleman who was called as a witness

131

The Wainwrights.

Mr. Besley here, who actually bore, or assumed to bear, the name of Edward Frieake. On the part of the prosecution they are endeavouring to suggest that, from October, 1873, there was a deliberate premeditated plan and scheme by Henry Wainwright to murder Harriet Lane. Now, I leave you to say whether you can reconcile that with the conduct of Henry Wainwright. It was put in evidence that there was a stern letter saying " do not come here "; but there is no evidence that the letter— which does not seem so very stern—was anything more than a request to Harriet Lane not to call at 84 or 215 Whitechapel Road, as the case might be, and a suggestion that they should meet elsewhere. That is the sole foundation that there was any other feeling in Henry Wainwright's mind than feelings of consideration, if not of affection, for the woman and children on whose behalf he was paying large sums of money.

Let us see how they endeavoured to make out this astonishing conspiracy between two persons, by which Thomas Wainwright was to be represented under the name of Edward Frieake—a person well known, be it observed, as he must be, to many in the East End of London, for he was continually fulfilling the semi-public functions of an auctioneer. They tell us that this conspiracy existed at the time of Harriet Lane's lodging with Mrs. Wells. Now, Miss Wilmore appears to have been a constant visitor there, but she does not tell us she ever saw there a person called Frieake; but Mrs. Wells says that Mr. King at one time brought a friend there with him, whom he called Edward. Now you are not to suppose that because a person is called " Edward " he is called Edward Frieake. There is no evidence that Henry Wainwright ever called " Edward " Edward Frieake; and the identity, if it can be said to arise, arises in the most unsatisfactory way from the evidence of Mrs. Wells, who had nothing to recall her attention to the fact of the visit of this person for two years, and who, remember, was unable to identify him in the ordinary way of selecting a person from a number of others. I submit that in this case there is a temptation for persons to rake up every little fact, and so to colour and exaggerate them unconsciously that they are really giving false evidence, though they believe themselves to be speaking the truth. It may occur to you that if Thomas Wainwright was not the " Edward " of the visit to Mrs. Wells, why should not the prisoner Henry produce that friend? But you must not assume that he is guilty because he is not able to produce witnesses to combat every little point. If he has forgotten that friend, he cannot call him. But whether true or false, you must remember that it is a necessary link in the chain

132

that at this time there was a cool, premeditated design between **Mr. Besley** the two brothers to murder that woman. Can you conceive any motive for selecting the uncommon name of Frieake when Brown, Jones, or Robinson would have answered the purpose equally well? Why should they choose a name which would at once attract attention, and arouse Harriet Lane to make inquiries? But did she make inquiries? No such thing. Is there a trace of a person named Edward Frieake? The fact is, Mrs. Wells has had her mind excited, and has been casting about for trifles, and, having got some trifle, has dressed it into an incident or a plot to murder, conceived long before it was put into execution. Mrs. Wells's evidence as to identity is such that the word "frivolous" is too dignified to apply to it. She said, in answer to the Lord Chief Justice, that she had not been able to identify him when she was shown him, and her sole description of the "Edward" who came to her house was that he had a slight moustache, but that he looked so much younger that she could not say whether he was Thomas Wainwright or not, as he passed under her view on but two occasions, and then only for a short period. That appears to me to be the most flimsy of evidence as to the question of identity. Although this is more essentially the case of Thomas Wainwright, I deal with it as the advocate of Henry Wainwright for the purpose of destroying the suggestion that these two men were in combination together long before September, 1874, to achieve a purpose which was achieved at that time.

We now come to her lodging with Mrs. Foster, which is from May, 1874, and I have to deal with the period of the four or five months following. The next three witnesses are Mrs. Jemima Foster, Miss Stanley, and Miss Wilmore, and they refer to the Frieake incident at that part of the story. They are the witnesses who spoke to these facts when before the magistrates; but Humphries is a supplemental witness, who is to establish the charge of joint action by the two prisoners. Mrs. Foster speaks, I believe, of one or two visits. It is almost impossible not to contrast her evidence with the evidence of Humphries, who is contradicted by her. If they were both speaking of the same identical champagne, they cannot both be speaking the truth, for Mrs. Jemima Foster has distinctly spoken to two occasions, on the first of which a pint of champagne was sent, and on the second a quart, and she also speaks of the borrowing of the glasses. She undoubtedly placed these two occasions at a period entirely distinct from that at which she was attracted to her door by the disturbance outside. Then she speaks of the identification of Thomas Wainwright as Edward

The Wainwrights.

Mr. Besley Frieake; and you will remember that on the first occasion she had only a very slight opportunity of seeing the person who came there, and certainly the non-recognition of Thomas at Leman Street police station is a signal and important fact upon the question of identity. Mrs. Foster failed to recognise him there, and I do not know that she was very strong in her recognition here. Miss Wilmore, the most trustworthy witness, almost negatives the suggestion that Thomas Wainwright was Edward Frieake the second, or the false Edward Frieake—and it is for you to consider whether there was not really another person who was entitled to use that name. Miss Wilmore said, when asked to describe him, that he was a thin man, with a light moustache—that when he came he did not stay long, and that it was in the evening time. She is asked whether she thinks either of the prisoners was the person, and she says, " I am not sure." When she is cross-examined she describes him as a person of youthful appearance, not very short, but in the most essential characteristic very different from Thomas Wainwright, viz., a person with a light moustache. She had the vaguest possible recollection of the person; and you must remember that the name was not given on the first occasion, but only on the second, after Harriet Lane had said that Edward Frieake was going to give her two rooms of furniture. That is quite consistent with the name being an assumed name, but it is also consistent with the person being entitled to use the name. It has been practically admitted by the Attorney-General that this was evidence upon which not much reliance could be placed, unless substantiated by other evidence. With regard to Miss Wilmore, she almost negatives the supposition that Thomas Wainwright was the person, and almost establishes the fact that there was another man going by the name of Edward Frieake. She is a person who is deaf, and persons with that affliction generally have their other senses sharpened to an unusual degree. She therefore would have been more likely to use her eyes than a person who could hear well, and was therefore a deal more likely to make accurate observation.

At Mrs. Foster's, as at Mrs. Wells's, from the time Harriet Lane was there, Henry Wainwright never entered the house. There is a story told about his being seen in a cab, but when it comes to be cross-examined it is entirely disproved. Mrs. Foster speaks of a disturbance in the street, and with reference to that there is no question but this, that if any date can be established without the possibility of error, it is the date of 1st September for that disturbance, because Mrs. Foster, who lets lodgings, said that the next morning she gave Mrs. King notice

134

Address to Jury.

to leave on that day week, and that day week was 9th Septem- Mr. Besley
ber. If she is right, it was on the night of 1st September that
this disturbance took place, and the fact is made more clear,
because Miss Wilmore and Mrs. Foster concur in saying that
two days' grace was given, and that 11th September was the
date on which she was to leave the lodging. Mr. Humphries
tells us a story which, when contrasted with the other evidence,
is improbable. I don't suppose, however, he wishes for a
moment to deceive any one, and, whilst making comments upon
the witnesses, I must ask you not to suppose that I want to put
you in the dilemma of having to say that any witnesses have
committed wilful misstatements. I refer to it only in contrast
with other witnesses who cannot possibly be deceived. Now,
here is a man who has four public-houses on his hand, and he
comes down here to lead a jury to believe that certain things
go on in one of his houses a year ago, which he remembers
accurately now. It was not even suggested that he could give
this evidence until November, the inquiry before the magistrate
having closed in October. What a lame story it is about the
champagne glasses. Mr. Humphries is taking stock somewhere
about that time, and he recollects the champagne glasses being
lent. Mrs. Foster may be mistaken, but if she be not mistaken,
they were obtained by a person who was not like Thomas Wainwright. And you will be asked to give credence to a story which
the Attorney-General himself has said he could not ask you
implicitly to believe, because it was so defective in reference to
identity.

Now gentlemen, in point of order, we come to the period
from 5th September down to the end of 1874. I have endeavoured, and I trust successfully, by argument and reason
to carry your minds with me, that at all events it is not satisfactorily established, and that the evidence rather leans the
other way, showing a fair ground for supposing that another
person other than Thomas Wainwright was the person known
to Mrs. King under the name of Edward Frieake. The letter
spoken to by Mr. Frieake, although it is dated 31st August,
I ought not to omit. Upon the receipt of that letter I make
this observation, that addresses are often inaccurate, and that
letters addressed to one place are sometimes delivered at
another. No one will set up the theory that no letter ever
has been delivered at the wrong house; and in this case there is
nothing to show how the letter written by Mrs. King, which
fell into the hands of Mr. Frieake, was addressed, for, as far
as we know, the envelope does not exist, and there is no evidence
with regard to it.

135

The Wainwrights.

Mr. Besley   The LORD CHIEF JUSTICE—The envelope was proved to be lost.

Mr. BESLEY—Your lordship recollects that the letter is evidence against Henry Wainwright, because it was called to his attention; but the envelope never was called to his attention. Strictly and legally I am therefore entitled to say that there is no evidence as to how that letter was addressed.

The LORD CHIEF JUSTICE—I shall tell the jury to draw an inference from the delivery of the letter to Mr. Frieake's place of business, that it was addressed to the place where it was delivered.

Mr. BESLEY—I am much obliged to your lordship for that statement.

The LORD CHIEF JUSTICE—I think it better when a counsel is arguing, and when I feel that there is an adverse view, to make him acquainted with it before his address is closed.

Mr. BESLEY—It may be fairly argued that you may infer that the letter was directed in full because it was delivered; but I must ask you whether that would be a fair inference, having regard to the fact that Mr. Frieake has never seen the envelope, and that the memory of the letter did not at once come to him. He had an interview with Henry Wainwright, and it never occurred to him at the time that he had received any such letter. If it is a question of memory we do not know, but it never made any impression upon Edward Frieake. Having regard to his position, and your ordinary knowledge of the careless way in which letters are directed, I shall ask you to reject the inference, and say that it was a letter addressed to the young man with no beard or whiskers who passed by the name of Frieake, and that it fell into the wrong hands. The letter reads—'' I trust you will pardon my writing to you. I ought to apologise for my rude behaviour last evening, after the kindness I have received from you.'' The letter goes on— '' I had been so worried and annoyed during the day, and I am sorry I lost my temper.'' I think it is an improper inference to come to that this letter refers to the scene in the street. It refers to some other incident. That she had come to an understanding with some person named Edward Frieake may be reasonably inferred from her refusal to live with Miss Wilmore. It is Mrs. King who makes this proposal to send the children to Miss Wilmore. Supposing a person had assumed the name of Frieake, and had given no address—it would be the easiest thing in the world for any one to suggest to her that Edward Frieake was an auctioneer, and that he might be the same

136

Address to Jury.

person. It is quite impossible that you can believe that if it is Thomas Wainwright who is personating Edward Frieake he would give the true address of Edward Frieake, 30 Coleman Street. The Attorney-General, in his reply, will have to give some explanation of this letter—that either it was intended for Thomas Wainwright or it was not. If it was intended for him, it is not likely that he would give Edward Frieake's address at 30 Coleman Street. This is approaching an important date, namely, 11th September, and the letter says—"I have been so worried and annoyed during the day, and I am sorry I lost my temper. I did not go out again, as you wished me not to." In reading that passage would you not yourselves come to the conclusion that the words "rude behaviour to you last evening, after the kindness I received from you," were written by a woman who received at her house the person she is addressing? It is quite clear, then, that it does not refer to the incident in the street, because the evidence is conclusive that on the occasion of the incident in the street no one entered the house with Mrs. King. She is brought in by Miss Wilmore, who sees no one in the street, but only knows what she is told by Mrs. King, as to the truth of which there may be considerable doubt in your minds. It is evident, then, that upon this night no man entered Mrs. Foster's house—certainly the young man with the light moustache did not.

The LORD CHIEF JUSTICE—Which is the part of the letter that shows the person she was writing to was not in the house that night?

Mr. BESLEY—I infer it from the words I have read, and there is further evidence in these important words, which I was omitting, namely, "I felt very sorry you left me so cross." This is a woman who, so far as we know, was simply the recipient of Henry Wainwright's money for a period of more than a year. And then she writes this letter to some person named Frieake, apologising for her rude behaviour, and stating, "I have well considered the subject you spoke of, and I think if Harry and yourself come and see me to-morrow evening we could arrange matters very satisfactorily. As the time is very short, write by return"; and she adds, "If I don't hear from you, I shall conclude I am not forgiven." The appointment was made by this letter, so that, in fact, it is not necessary to suggest that 31st August was not the real date of it. The next day would be 1st September, which is the day fixed upon by both Mrs. Foster and Miss Wilmore for her being intoxicated in the street, because notice to leave was given next day. Thus the letter

The Wainwrights.

Mr. Besley itself supplies internal evidence of a proposed meeting between herself and the person named Frieake. Whether the other Mr. Frieake, who is not a witness, ever met her, where the meeting took place, what led to the scene in the street that particular night, are matters upon which we have no evidence, and there is no satisfactory evidence that Henry Wainwright was there at all. Mrs. Foster says she put her hand on his shoulder and said, " Mr. King, try and get her in," and she deposes that this was the Mr. King she had formerly seen. Faces often resemble each other, and identity is a matter of difficulty. The witness's attention was evidently more directed to preventing a scandal outside her door than to deciphering countenances. Then she was there only for a short period, and, having heard Mrs. King say, " What do you mean by interfering with my husband? " she would be naturally led to the conclusion, without minute investigation, that it was the Mr. King who had taken the lodgings some months before, and whom she had not since seen until that moment. I think the contents of the letter require some theory on the part of the prosecution. Any theory inconsistent with there being another lover going under the name of Frieake would be entirely out of the question. I do not know how it can be argued before you upon that letter that there must have been an interview in Mrs. Foster's house between Mrs. King and some other person, who is neither of the prisoners, either on 30th or 31st of August. It has not been conclusively proved that either of the prisoners was in the street on the night of this incident; on the contrary, a review of the evidence rather establishes the view that there may have been persons there who found her at some place and made her acquaintance.

Coming now to 10th September, Mr. Besley disputed the evidence of Mr. Baylis that the chloride of lime was bought on that day. It was not clear that the entry was made on the day in question. Moreover, it was unlikely that a man desiring to conceal what he did would go to a person who knew him, in his own neighbourhood, to purchase the means of that concealment. A police contract with the prisoner was signed on 27th September, 1874, and for its execution chloride of lime was required. No witness had traced the chloride of lime to No. 215 Whitechapel Road. There could be no identification of the lime found in the grave with that delivered some time or other at No. 84. The smells at No. 215 were perceived before 11th September. The hour alleged by the three witnesses as that when they heard three shots fired, namely, between five

Address to Jury.

and seven o'clock on the evening of 11th September, was utterly untrustworthy, as half-past six o'clock was the time when there must have been a van at the door of No. 215, which Mr. Martin had sent in order to remove goods to his salerooms. The supposition that the men heard three shots fired was entirely a result of questions being put to the workmen by a reporter of the press after they had heard of three bullets having been found in the remains. Their notion of the date was vitiated by Mrs. Trew's evidence that the entry in her father's book was 9th September. All the probability was that Mr. Pinnell was on the 9th trying how fast he could fire off his pistol a number of times in succession, and that day it was beyond question that Mrs. King was at 3 Sidney Square.

The evidence of the interviews of the Lane family and the friends of Henry Wainwright was untrustworthy, as such evidence always was when it related to conversations of which no memorandum was made at the time. So far as we know, all the statements made by Henry Wainwright were truthful; there was no proof that they were false. It was not shown that the prisoner knew anything of the Charing Cross letter until it was put into his hand; nor did the prosecution prove who despatched the telegrams from Dover. It certainly was not a fair inference that Henry sent them; and yet a guilty person would be very likely to go to a distant place to do such a thing. His (Mr. Besley's) theory was that the telegrams were genuine, sent by the person who was in the cab with Mrs. King when Miss Wilmore saw her drive past near the Bank of England.

As a motive for the charge in the indictment—that the prisoner had immoral relations with other women than Mrs. King—the prosecution had utterly failed. Whether it had been intended to establish that point by Alice Day, he (Mr. Besley) did not know; but not a scintilla of evidence had pointed to any such relation. We find, then, after the fire, business is being carried on at No. 215 only, and that on the part of Henry Wainwright the struggle would necessarily be a great one; but still he pays to Miss Wilmore as much as could be demanded of him, and even more, for the support of his children. You find that he is paying £5 a month regularly down to June, and in no way is his conduct that of a man who desires to shirk his responsibility, though he might well have said, " I am no longer in a condition to pay what I have done." When Miss Wilmore suggests, " If you cannot pay 25s. a week, I will take 20s.," he said, " No, I do not wish to alter the arrangement; I am quite content," and by his words and acts, in every

The Wainwrights.

way, shows that he desired to provide most handsomely for those who had claims upon him.

Having, as I hope, disposed of that link in the chain of evidence which sought to establish the death of Mrs. King on 11th September, I now come to an incident of immense import-ance, and that is Miss Wilmore's statement, in cross-examina-tion, that about Christmas, 1874, when near the Bank of England with the eldest child, she saw a person in a cab with a gentleman, who, she believed, was Mrs. King. The cab was stopped by the traffic, and she had an opportunity of observing the peculiar tint of the lady's hair. She made no attempt to reach the cab, as it was enabled then to move on, and, being hampered with the child, she was unable to reach it. But so strongly did she believe she had seen Mrs. King that she stated she had seen her, and she has since shown her *bona fide* belief that it was Mrs. King who was in the vehicle on that occasion. There is no evidence whatever to set that aside. It is all very well to say it is not proved where Mrs. King is now; but I submit that she may be in Australia or New Zealand or some-where; she cannot know the question that is going on about her now in London. Anyhow, there is the fact. She states her belief of it, and that is repeated by Henry Wainwright. Why should he disbelieve Miss Wilmore? There are other statements of his, that his foreman, or porters, or workmen had also seen Mrs. King. It was stated that he had said Rogers had seen her, and when Rogers is asked he says, "No, I did not." But there is the other statement that his porters or workmen had seen her, and I would submit to you that, when Titiens was in the box, this question was not put to him, while Vostius was not called at all for the purpose of showing that Henry Wainwright's statements in this respect are not founded on fact or are con-trary to the real truth.

Coming now to the question of Rogers' evidence, if the fact stood alone that he never before Thursday said a word about that story of seeing Mrs. King at the shop at No. 84, when he described the fainting scene and the snatching at the letter, I should ask you to discard altogether his evidence. I contend that the story is the fruit of his imagination prompting him to say that which is false, regardless of the consequences; or that he knew these facts, and that, knowing their importance, he concealed them. In either of these points of view, his evidence is evidence upon which no jury ought, in such an issue, in any way to rely. Having commented on the singular features of this witness's story—his marriage at fifteen, his employment, and the bigamy which he admitted having committed, Mr.

140

Address to Jury.

Besley said Rogers was the only person who had been called who had suggested that any time previous to September, 1874, there was the slightest disagreement between Henry Wainwright and Mrs. King. He is the person who introduced the topic of that letter; but do you think there is any truth in it? Then the "Don't, don't" of the witness Jane Rogers! Why, I thought it meant that there was a struggle and a blow. But what does it mean? It was spoken while the wife was sitting with her husband. Yet he does not hear it, and he does not come downstairs till he is called down by Henry Wainwright! And when he does come down Mrs. King is standing up. I contend it is an account which is perfectly incredible. You remember that Rogers and his wife were living upstairs. Is it likely, therefore, that when the shop was shut Wainwright was likely to bring Mrs. King there, and that on one occasion only? While if she came unexpectedly, what would have been easier than for him to return to the room and request them to tell her to come another time? Pray, gentlemen, also recollect that we have no explanation how she came there. She seems to have dropped from the clouds. At any rate, we have no information how she came there. Then we have this extraordinary story that a letter is ready written and at hand directed to Mrs. Henry Wainwright at her residence, and that her husband is despatching a note; that "Don't, don't," is heard by the husband; that he has handed to him a letter which says, "I am going to commit suicide"; that it is torn violently out of his hand, and Mrs. King goes off into a faint, and that is the matter you are asked to believe. Rogers reads his master's letter when he gets outside, and thinks it such nonsense that he says nothing about it, and throws it into the fire, and that fact entitles him legally to tell us the contents of the document. That is a marvellous incident—so marvellous as to arouse the attention of the Attorney-General, who had no notice of it, and in our ignorance of the existence of any such paper my lord did not allow the contents to be made known on the first day, as we had not had notice. Really, gentlemen, when you come to think of it, do you for a moment believe there ever was such a paper? If there was no such paper, a thousand times stronger is the reason why you should not believe Rogers. Not one word did he say in his examination-in-chief of this. He did not tell us of his wife, nor did he say that he was called downstairs.

The LORD CHIEF JUSTICE—He certainly did say that.

Mr. BESLEY—I was pointing to the fact that the whole thing was left out in the examination-in-chief. Mrs. Rogers stands on a different footing, but she cannot be entirely free from the

141

The Wainwrights.

Mr. Besley observations I have made on Mr. Rogers. It seems to me to be the innate nature of man to screen as far as possible the acts of a woman—to avoid giving her pain. It is the natural promptings of one's heart to save them from any reflection which may cause them to be less esteemed by their friends, and I therefore simply point out that my view with regard to Mrs. Rogers is, that the question of " Don't, don't " was an afterthought—did not form an original part of the case, and was not spoken of or remembered till the grand jury had returned a true bill. We have no evidence of there having been quarrelling; and I refer to this and the entanglement with other women to show that both these motives have failed, and yet you are asked to rush blindly to a conclusion, because something revolting has occurred in dealing with the body of a person who is dead.

With regard to the circumstances occurring between Christmas, 1874, and September, 1875, there appears to have been very nearly, if not entirely, a cessation of any expectation of Harriet Lane's return. This is perfectly consistent with the facts submitted to you as proving that she had arranged or contemplated the withdrawal of herself from this country in the company of a man whom she supposed to be rich, having received from Henry Wainwright as much money as she could previous to her departure.

We now come to 10th September, 1875. With reference to the subsequent discovery made by the police that there was a grave at 215 Whitechapel Road, it would be idle for me to deny the fact; but that it was the grave of Harriet Lane is quite another question, because that must be a matter of identity to which I shall presently draw your attention. When was that grave prepared? We know not. We know not if it be the body of some other person than Harriet Lane; we know not when that person died; or how it came that the body so dead was put into the grave. We do know that the remains found in the possession of Henry Wainwright were at one time there; but as to the mode of preparation I think the learned Attorney-General went so far in his opening speech as to say that the grave was dug either before or after Harriet Lane's death—that it might have been in preparation of her death, and it might have been afterwards. There is no proof of these matters. They are really speculations—theories; and because a theory comes with importance from one of the law officers of the Crown, you are no more compelled to accept it than a theory that comes from the last-called barrister of yesterday. There is nothing to show when this grave was prepared, but there is sufficient

142

Address to Jury.

to show that it must have taken time in preparation. The sawing of four joists in three places is not an operation to be disposed of in three minutes. It is a peculiar noise, a noise that is as likely to attract attention as the noise of the explosion of a pin-bullet of the size of the top of a child's little finger, a bullet which makes very little noise indeed. There is no one who comes forward to say that they ever heard in 1875 or 1874 the noise of the saw in the paint room of 215 Whitechapel Road. That it was done is indisputable, but you will recollect that for a considerable period, so far as Henry Wainwright is concerned, he is not seen either in any way tampering with these premises or going about them at extraordinary hours, unless those of business. The only indication, which is an indication not trustworthy, of there being a body there at all is an odour arising some time in April, 1875, and that may be easily confused with the smell from the heap of rubbish which one witness said contained vegetable refuse, although many others spoke of it as ashes. That odour is laid by a sprinkling —of what? Why the very chloride of lime, a quantity of which was found a short distance off in the grave. No indication of that grave was found until a period of time had elapsed, when Henry Wainwright had no more control over the premises as to the mode of access. The key was produced for the extreme purpose of justifying the observation I have before expressed, namely, that the key is one of the most ordinary pattern—that there are hundreds of keys of a similar kind, one of which would open this door at any time and permit access into the premises against the desire of the person who had control of them.

There is a circumstance introduced by the prosecution of so trivial a nature that I must really apologise for calling your attention to it. Mr. Johnson was called to prove the stippling of four panes of glass in a window. It must have been that Mr. Johnson was thought a desirable witness from his hearty English bluff manners, one who would commend himself to a jury. Otherwise there could be no pretence for occupying your time by placing him in the witness-box; and, as I contrast the absence therefrom of the man who drove the van to No. 215 on the evening of the 11th of September, 1874, the triviality becomes more apparent. Mr. Johnson said the windows were stippled, as he supposed, to prevent a person living in the house from seeing into the warehouse. Really what does it come to? Henry Wainwright was looking out for a person to occupy the house part of the premises, No. 215, and he no doubt thought it

143

The Wainwrights.

Mr. Besley desirable if a stranger were introduced that the windows should
be stippled, and Mr. Johnson thought the idea was a good one.
This is only an attempt on the part of the prosecution to force
as distinctly as they can all the points which are necessary to
make out a case to their minds.

Up to June, 1875, when, pending a settlement with the fire
office, Henry Wainwright was made bankrupt, he never shrunk
from the liability he incurred to Miss Wilmore. Then his
money became scarce; but it by no means follows that, prior to
this time, he was in want of funds. It is only by separating
the facts and taking a just view of these circumstances that you
can get rid of the effect of a general statement by the Attorney-
General, to the effect that this man was so persecuted by this
woman Harriet Lane, at a time when he wanted means, that
he would resort to any expedient in order to dispose of her.
That, I submit, would be a very unfair reading, not only in a
matter of life and death, but even were it a small case in a
County Court, where the question of Henry Wainwright's
liability was in dispute. The arrangement made with his
creditors for the payment of 12s. in the pound was a mode of
doing business not at all discreditable to Henry Wainwright
when it is contrasted with the present mode of offering 1s. in
the pound. His struggle to pay the last 3s. was carried on
until he was made bankrupt in June or July, 1875.

Speaking of the transaction of 10th or 11th September, I
have already mentioned how facts grow when a celebrated case
is in the mouths of every one, and the attention of every one
is called to the particular persons involved. Who shall say
that Stokes is right, and that Henry Wainwright had talked
of the disposal of an axe and shovel before they were bought?
Stokes seems to think it was on a Thursday evening or Friday
morning when he was applied to for the purpose of selling an
axe and shovel. We know as well as we know any fact—and
really very few facts in this case are positively proved—that
Mr. Pettigrew sold them on 10th September, 1875, to Thomas
Wainwright. That they ever reached the hand of Henry is
mere speculation, although I in no way cast any reflection upon
the prisoner Thomas. But I say there is not a scintilla of
evidence that Henry even touched the axe or spade before what
is called the mutilation took place.

The LORD CHIEF JUSTICE—Henry Wainwright wiped the axe
and put it in paper on the 11th.

Mr. BESLEY said he was confining his remarks to the 10th,
and his argument was that nothing whatever in the case con-

144

Address to Jury.

nected Henry Wainwright with the mutilation of the body. That he bought the American cloth and cord of a similar kind to that in which the remains were wrapped I at once concede. But this is a long way from saying that he had anything to do with the mutilation of the remains. That he knew the remains were there on the next day is also, I think, indisputable. It is not my duty by any false reasoning to say that Henry Wainwright did not become aware that there was in the grave a body, that he did not become aware it had to be removed. But this does not, of course, imply that he had the least idea that it was Harriet Lane. If it were the remains of that woman that were deposited there he would be perfectly conscious, from his knowledge of the inquiries proceeding as to Harriet Lane's disappearance, that if they were not at once removed from premises occupied by him, upon him would fall the burden of proving why those remains were there. That supplies the whole key to his conduct the next day. Thomas Wainwright made a confession when taken into custody that he had bought the axe and spade for his brother at Mr. Pettigrew's. It does not follow that he did; there is no confirmation of it. It is a statement made for his own exculpation, and does not inculpate the other man. There is no attempt to show that the knife found belonged to either of the prisoners. That Wainwright became aware on 11th September that in the possession of this body he was deeply compromised is beyond dispute, and that explains sufficiently all that took place afterwards. Knowing that Harriet Lane was missing, he would feel that he would be made responsible for her, and be called on to explain where she died and under what circumstances.

I pray you once again to separate in this case what is painful and revolting, and keep your minds on the facts. The prosecution have to prove mainly that Harriet Lane died by violence, and that Henry Wainwright was the person who caused her death. He goes with Stokes, and it seems to me that if he had been conscious of crime, a person like the prisoner, with powers of reasoning equal to any of us, the last thing he would have done would have been to ask Alice Day to ride with him in the cab. Alice Day is a person for whom we must all feel the deepest commiseration, because, by no fault of her own, she has been placed in a false position, where the tongues of the malevolent may affect her good name. Surely if the prisoner had been conscious of having committed a crime he would not thus have multiplied witnesses against himself by allowing her to ride over to the Borough with him in that cab. Again, if

The Wainwrights.

Mr. Besley he had been conscious of crime, would he not have sent Stokes for the cab instead of going himself? Why, the very discovery arose from the carelessness of innocence. If he had been conscious of guilt, would he have left Stokes in possession of the bundles which contained such damning evidence against him? And as to the great smell, you may well believe, gentlemen, that there has been great exaggeration from first to last. It is just like the police. They had got a fact, and they made the most of it. Do you think that Alice Day would have remained in that cab if there had been such a stench as the police have described, or anything more than she could attribute naturally to the American leather?

I quite acquiesced in the remarks of his lordship about the key when my learned friend (Mr. Moody) was cross-examining respecting it. Henry Wainwright was seen to open the door, to leave one parcel there, and go back for the other, and therefore the possession of the key was a matter of no moment whatever. All that the prisoner then did—his pretending to bribe the police into silence, I pass by. The fact of his being compromised fully accounts for his conduct, but you must not assume from that that he is guilty of murder. It has been done over and over again by men who have suddenly found themselves placed in difficult circumstances.

I now come to a question quite distinct from the others, namely, the identity of the body found as that of Harriet Lane. It is identified by two classes of evidence, which I may divide into material and corporeal. The Attorney-General pressed twelve points of identity, viz.—(1) Slight build; (2) 5 feet in height; (3) small hands; (4) small feet; (5) hair of light colour; (6) pad, with a number of hairpins; (7) decayed tooth; (8) age; (9) woman who had had children; (10) scar; (11) wedding ring and guard; (12) two buttons. There you have twelve points of resemblance, and there was at one time another point, that of earrings. When those were supposed to have belonged to Harriet Lane they were remarkable, and looked nice, though not of gold; but when found to be Mrs. Izzard's they were common and of no value at all. If Mrs. Izzard had not been forthcoming you would have had a thirteenth point of identity. I will soon dispose of two others also. There is not a word of evidence of those buttons having passed through the fire. It was opined that Henry Wainwright burnt the clothes, but that is entirely unproved. Miss Wilmore is a milliner, and knows all about buttons, and she point blank said she would not say the two produced from the stay-box were the same buttons.

Address to Jury.

If the clothes were burnt, where are the other buttons, and can you attach any weight, therefore, to that point? I must, however, express my regret, though I don't complain, that Mrs. Lane, in whose custody that stay-box was for a year, was not called to prove that no other buttons had, during that time, been put into the box.

The LORD CHIEF JUSTICE—The buttons were taken out of the box the first time it was opened.

Mr. BESLEY—I think the evidence does not go that length. There is no proof that scores of buttons might not have been used out of that box by the lady who had it in her custody all that time, and who is not called. Then that decides the question of buttons. As regards the wedding ring and keeper, they are not identified; and there is a significant fact that there was no furrow on the finger indicating that the deceased had ever worn a wedding ring. Now, we come to the corporeal resemblance. (1) and (2), "slight build and 5 feet in height." We have 3,500,000 of people in this metropolis, and if all the women of 5 feet high were mustered there would be an exceedingly large array; and therefore there is nothing peculiar in "slight build and 5 feet in height." As regards 5 feet we are theorising again. Mrs. Allen said that her sister Harriet Lane was the shorter; but Mrs. Allen measured without shoes 5 feet $\frac{1}{8}$ inch. From all that appears Harriet Lane was 5 feet $\frac{1}{4}$ inch; and if so, the body in this case, 4 feet 11$\frac{1}{8}$ inches, could not be that of Harriet Lane. Now, with regard to the hands and feet, they are said to have been small. We have no measurement of the hands, but we have a measurement of the feet, and instead of being small, they are quite of the ordinary size. They are said to be 8$\frac{1}{2}$; but is that very small, as Harriet Lane's were said to be? It was said the boots were 9 inches, therefore the feet must have been something less, for ladies with fine feet are not generally satisfied with a margin of only half an inch. I say that there again the discrepancy between the facts and the evidence destroys the value of the testimony, and if a matter is left in doubt you at once get rid of the identity of Harriet Lane, and, if so, of all motive for Henry Wainwright getting her out of the way. Coming now to the hair and the pad, you must put them together, and on them I will remark that, while the hair of Harriet Lane is said to be "frizzy," it is not frizzy in the hair which has been submitted to you; but of that you will be able to judge, and I shall call medical men who examined the body, who will tell you the hair was not frizzy or curly, and that to call it so would be inaccurately to describe it. Then,

The Wainwrights.

again, we hear that chloride of lime is a bleaching agent, and therefore you must look to the fact of this hair having been altered in colour by contact with this agent, and different from what it was on the individual in life, and if you find no trace of light auburn, as Harriet Lane's hair is described, I think the question of the hair will have been disposed of. As regards the pad, it is monstrous to suggest that there was any mark upon it by Miss Wilmore, by which she would be able to identify it. And as to the number of hairpins found in it, I am not aware that there is a standard number, so that by going beyond it there is an abnormal number. I trust, therefore, you will have the good sense to disregard everything which has been said about the hair or the pad. Then, again, with regard to the decayed tooth. It is a little remarkable that these trustworthy witnesses have given two descriptions of Harriet Lane's teeth. Miss Wilmore said she had teeth which projected on each side, but not so as to disfigure her—not the incisors, they were not prominent.

The LORD CHIEF JUSTICE—What she said was, "She had no disfigurement of the teeth, but they projected a little in the upper jaw."

Mr. BESLEY—Very good, my lord. Let us then pass on to see how far this is consistent with the doctor's evidence that there were two teeth projecting, and those in front. Now, not only were there five teeth missing when the body was discovered, but after the discovery of two in the original parcel, and after sifting the earth of the grave, there still remained two missing. I contend, therefore, that is a proof that this was the body of a woman who had lost two teeth in her lifetime, in spite of the opinion of the medical men. As to the decayed tooth, there is nothing extraordinary in a decayed tooth; it is the commonest thing possible, and can that possibly be a ground on which you are to say that this body has been identified? Then, again, the age of the body cannot be spoken to within ten years, though that was made a great point in the speech of the Attorney-General. Now, as to whether it was the body of a woman who had borne children, I tell you at once that the evidence will be conflicting. Mr. Larkin yesterday persisted in the error that what he called the thinness of the walls of the uterus was an indication of the woman having borne children; but when the more experienced Mr. Bond came into the box we have the correction made. I shall supplement that by the evidence of two similar medical men, who will tell you distinctly that this is not the uterus of a woman who had borne children;

Address to Jury.

and, if not, it cannot be the body of Harriet Lane. Next, with regard to the scar, Miss Wilmore says she has seen it from time to time, while Mrs. Taylor had not seen it for five or six years; but that those scars are indelible must not be accepted for a moment. Besides, such a scar may have arisen to a dozen children from so common an incident as a poker dropping out of a fire, and if there are two scars, one on each leg, in this case, as I shall show, then what becomes of the value of the scar in regard to identity?

Let me impress upon you that though you may have the concurrence of two or three points of identity, yet if, on the whole, you think the identity is unsatisfactory, you will not find Henry Wainwright guilty of the murder of Harriet Lane.

But, then, there is another count in the indictment, which says that you may find him guilty, and deprive him of life— for that will be the effect of your verdict—of the '' murder of a woman whose name is to the jury unknown.'' But would that be a satisfactory thing to do? The explanation of the presence of this count is clear. The prosecution could not trust to the identification of the body of Harriet Lane. But if you charge against him the murder of a woman unknown, no one knows the circumstances under which the murder took place; and if you exclude Harriet Lane, what evidence is there that it is not a suicide? Mr. Bond would not swear that the cut in the throat was inflicted during life. I do not put forward the monstrous theory that the woman shot herself first and then cut her throat afterwards. I admit that the cut throat must have been the result of mutilation. But I do contend that it might be possible for a person committing suicide to fire more than one shot. There is nothing to show the order of the shots. A person might miss the first shot, and then, when one had taken effect, there would be time before the heart stops to fire again before falling to the ground. I say, then, before you charge Henry Wainwright with the murder of a female unknown, you must have proved that it is a murder. I say that you cannot prove that it is a murder—that it may be a suicide, and, if it is a suicide, would you for that take away a man's life? It is in that case that I have ventured to make these observations to you.

The LORD CHIEF JUSTICE said he should be glad to know the learned counsel's theory, or he should be obliged to put to the jury that no man of common sense could accept the idea that a suicide had dug his own grave and buried himself.

Mr. BESLEY—I am very much obliged to you, my lord, for the suggestion. I have dealt with the defence of Henry Wain-

149

The Wainwrights.

Mr. Besley wright as against the charge of murdering Harriet Lane upon two points—first, that the case has not satisfactorily been made out; and, secondly, that there is a want of identification. It is for the prosecution to make out that it is Harriet Lane. But, then, they charge the murder of a female unknown; and as regards the second count I can well conceive circumstances in which a person, young and unmarried, with a brain overstrained by trouble, who might commit suicide with the idea of appalling and punishing the person who had wronged her. Imagine such a man confronted with the body! It is easy to imagine that it would be wiser to call in the police, but does it inevitably follow that such a man would always do the wisest thing? Such a man might say that she is out of the world, it matters very little where she lies, and he might be induced for his own protection to place in an improper place the person who had committed suicide. I have submitted that as applying to the second count of the indictment; but if you, gentlemen of the jury, in your judgment, think it applicable to Harriet Lane, it is not my doing. I do not suggest the argument in that way. I argue that it is not Harriet Lane, and therefore he has not committed wilful murder. If it is the suicide of a person unknown, the possession of the remains is not enough to deprive the prisoner of life by your verdict.

Evidence for Henry Wainwright.

Dr. Meadows Dr. ALFRED MEADOWS, examined by Mr. STRAIGHT—I am a Fellow of the Royal College of Physicians, a lecturer on midwifery at St. Mary's Hospital, and physician to St. Mary's Hospital. I have made obstetrics a considerable subject of study. I was present in Court yesterday during the examination of Mr. Larkin and Mr. Bond. I examined the uterus at my house on 3rd September, in order to form some opinion as to whether it was that of a person who had borne a child. The points are principally two to which I look for the purpose of forming that opinion to determine the question, and they are the size and as to the cavity of the walls, but more particularly the shape of the uterine walls. The walls in the present case were exceptionally thin, instead of being, as I should expect to find them, somewhat thicker than an unimpregnated uterus. At the time I saw the uterus it was in a liquid of some kind—I believe spirit and water. With regard to the second point, I found the walls of the uterus projected in a convex manner into the uterine cavity. It is not possible to express any distinct

150

Henry Wainwright.

Evidence for Defence.

opinion as to whether the uterus had been pregnant or not; my
opinion, after considering the points mentioned, is that the
uterus had not been pregnant. It is not possible, with any
accuracy, to form an opinion as to the age, owing to the decomposition and the long time the body is supposed to have been
buried. Chloride of lime is called a decolorer; I have no experience as to its effect. I think it possibly might reduce black
hair to a light shade. It would undoubtedly have a bleaching
effect.

Cross-examined by the ATTORNEY-GENERAL—I did not
examine the body of this woman at all. I should probably
endeavour to find out the age by the teeth; I am not aware
that it could be found out in any other way. Wisdom teeth
make their appearance from twenty, perhaps a little before, to
twenty-five or twenty-six; they vary a good deal. I am not sure
that I should come to the conclusion that a woman was not
over twenty-five if I saw her dead body, and from whose jaw
the wisdom tooth was just protruding, but probably I might.
I do not think it could be stated with certainty that the uterus
of a woman recently dead had been impregnated. The walls were
convex, which is certainly not due to the muscular degeneration.
There was muscular degeneration very considerably; the whole
mass was very flaccid, but not at all difficult to measure; I
measured it. The uterine cavity was 2½ inches. I only speak of
two measurements. The other was 1 inch and a third in depth.

Re-examined by Mr. STRAIGHT—I measured each wall
separately; the anterior wall was a little under a quarter of an
inch, and the posterior wall a little over a quarter of an inch.
I should expect to find the uterus of a woman as large twelve
months after death as just after. I have not had practical
experience of the inspection of a uterus twelve months after
death, but I have had experience of the examination of the uterus
in bodies a few weeks after death, and I am able to express
an opinion that the measurement would be the same after the
lapse of twelve months. I think there is no shrinking of the
uterus after twelve months, but probably there may be of the
whole body. I think, as regards the uterus, it would be in-
finitesimal. A virgin uterus is subject to considerable variations,
even in what we call the normal state. If a body shrinks the
uterus might participate to the extent of the sixteenth of an
inch, which I think would be a fair proportion, because it has
been found that after the womb has been developed it very
seldom returns to its original shape again; it is exceptional if
it does. I was not speaking of it as an invariable rule, but it

151

The Wainwrights.

Dr. Meadows is regarded as an indication of a nulliparous uterus. I do not know in what way the uterus had been treated when it was taken from the body.

F. G. Aubyn FREDERICK GEORGE AUBYN, examined—I am a member of the Royal College of Surgeons, and practise at 519 Commercial Road. I have been eighteen years in the profession. I was desired to inspect the remains on 24th September by the solicitor for the prisoner. I attended at the mortuary at St. Saviour's Church on the following day. I made an inspection on three or four different times, in company with Mr. Bond. The body was in a very advanced state of decomposition. From examination I thought the age of the person would be from twenty-five to thirty years—I should say not more than thirty.

By the LORD CHIEF JUSTICE—From what can you judge?— Because the sutures in the interior part of the skull were not invisible, and we expect to lose them after thirty.

Examination continued—I examined the legs. I agree that there was a scar on the right leg. I examined the left leg also, and discovered a scar upon it. I cut that scar out.

Can you produce it?—I can.

[The witness produced a small piece of the decaying flesh or skin, about an inch and a half square, wrapped in paper, which he handed to the Lord Chief Justice.]

By the LORD CHIEF JUSTICE—In what you have handed up to me there appear to be two colours. One portion is darker than the other?—Yes, the darker is the scar.

What do you say it is the scar of?—I can only say it is a scar, but how caused I cannot say.

Are you sure it is not the result of the decomposition?—I would not swear positively, but my opinion is that it is a scar.

Examination continued—There was one decayed tooth, and several others were missing. I would give no opinion upon dental surgery, and therefore I cannot say whether one tooth decays more rapidly than the other.

I examined the uterus with care for the purpose of forming an opinion as to whether the woman had been pregnant or not. The signs to which I looked were the length and the size of the cavity, the general appearance of the womb, and the thickness of the walls. I also observed the shape with Dr. Meadows. I do not give a decided opinion as to her having been pregnant, but my opinion is that she was not pregnant, that the womb had not been gravid, that she had not borne a child. I

152

Evidence for Defence.

examined the hair, and did not detect any curl in it. I produce some of the hair which was taken from the back of the head by me.

[The hair was compared with the other hair cut from the head of the dead woman. It was dark in colour, but this the witness attributed to its not having been washed, and that there was chloride of lime on that portion which he had taken off.]

I measured the woman's body with great care, in presence of Mr. Bond. It measured 4 feet 11½ inches. The feet were not unusually small in comparison with the size of the body.

Cross-examined by the ATTORNEY-GENERAL—I formed my opinion as to the age of the woman from the sutures and the teeth. When I saw the wisdom tooth just appearing Mr. Bond told me he had cut it, and therefore I could not very well say decidedly what her age was from this source of information.

By the LORD CHIEF JUSTICE—Allowing for what Mr. Bond had done, I could not judge the age, owing to the decomposed state of the body.

Cross-examination continued—Suppose the tooth had just been making its appearance?—Then the age might have been twenty-five or twenty-six. It appears sometimes earlier, sometimes later.

Between what ages do the wisdom teeth usually make their appearance?—From twenty years to twenty-five or twenty-six years.

And your principal reason for fixing this woman's age is what?—The fact that the anterior sutures had not disappeared.

By the LORD CHIEF JUSTICE—You say her age was between twenty-five and thirty years. What makes you begin at twenty-five?—Because at that age we lose the posterior suture.

Cross-examination continued—Is it not a fact that the posterior sutures remain until middle age?—No; I believe they go at the age of thirty.

The posterior suture remains for a long time, and this anterior goes at an early period?—(After a pause)—Just so.

Which were left here? Can you not tell from recollection? Had the anterior sutures disappeared?—No, they had not.

Why, then, do you come to the conclusion that she was twenty-five years of age?—(The witness did not reply).

Had the posterior sutures gone?—No; I judged the age by the sutures as they remained.

You say that the wisdom teeth make their appearance between twenty and twenty-five. Why, then, do you think the

The Wainwrights.

F. G. Aubyn woman was twenty-five years?—Because she had cut the other wisdom teeth. I did not hear that she had cut three, but I came to that conclusion, because she had cut one.

Have you any other reasons to give me that the woman was this age?—No. I only found the scar on the right leg on the last examination. I conducted that examination with Mr. Larkin and Mr. Bond. We scraped the legs on the first examination, but did not find a scar on either, but we did ultimately find one a little below the knee on the Tuesday. I have no doubt about it being a scar, and I think it might have been produced by a burn. We did not discover it on the first or second examination—not till a fortnight afterwards, the day before the remains were buried. They had then been removed to a dark vault under the church, and we went down with a lighted candle. I did not notice whether we had one or two candles. I did not notice dark patches here and there, but there was one patch on the leg which struck me, though not till the day before the body was buried. Mr. Bond looked on the left leg, and I looked on the right. I did not look at the left leg till the next examination, and then we had two examinations before we found either of the scars. We cut out the piece of flesh containing this scar. I will not swear what the scar was produced by. If the woman during life had received a blow on her leg she might have had a scar. A blow inflicted on the leg would produce such an appearance if it suppurated. I will not swear that this is not an appearance produced by decomposition. I examined the uterus with Dr. Meadows.

E. Martin EDWARD MARTIN, examined by Mr. DOUGLAS STRAIGHT—I am a corn merchant, and in September, 1874, I carried on business in the New Road, Whitechapel. I had two vans, a large and a small one, and I frequently had them repaired at Mr. Wiseman's. I have my books here, which are kept by myself and my clerk. I know nothing from memory, but I have a bill and receipt here for £3 10s. on account, for repairs to my vans on 4th September. The two transactions were somewhat mixed up together, for the small van and the large one, and there is a balance left. This is his name at the bottom; it is " Repairs to van, £5 10s.," and you will see that it is agreed as £5 10s. in the corner. This is an August bill, and on 4th September I paid £3 10s. ; that was for the little van. By my cash book I paid, on 4th September, £3 10s. on account, and on the 9th £3 15s., which was the balance on the two vans. This is the entry corresponding with the receipt. You will afterwards find on the credit side £1 paid

154

Evidence for Defence.

for some more work done. On the first receipt I have produced E. Martin
of 4th September, £3 10s. was paid on account. The small van
being completed, Mr. Wiseman would bring the bill round. The
£3 10s. paid by me to Mr. Wiseman on account on 4th September
was on the small van. The repairs were £5 10s. The £3 15s.
was on the settled bill for the two. This was in part payment
of £7 5s. for the small one and on the large one. The small
one was £3 15s. and the large one £3 10s., but I have no bill for
the large one. We always pay cash when it is finished, immediately the job is done. Wiseman is told that if he does not take
the money then he will not get it. Those small accounts are
always paid cash. I paid him £3 10s., but perhaps I had not
seen the van then to see that he had done me justice. We
call payment on Saturday, cash. This is my day-book, by
which I find that on 10th September the big van was actually
in use. Here is an entry of 116 bags of rice shoots fetched
from the mill at Wapping at one load; the big van would be
required for that, and on the same day the small van had to
fetch one load of 58 bags, and another of 22 bags. On 11th
September I find in the sold day-book an entry of three tons of
rice from my premises to Ems' wharf, which the one-horse van
could not have carried at one load; that is, I should say, 2 miles
from my place, and it would occupy half a day I should say for
the van to go there and back. I should like to look at Mr.
Wiseman's workmen's book; it is a very singular thing, if you
put the two payments together for the small one and the large
one, whether they will come to the amount which he has charged.
You see I am not speaking from memory, but from my own
books. Mr. Pollard, from the Treasury, came and examined my
books.

Henry Wainwright entered my service in May or June, 1875,
and was in my employment as manager when he was taken in
custody. He was very steady and well conducted. He was very
regular every morning at eight o'clock, and he commonly went
away about 8 p.m. I recollect his being taken in custody on
11th September, 1875. He was at work on my premises in the
usual way on 10th and 11th September. On Fridays he had
to make the accounts out for wages, and on Saturdays he had
to pay them. I left it entirely to him; I had my own business to
attend to. I have known his father thirty years, and himself
about two years. I met him at a party at Tredegar Square.
During all the time I have known him he has borne the character
of a kind-hearted, humane man.

By Mr. Moody—I do not think I have seen Thomas above

155

The Wainwrights.

E. Martin twice in my life. I have no recollection whether I saw him on Friday, 10th September.

Cross-examined by the ATTORNEY-GENERAL—I know that the father was in a good position, but I do not know that he left property. I live at Carlton Villa, Upton. I take the 7.50 or 8.50 train at night. I have only two places of business, a rice and a corn establishment; they are opposite one another. I have the means of living even without business, and I only carried on the brushmaking establishment for Mr. Wainwright; it was more for him than for myself. I was not one of his creditors. I never had transactions with him before meeting him at this party. He was very much embarrassed, so that I did my best to assist him. I paid him £3 a week wages. He managed the brush business and the shipping house, and he gave orders for £100 to £150 at a time. He carried on the business as my manager at the upper part of 78 New Road, and 109 opposite. It was a profitable business to me. I received the profits and paid him £3 a week. He was with me from May or June to Saturday, 11th September. My view was to carry on the business until I got back my money, and then he would have had the business. I had not lent him money, but the profits of the business would have paid me what I had laid out in the business, about £300. Afterwards I would have handed it over, and Dr. Naggleton would have let him have the house again. My real business is the corn and rice business. The corn business is on the ground floor; there is a warehouse at the back, and the brush business has a side entrance to the two top floors, quite distinct. I closed my business premises at 8.30. I left the brushmaking to Wainwright, who generally left about eight o'clock, if I was not going by that train, but if I went at 7.50 I went before him. His train went at 8.10.

I showed Mr. Pollard my books, and told him that the vans were paid for before. I have not said that my books would throw no light on the matter; I said that I would find the bills, and let Inspector Fox have them next morning. I offered every assistance to the police, and Inspector Fox will tell you so. This first bill, dated 29th August, 1874, is, I should suppose, for repairs done to the small van. Not a farthing was due from me to Wiseman on 29th September, 1874. I should have paid it if there had been. He would not have let it rest an hour, and I always pay a bill at once, and never have credit of anybody. This bill is £3 10s., and not £3 15s., because Mr. Wiseman agreed to take off 5s. We enter the cash on the day we pay the money, and always make

156

Evidence for Defence.

the entries at the time. On 4th September I paid Wiseman
£3 10s., leaving £2 10s. unpaid. Probably the van had not
been sent home then. If he had come for £3 10s., I should
have given it to him. I think I have paid part before the
work was delivered. I think you will find that the two
amounts in the cash-book were sufficient to pay both these bills.
The next payment was on the 9th. My clerk looked nearly
all night for the bill for the large van and could not find it,
and I have tried to find it myself. I do not know whether I
had a bill. This (produced) is the bill for the work done in
June, which was delivered on the same date as this one of
29th August. I did not produce these two bills before, because
they were both shut in the books. All these things were paid
for at the time; we never let a thing like this 8s. 6d. stand;
it would not be entered. I do not say that we never enter
such amounts, but in this cash-book it is very rare. £5 10s.
was the whole amount due from me on 4th September, and this
£3 10s. on account was the whole amount I owed him at that
time. That included everything up to that time, and the
£1 5s. for repairs to the big van and the work done to the
little van. We have thousands of papers in the course of a
day; they are kept on a large file; we have searched three or
four large files on several occasions to find the bill I paid Mr.
Wiseman. We probably did have a bill for repairs of the large
van. I did not usually hire vans when my own vans were being
repaired, but I do now, as we are busy. If my vans were
being repaired, I should make shift with a one-horse van till
mine was repaired; he would not keep it more than a day or
two. Mr. Wiseman has been told by me always to take his
money as soon as he has done his work. I don't suppose I
should pay him for it until I had seen what he had done to it.
I probably paid him £3 10s. because I saw what he had done
to it. I only speak from my books; I have no memory of the
transaction. The small van did go several times; it did two
loads on 10th September, and the big one one load. The
small one would have to go, I suppose, 3 miles. It was generally used for all purposes, taking out corn and all small loads,
but it would not carry 116 bags of rice at the same time. I
had the little van oiled in September; it was generally paid
for when done; it was only a shilling.

By Mr. BESLEY—The £300 was money used for carrying
on the brushmaking business; it was not money that went into
Henry Wainwright's pocket. It was capital.

The Rev. JOHN THOMAS, examined by Mr. DOUGLAS STRAIGHT

The Wainwrights.

John Thomas —I am an Independent minister. I have known the priso
Henry Wainwright, about eighteen years, and during all
time he has borne the character of a humane and kind-hea
man.

W. T. Good WILLIAM THOMAS GOOD, examined—I reside at 213
chapel Road, and am a tailor. I have known prisoner a
sixteen years, and during all that time he has borne
character of a humane and kind-hearted man.

D. Monroe and others Mr. DONALD MONROE, a member of the Metropolitan B(
of Works; Mr. JOSEPH MYERS COLE, Mr. EDWARD LACY, che
Mr. SAMUEL LUDBROOK, brushmaker; Mr. WILLIAM VI
BARDON, manager of chemical works in Whitechapel,
similar evidence.

Evidence for the prisoner Henry Wainwright closed.

Adjourned till Monday.

Seventh Day—Monday, 29th November, 1875.

Closing Speech for Henry Wainwright.

Mr. BESLEY said—Gentlemen of the jury, of course you will not anticipate that I am about to address you on the very many topics to which I drew your attention on Saturday. It would be no compliment to you to suppose that the effect of the arguments and facts put before you was so ephemeral that you could not retain it for forty-eight hours. When the Legislature gave the privilege of summing up to a prisoner's counsel, I have always understood its true object was that, when other evidence was put before a jury on behalf of a prisoner, it was advisable that his counsel should make some remarks on the new witnesses called.

The LORD CHIEF JUSTICE—If anything occurs to you, by no means restrict yourself to that. I have always held the contrary opinion. I think the Legislature intended that, when the whole case was before the Court, the counsel for the defence should be entitled to treat all its facts as one, and discuss them from the beginning to the end. I quite agree with you that it would be unnecessary to go over the same ground again, considering the great attention the jury are paying to this case; but if anything should occur to you, you need not feel yourself tied down by any restraint on that point.

Mr. BESLEY—I am obliged to your lordship, but I feel that comparisons might be made as to the way in which the case was treated on Saturday, and I don't therefore intend to go over the same ground again, except so far as it may be affected by the new evidence. I am unconscious of having omitted to deal with any matters before the Court previous to the calling of my witnesses, and I therefore briefly recall to your minds the grounds on which Henry Wainwright is defended. In the first place, in a case of circumstantial evidence it is necessary that every part of that evidence should not only be relevant and consistent in all its parts, but that if one link only is snapped asunder by argument or cross-examination, it is your duty in a case like this to give a favourable verdict to the accused person. One very essential part of the case is the date on which

159

The Wainwrights.

Mr. Besley the person dead is said to have been deprived of life. There are cases in which dates are of no value whatever, but in a charge of wilful murder the time of the alleged deed is the very essence of the charge, and if on that particular link in the chain you are led irresistibly to the conclusion that the prosecution has not proved their case, then you must give the prisoner the benefit of the doubt, as it is called, and you will say by your verdict of not guilty that the prosecution has failed to bring home the charge. If 11th September is not the true date of death of the person so killed, if it be any other time—weeks later or months later—the whole theory of the prosecution is shattered, and it is of no value, because it must be consistent from the beginning to the end. Miss Wilmore and Mrs. Foster swear that they last saw Harriet Lane on that day—that is, assuming that these remains are those of Harriet Lane, which I by no means concede. The prosecution, however, fix the day as that on which Harriet Lane withdrew from her lodgings at Mrs. Foster's, viz., 11th September, 1874, and they also fix on a particular period of that day, viz., between five and seven in the evening—and also on the back premises of 215 White-chapel Road as the place.

With reference to these vital points, if the day of hearing the pistol shots is entirely disproved, how can you find your way to bringing in as your verdict that Henry Wainwright murdered Harriet Lane on 11th September, 1874? Whitechapel is a densely crowded neighbourhood, inhabited by numerous families at home at all hours of the day; and if you know any-thing of this class of the population of the East End, you are aware that on Saturday night they would be in the streets between five and seven, providing for the comforts of their families on the day of rest. You must remember, too, how many families and persons live within a few yards of the very spot where it is said a pistol was fired three times. I have already spoken of the evidence of the two Kays and the younger Wiseman. If you could have had a lingering idea in your minds that those three witnesses had told a truthful story, that idea must have been entirely removed if you paid attention to the evidence of Mr. Martin. Mr. Martin had been waited upon by the Solicitor of the Treasury. They examined his books, they examined him and questioned him, who certainly has in no way behaved himself in such a manner that his evidence should be mistrusted in any way, and yet he is not called by the Crown. What is the inference? Why, that you may dismiss from your minds the theory that between five and seven that evening three

160

Addresses to Jury.

shots were fired at all. It is swept away by Mr. Martin's testimony. We heard of the "big job," but can you doubt for a moment that that "big job" was finished before 9th September? According to the evidence, the work is not entered until after it is finished; and Mrs. Trew says the entry in the book is 9th September, and that is confirmed by reference to Mr. Martin's cash book. Work was being done on the small van, and a payment was made on 4th September, 1874. That was a Saturday, and that is a material point for you to remember; and Mr. Martin paid the balance, together with what was due for oiling the big van, on the following Thursday.

The FOREMAN OF THE JURY—I beg pardon, my lord, but is not the learned counsel quite wrong in his dates? In 1874, the 11th was a Friday.

The LORD CHIEF JUSTICE—That is so. It is, however, a natural mistake to make, as Saturday, the 11th, 1875, is an important date in the case.

Mr. BESLEY—I beg your pardon, gentlemen, you are right, but that only makes my point the stronger, for the second payment in that case must have been on the Wednesday, and Wednesday, the 9th, must have been the date when the big job was done. It does not rest only on the payment of the account on that day, because there were other reasons, viz., reference to other books. On the 11th bags of rice were conveyed by the big van from a warehouse to 78 New Road, for there is an entry of it, and Mr. Martin says, and will swear now, that on the 10th he had the big van in use, and on the 11th he had it in use, for on the 11th he sent three tons of rice to Queen's Wharf in it, while the small van was engaged in carrying other quantities. It has been attempted to show that Mr. Martin might have hired a big van, but he declares that at that time he never hired.

I will now pass on to treat of the question of identity as now affected by the evidence of Dr. Meadows and Mr. Aubyn. Dr. Meadows is one of the highest authorities, if not the highest, upon obstetric medicine. He has made that a specialty. He is at the head of his profession, and the Attorney-General cannot gainsay either that or the fact that he is a fair witness, not concealing the difficulty of the inference when he says, "My mind was and is inclined to the belief that these are the remains of a woman who has never borne a child." Mr. Bond and Mr. Larkin had given a different opinion, but Mr. Bond, in committing himself to an opinion unfavourable to the defence, shows how little satisfied he is with his opinion, because he goes through

M

The Wainwrights.

Mr. Besley another operation after he has given his opinion. Dr. Meadows frankly states to the jury that no one can with certainty infer the fact from an examination after death. It is a fact known in every medical school in London that it is so. But mark, Dr. Meadows says that lapse of time makes no difference, and that he can judge as well now as he could have done a twelvemonth ago, that it does not affect his opinion in any way. We get, therefore—first, that there is no certainty if you examine the moment after death, and you know his conclusions; that, contrary to Mr. Larkin and Mr. Bond, he infers a state of facts exactly opposite to that necessary to support the prosecution. He also tells you with reference to chloride of lime that it is a bleaching agent which would render the colour of the hair lighter. I call your attention to that because it is of importance when you come to consider the evidence with regard to the hair.

Passing now to the evidence of Mr. Aubyn, unfavourable comments no doubt will be made upon his demeanour in the box, but remember it is a very trying position to be in on such a trial as this for a witness to be examined by the Attorney-General, and that Mr. Aubyn was excessively nervous. No one can doubt that for a moment, for, with reference to the question of the sutures, he went backwards and forwards until the matter was involved in such confusion and absurdity that it would be absurd to suppose that you could give him the credit which is really due to his scientific attainments and observation. But what does Mr. Aubyn do with regard to the hair? He produces some of it which has not been subjected to the washing and cleansing process, but in the state it was when the relatives of Harriet Lane saw the remains. Now, if washing and cleansing were necessary to produce the appearance of the true hair of Harriet Lane, all that those witnesses saw was the hair which had been cleansed, and there is not one of them who says, " I recognised the hair directly because it was like hers, only a little darker in colour." Those words, " only a little darker," had not proceeded from the mouth of any of the relatives of Harriet Lane. They all say, " That is the colour "; not " that it is the colour, only a little darker." But if that is the colour of the hair of the human remains, the hair must be that of a woman who had lighter hair than Harriet Lane. Then, again, the hair of Harriet Lane is said to have been wavy or " frizzy." I think that those were the terms used.

The Lord Chief Justice—Miss Wilmore talked of her " frizzing " her hair over her pads.

Mr. Besley—I understood that the hair of Harriet Lane was

162

Addresses to Jury.

of a curly nature, that it was not long and perfectly straight, as we find it when hair has been washed, or when produced unwashed by Mr. Aubyn. There it is, and that hair turns out to be not frizzy, or wavy, or curly, or anything of the kind. Again, I say there is a marked discrepancy as to identity with reference to that particular point of the hair.

The LORD CHIEF JUSTICE—I think the expression was she " used to ' frizz ' her hair over the pad "; but if any witness said that the hair was " wavy " or " curly,'' and you call my attention to it, I will take care that the fact is brought to the notice of the jury.

Mr. BESLEY—Thank you, my lord. Well, then, again, if washing produces a lighter colour of hair than that of Harriet Lane, you must not forget that there has been a further process of lightening by the hair being in contact so long with such a bleaching agent as chloride of lime. We have therefore a double process of lightening going on before you get the colour of the hair which is placed in your hands, so that the natural colour must have been much darker than that which is spoken to by the members of the same family.

I now pass to what I submit to you is of less importance, viz., the age. Incidentally, I may say that I have given up Mr. Aubyn on the question of age, for his answers with regard to the sutures left my mind in such a vague state that I did not know which of them remained, or if either remained. I thought I gathered from him that one suture disappeared from twenty-five to thirty, and that that had actually disappeared in the remains. But in this question of age, I don't think the sutures are an important test question; and remember that the other medical witnesses say that they cannot swear to any period within ten years. But the question of age involves a question with regard to the teeth. Mr. Meadows said—'' If I were to make a guess at the probable age of the remains, I should look at the teeth, and, if the wisdom teeth were not cut, knowing that they usually cut at about twenty-five, I should place the age at about twenty-five.'' But all this is mere guesswork. In the case of these remains, three of the wisdom teeth had appeared, though Mr. Aubyn was so nervous that he seemed to forget that there were four to cut—two in each jaw. This rather favours the age being more than twenty-five, as the cutting process may last a considerable time, and you probably know within your own experience that sometimes they are not cut till late in life, and sometimes they are not cut at all. I must therefore, as I do not propose to call a dental surgeon,

The Wainwrights.

Mr. Besley leave the matter to you. All I submit is that, assuming twenty-five to be the normal period, the correspondence of age between these remains and the age of Harriet Lane in September, 1874, immediately disappears.

With the decayed teeth I have already dealt. I do not propose to revert to it again; but there is the question of height, and that is of much importance. I have already stated that the height of the remains is established by concurrence of measurement between Mr. Bond and Mr. Aubyn at 4 feet $11\frac{1}{8}$ inches. Now, that is an absolute fact. But you have it in evidence that the height of Harriet Lane was perceptibly greater than that of Mrs. Allen, and she, measured by Inspector Fox, without her boots, was 5 feet $\frac{1}{8}$ inch. That would give for Harriet Lane, at the very lowest computation, for the difference might have been as much as half an inch, a height of 5 feet $\frac{1}{4}$ inch, so there is a difference between her and those of the remains of $1\frac{1}{8}$ inches. How, then, can you believe that these are the remains of Harriet Lane?

With regard to the scar, I labour under the disadvantage of having a nervous witness in Mr. Aubyn, and he said in cross-examination he would not be positive that the appearance of the piece of skin, which he thought bore a scar, was not produced by decomposition; but the fact still remains that he is of opinion that it is a true scar. If so, it is a mark which has never been noticed by any of the Lane family, and if there is a mark or scar on both legs of these remains, what reliance or importance can you place on the scar on the right leg, of which not a syllable was said by the medical men until its existence on Harriet Lane had been referred to by members of the Lane family?

I believe I have now treated all the real points involved in the medical testimony as to identity, and I say no more than again repeat, that if you find that, although there are one or two things still capable of being proved, there remain some one or two even that have been answered, you will not come to a decision unfavourable to the prisoners.

I now pass to the evidence given by Mr. Martin. He speaks of Henry Wainwright being at his ordinary duties from eight o'clock in the morning till eight at night on 10th September, and from eight in the morning till eight at night on the 11th. These are the dates of the purchase of the axe and spade, and of the employment of Stokes, which led to the apprehension of Henry Wainwright. Upon both of these days he was engaged—on the first in making up the books, and on the Saturday in paying the men—and it is suggested that the mutilation took

164

place between the afternoon of the Friday and Saturday. His **Mr. Besley**
character has been spoken to as of a kind and humane man,
and as to that it is for you to consider how far his conduct is
consistent with a person who has been guilty of this crime.

I am now about to close my task. You will retire to your
room at some period now approaching, and there quietly amongst
yourselves will have to say, first of all, if this crime has been
conclusively proved to be the deprivation of the life of a woman
by another or by herself; and, secondly, you will have to
consider, are those remains the remains of Harriet Lane beyond
any reasonable doubt?

Speech on behalf of Thomas George Wainwright.

Mr. Moody said—My learned friend, in adverting to the **Mr. Moody**
solemn nature of the duty devolving upon all engaged in this
trial, has treated the subject so well that I can add nothing to
what he has said, and to travel over the same ground again
would only be to show my inferiority. I shall therefore only
allude to it on behalf of Thomas Wainwright. One of the charges
is that of being an accessory before the fact, and the other that
of being an accessory after the fact. The former is most serious.
The Attorney-General has said that the charges of being an
accessory before and after the fact are very different, and that
is so; for whilst the latter can be visited with the heaviest
penalty the law can give, short of sentence of death, on the
former the more grave sentence can be passed. My learned
friend at one time appeared to anticipate that I might, in
the course of my address on behalf of Thomas, take views which
might appear antagonistic to his client Henry; all I can say on
that matter is, nothing can be further from the wishes of my
client, or further from my intention, that I should adopt such
a course. There may, however, be reasons why I should address
you upon the point whether or not Thomas Wainwright, if
there has been murder committed, aided and abetted it. If
it should be left to you to decide that these remains are the
remains of an unknown person, then, so far as Thomas Wainwright is concerned, there will be nothing to answer in the
Frieake episode, and the telegram and the letter would fall to
the ground. There would still remain the question of the shovel
and axe, but that would be far too trivial a matter to justify
a man being put on his trial as an accessory.

The case as opened on the part of the prosecution presents

The Wainwrights.

Mr. Moody the charge against Thomas to you in this way, that the prisoner Henry Wainwright, having been on terms of intimacy with the woman, became tired of her, and was most anxious to break off the connection, and on this account entered into a plot with some person that the woman should disappear. But it could hardly be conceived that he would have taken such complicated measures to guard against inquiry, which there was no ground for supposing would ever be made. Then, again, the prosecution allege the existence of a plot for a long time, and they call before you Mrs. Wells to say that it had been conceived and entered upon within a week or two of Christmas, because she said that a man who answered to the name of Edward came within a week or two after the second confinement of Mrs. King, which she fixes at December, 1873. Therefore, according to that, this plot must have been conceived so far back as December, 1873, when there was no ground for saying that there was any reason for such a thing. The only ground set out at that time was that there was a difference and a coldness between them; but you ought not to take that into account. Henry Wainwright has been proved to be a kindly and humane man, who has won the respect and esteem of every one with whom he came in contact, and if he be a man of that kind, may it not have been that he paused and hesitated in the course he was following with Harriet Lane? It seems to me that that is a reasonable supposition, especially when it is seen that he takes care of her welfare and supplies her with money. If that be so, is it at all likely that any such plot could have been entered into at any period before the actual pressure for money arose? If my theory be correct, there was no other cause, there could be no other cause, and that appears to be one of the difficulties which the prosecution have to meet.

Then, again, if such a plot were to be entered into, it would not be probable that a person so well known as Mr. Frieake would be selected as the man to be represented, or that the man to represent him would be a young man without either beard or moustache. If this woman was to be deceived by a person with a false name, the last person selected for that purpose would be one who would probably often be seen in the company of Henry. From time to time this woman went to No. 84, and if this was the case, why should she be asked to believe that he was Frieake? She might have heard him there addressed by his own name, or be told by any person in the establishment that it was Mr. Wainwright's brother. This is a strong reason for believing that this plot was not formed, but

Addresses to Jury.

merely evolved from the minds of the various parties interested **Mr. Moody**
from what took place after the disappearance.

I think I shall satisfy you that the proof of Thomas Wainwright being in the several places in which he was alleged to
be is of the flimsiest and most unreliable description. In the
first place, I shall draw your attention to the evidence of Mrs.
Wells. It is clearly evident that Mr. Frieake and Henry Wainwright were upon terms of intimacy and friendship for years,
and that they were in the habit of addressing each other by the
respective names of Teddy and Harry. Mrs. Wells says that
some time by gaslight Mr. King came to her house, and brought
with him a person whom she showed into the parlour, and
then she went into another room about her own business. She
had no occasion to pay any special attention to this occurrence,
and therefore the visit was not in any way calculated to greatly
impress her. The parties remained in the house for some time,
but she did not speak to having seen him again. She heard
a voice from upstairs saying, " Edward, will you come up ? "
It is clear that Henry Wainwright never addressed the real Mr.
Frieake by the name of Edward. Therefore, if he were talking
to a man who was trying to pass off as the real Mr. Frieake
one would think he would act towards him as if he had been
that person, and not some one else. If he had taken a person
there to represent him as Mr. Frieake, the natural thing would
have been for him to go downstairs and speak to him, asking
him then to walk up. This is rather the language of a master
to his servant, or the manner in which a tradesman who called
upon a matter of business about furniture or such like would be
addressed. There was another interview equally transient, and
in which it was equally impossible to form any satisfactory
opinion. One night when the gas was burning a cab came to
the door, and Mrs. King came out of it, followed by the man
said to be called Edward. As regards the operation of the
identification of Thomas Wainwright, the whole time spoken
to by the several witnesses may be comprised in as many
seconds ; and out of the eight or ten descriptions of the prisoner,
none of them exactly agreed. Mrs. Wells said, if he had a
moustache at all, it must have been a very slight one. If a
person came to speak to the identity of another, and was not
certain as to the existence or non-existence of so prominent
a matter as a moustache, what reliance would be placed on the
identification at all ? The witness had never been called upon
to exercise her memory in regard to this man, and this interview, taking place in January, 1874, and the witness not seeing

167

The Wainwrights.

the prisoner until October, 1875, a period of about one year and eight or nine months, that is rather a long period over which to carry one's recollections and to remember either faces or names. When she did venture to say she recognised him, it is when she sees him in the dock, knowing him to be charged with representing himself as Frieake, standing beside a man whom she knows to be charged with a serious crime.

We now come to Miss Wilmore. She must recommend herself very much to your feelings, because she is a person who, for months after the disappearance of Harriet Lane, discharged the duties of a mother to the children left behind. She was the constant friend and companion of Harriet Lane from the date of her apprenticeship until she was last heard of, and she was, it seems, always in her confidence. If, then, any one presented himself to her friend as being called Frieake, she would be likely to take a searching look at the person. From the deficiency of the sense of hearing, her perception would in all probability be the more acutely developed, so that she was more likely to take a keener observation of this person than either Mrs. Wells, Mrs. Foster, or Mrs. Stanley. Miss Wilmore gave a description of this Frieake at the coroner's inquest, at the Police Court, and during the present trial, a description to which Thomas could never have answered. She said he was very young-looking, well dressed, of light complexion, had light hair, light moustache, and was rather fair and long. That was given from her memory, and upon the several occasions specified her account was substantially the same. You will bear in mind those words, "rather fair and long," because they differ in many respects from the evidence given by Mrs. Foster.

This latter lady is the next witness to whom I shall call your notice. She says this person came to her house at most upon three occasions—two or three times. Upon the first occasion Mrs. Foster opened the door. Mrs. King, who was standing at the stairs, said, "Mr. Frieake, will you walk up?" which he, without comment, immediately did. The other occasion was when Mrs. Foster let him in and announced him upstairs. A very short space of time was then occupied, and the only words that passed were those conveying the information that he was Mr. Frieake. On the night of the disturbance in the street she could not be expected to pay any attention to this man, even if he were present. She addressed him whom she supposed to be Mr. King, and then ran into her house, seeing no more of the parties outside. You will, I think, agree with me that those three transactions could not have occupied more than

Addresses to Jury.

a couple of minutes. This took place on 1st September, 1874, and she did not see the prisoner until he was in custody on 2nd October, 1875—a period of thirteen months—she was shown a number of men, and told to select the person whom she had formerly seen. This was the only witness to whom this test was applied, and she failed to recognise him. She next saw him in the dock at a time when he was alleged to be the man who called at her house. Under those unfavourable circumstances, she said, "He is about the size and stature of the man; very possibly he is the man. He had only a little moustache." How does that description accord with the others? She added that he had very little whiskers, very light; she was the only witness who imported the whiskers into the case. It would therefore be absolutely impossible to rely on the evidence of this woman when she failed to recognise the prisoner when the surrounding circumstances were favourable to him. There was a Miss Foster living in this house, and he would like to ask the prosecution why she was not called. Had she no opportunities for seeing the person who alleged himself to be Frieake?

We now come to Mrs. Amelia Stanley. She knew Mrs. King merely as a lodger, and she could not be specially attracted by any one calling to see her lodger casually. The visitor stood in the passage while Mrs. Stanley went upstairs to announce him as Mr. Frieake, and to return with the answer of the lodger, Mrs. King, "Show him up." There was no time allowed here for any close observation, for the visitor at once proceeded upstairs. It is on such an identification that you are asked to believe that Thomas Wainwright went to the house and represented himself as Frieake.

I will now advert to an observation of the Attorney-General. He said that all these witnesses gave their evidence with great doubt and hesitation when at the Police Court as to the identity of Thomas Wainwright with Frieake, and, if it depended upon them, he should not himself be satisfied with their testimony in his own mind without strong confirmatory testimony. But of what did that testimony consist? Of one witness only, Mr. Humphries, and he stands before you in this position. Before he left the box his lordship told him there were grave doubts as to his accuracy, as he had fixed upon a time incompatible with the other evidence in this case. It is the theory of the prosecution that these two prisoners were plotting the murder of Harriet Lane, and that in pursuance of that plot they went to a public-house kept by a man who knew him, exactly opposite the house of their intended victim, and were smoking

The Wainwrights.

Mr Moody and drinking there in the bar, where they might have been seen by any one from Harriet Lane's house, or, perhaps, by Harriet Lane herself. Could anything more improbable be imagined? But that is their theory, and Mr. Humphries came to prove it, and he brought his book, which was undoubtedly wrong, to prove that it was Saturday, 5th September. But that was not the only error, because it was more than probable that the pint and quart of champagne he deposed to selling were had on different days. Mrs. Foster went and borrowed three glasses, and only two were used. There were only two persons for whom the wine came, and why did she get three? Possibly she thought they would ask her to take a glass.

The LORD CHIEF JUSTICE—The same thought occurred to me.

Mr. MOODY—I am happy to be confirmed by the Lord Chief Justice. Mrs. Foster was not asked to drink, and whether or not she thought the rising generation less polite than in her younger days, the disappointment was one likely to impress the matter upon her memory, and she said the two bottles came upon two several occasions, thereby flatly contradicting Mr. Humphries' evidence. Again, he said it was on the 5th that the disturbance took place. Afterwards Mrs. Foster did not put either of the nights when there was champagne as that of the disturbance. When the woman came there, contrary to her usual habits, in liquor, and the disturbance took place, she had had her drink away from the house. Humphries therefore was indubitably wrong on that point also. His conduct as a witness is open to just remark. Mr. Frieake at once, when he heard of the affair, gave information, and told all he knew, but Mr. Humphries, although he admits reading Mrs. Foster's evidence before the magistrates, kept all he knew to himself till 23rd October.

I will now refer to the letter of Mrs. King to Mr. Frieake. It is dated Saturday night, and Mr. Frieake thought he received it on the last Monday in August, which would make it to be written on Saturday, 29th August. I shall present it to you from a different point of view to that given by Mr. Besley, though with no intention of prejudicing his client in the least. The contents of the letter showed that it was not written with a view to some arrangement for transferring herself from Henry Wainwright to the person addressed. He was rather above her in position, from whom she had received benefits, and looked for more. I have shown you that there are great

Addresses to Jury.

doubts as to the reality of this Frieake episode at all, but if it did take place, its object was, I think, quite different. The letter, which has been often read, begins, " I trust you will pardon me for writing to you," and concludes with the words, " As the time is now growing short," and " In future I will promise to behave more ladylike." As a matter of fact, this letter has never been brought to my client's knowledge at all. It seems to me that this matter affords ground for the belief that peace was the reason of this design. We know from evidence that in May Henry Wainwright was in pecuniary difficulty. I have adverted to reasons why the prisoner Henry should be desirous of placing his relationship with this woman on a different footing. I can conceive Henry Wainwright desiring that she should suffer as little inconvenience as possible, and still finding it impossible to continue the relationship which had existed between them, and desiring to make some permanent provision for her, so that she might contribute to her own support, it might be by reverting to dressmaking, while he was oppressed with difficulties. At the same time it would have been inconsistent with him in this state of pecuniary difficulty to appear to be advancing any considerable sum out of his own means. He may have naturally concluded, " If she receives this money from me, she will think I have been deceiving her as to my position; and if, therefore, I can get together a sum of money, it will be better to represent it as coming from a friend, and as being in the nature of a loan, and through that friend to make arrangements for terminating my ambiguous position with her." He may thus have obtained the aid of some friend, but certainly he was not likely to take his brother, as he was the very person who would be most likely to be found out by Harriet Lane. If he were to represent him as his good friend E. Frieake, who was advancing the money, on such a supposition as this, I say the letter of Harriet Lane is precisely such a one as would be written by a woman to a man who had been at first, it may be ungraciously, the negotiator of the prisoner Henry, but who afterwards wished to reopen negotiations. If that is consistent, what becomes of the value of the Frieake theory, as something prepared and leading up to what, for the purposes of argument, I will call a murder? I may have to advert later on to the charge of Thomas Wainwright being an accessory after the fact.

I now propose to sum up shortly what I have been endeavouring to impress upon your minds. First I submit that from the character of the man, with regard to the principal

The Wainwrights.

Mr. Moody charge, there is every probability that he never could have been engaged for any length of time in so cruel, so cold-blooded, and so treacherous a design as the prosecution have alleged against him; that if such a design was ever present to his mind, it could not have been carried out by such a person. There is the greatest improbability that the prisoner Henry Wainwright should have selected his brother, with whom he might at any time be seen in contact, to act the part of this simulated Mr. Frieake. In no way has the evidence in the case tending to the identity of Thomas Wainwright as Mr. Frieake been strengthened as compared with what it was at the Police Court, although on one point the Attorney-General observed to you that it would not be safe to rely upon it. I have submitted grave reasons to you why I say that Mr. Humphries has not strengthened the case, and therefore I ask you to rely on what the Attorney-General said in his opening on the point. I have endeavoured to show further, that even if you should be of opinion that Thomas Wainwright did take part in any portion of this Frieake episode anterior to the disappearance of Harriet Lane, even then his conduct is consistent with the theory I have presented to you, and is not only inconsistent with the evidence of a guilty design, but is consistent with a truly laudable motive, for the advancement of the comfort of this woman. I shall address you in a subsequent part of the case on the whole facts extending over the whole transaction.

Before finally leaving the subject of accessory before the fact, I may call your attention to the fact that the last time Frieake was seen in the house was clearly before 1st September, and there has been no evidence produced to show that Frieake ever was there afterwards. From that time he disappears from the case till somewhere about 9th or 10th September, 1875, and the only connection of his with the case is the letter and the telegram. Therefore, for twelve months there is no evidence of his having taken any active corporeal part in the matter. Even as regards the one or two facts which the prosecution allege, there is considerable space intervening between 1st September and these occurrences. The allegation of the prosecution is that, contemplating her disappearance, and in order to form an excuse for it, Frieake is introduced before her disappearance, and facts are created in order to lay the foundation of the theory that she had gone away with him. If persons prepare an elaborate scheme to meet an emergency, they would be expected to use it when the emergency arose. The scheme having been elaborated with such care and prepared to meet

172

the emergency, it is not used at the time when it would naturally **Mr. Moody** be expected that it would be used. Reasons may be put to you for this. I must ask you to bear in mind that such reasons can only be speculation, as there has been no foundation of any fact for them. Another view to be taken is that if this plot was prepared for this 'purpose, one could have imagined that there would have been communications between the prisoners taking part in it immediately after the inquiry was set on foot, as their object would have been to prevent inquiry. Under such circumstances the reasonable course would have been, when the disappearance took place, that there should have been a communication forwarded in order to prevent visits from Miss Wilmore to the house.

Now we come to the Dover letter. That letter was received before 17th October, the date on which the telegrams were sent, and taking the limit the other way, one of the witnesses had said it must have been received three weeks after the disappearance. That would put the letter in any case at a date not before October, 1874. That letter is used, and you will observe that upon it I have not founded a single question in cross-examination, the only question put being to Mr. Chabot, as to whether the writing was not an undisguised writing, and he replied that as regarded the writing it was an honest letter. Do you not believe that the first impulse of a man called upon to execute such a task would be in some way to disguise his handwriting?

Of course it may be said, "How, then, came it to be written?" and then, undoubtedly, does arrive a difficulty, which has been present to the mind of the Attorney-General. When Henry Wainwright was taken into custody, the charge was no doubt a matter of surprise and astonishment to Thomas, but when the matter came before the Police Court it could not have been long before the name of Frieake was called to his attention; but you have him remaining in London, liable at any moment to be arrested, whilst he had the means of escape at hand. If there were any consciousness of guilt in Thomas Wainwright's mind, would he have abstained from flight? Then he has spoken of the spade and the axe, which he says he did buy; but no one would have expected him to come forward against his brother. Then he said when taken into custody, "I have done no more than one brother would do for another," and really I do not think that the prosecution would attempt to strain that into an admission of guilt. It is not improbable that the one brother might have gone to the other and said, "She has disappeared, and her friends have a notion I am

The Wainwrights.

with her, and they are coming here and making a noise, and I want to stop it. I know the person with whom she has gone away. Will you write a letter?" One can conceive the possibility of men whose lives were devoted to works of piety even doing such a thing as this to relieve a relative from some temporary trouble, however much they might regret that he had fallen from the right way.

Connected with this branch of the evidence is that which refers to the telegram. There is nothing to prove that it ever reached the hands of Thomas Wainwright. Three telegrams appear to have been sent consecutively by the same person—one on 17th October, one of them being to some place at Fulham or Walham Green. The prosecution have failed to prove that at that time Thomas Wainwright was actually residing at Walham Green. If there had been a real residence there it would have been the easiest thing in the world to have adduced proof in regard to it. From other circumstances in this case you will understand it was not in that house that his wife and family resided. The telegram being the last entered in the book of the Walham Green Post Office it would appear to have been the latest received, and it is not improbable that instead of punctually delivering it, the tired message boy went home for supper, and the dispatch may never have reached its destination.

Another circumstance of importance is that while in the letter from Charing Cross Hotel the name is spelled "Frieake," yet in this telegram it is spelled "Freeke." If those telegrams were sent as a means to deceive and mislead Miss Wilmore and Mrs. Taylor, they could never have been sent by any person actually cognisant of the purpose for which they were sent. There is nothing whatever to connect Thomas Wainwright with these telegrams, and it is an absurdity to suppose a man would telegraph to himself facts with which he is supposed to be familiar. Supposing a man had consented to write the letter to which I have referred, might not something of this kind happen—he would say, " I hope this business is all right," and receive for answer, " No doubt there will shortly be an intimation from them, and very likely there will be a telegram to say it is all right, in which case you shall know." In some such way as this the telegram may be capable of explanation. No other explanation can be given of a document which has never been seen, and which is in no way brought before us.

That concludes the connection of my client with this case. During the subsequent transaction in the following months he

Addresses to Jury.

had nothing to do with it. According to Mr. Pettigrew, on or about 10th September, 1875, he purchased a hatchet and spade, and these from Mr. Pettigrew, a man who has known him for years. He tells for whom he wants them, and, going back, delivers them, making a profit on the transaction—a thing which, if he were conscious of the fearful crime, would scarcely be present to his mind. Besides, being in the trade, he could have obliterated all trace of the purchase by erasing the trade marks.

The interview on 11th September is one of those instances of unsatisfactory evidence, of which there have been several in this trial. The man Alfred Young said he saw Henry and Thomas Wainwright on 11th September in conversation outside of Mr. Martin's door. Why did the witness not come previously forward to say so, until, one or two days before the prisoner Thomas was expected to be put on his trial, he said he talked the matter over with his father? The discovery took place at five in the afternoon on the other side of the water, at a distance from the house of the witness, and was not generally known until the publication of the morning and evening papers on Monday following, the 13th. This, therefore, I take to be a second instance of defective memory. With regard to the date, I think this conversation may have taken place on the morning of the 10th, when Thomas was in the neighbourhood, rather than on the morning of the 11th. The two brothers were seen talking together. One was observed to be rather unwell, and his moustache appeared to be shaved off. It is upon that that the prosecution endeavour to build up some vague suspicion of a man having been employed for hours during that night in performing this fearful and ghastly work of mutilation. If this fearful work had to be done, was it likely a third person would be brought needlessly into the matter? If Thomas had assisted in this cutting and chopping, why did he not take part in the removal? Why, under such circumstances, should the chances of detection be multiplied? Surely if Thomas had been engaged in this work, it was madness to needlessly enlarge the area of discovery by bringing in the agency of Stokes. In fact, there is nothing on which to base this supposition but surmise, arising from his having a pale and haggard look while talking to his brother outside the shop on 11th September.

As regards the keys of the Hen and Chickens, you will have seen that they were taken possession of in the ordinary course of business by their lawful owner. It is alleged that the key

175

The Wainwrights.

Mr. Moody was handed by Thomas to his brother Henry, but there is no evidence on that point. You have seen the key and padlock. It is as ordinary a piece of ironmongery as any that can be seen. The locksmith said the key found on Henry Wainwright was the one which properly would go with the padlock, but, supposing it did, these locks are sold by thousands, and the key of one will easily unlock another. But if it were admitted that it did pass from the one brother to the other, what proof is there that it was for any criminal purpose? At any rate, the tenure by Thomas of the premises in Southwark was as insecure as that of Henry at Whitechapel Road, and if he were a party to such a concealment, is it at all likely that he would consent to the body being placed where he might have to give up the premises very shortly?

I have now gone over all the circumstances which followed 11th September, 1874. I think I have shown that in each link of evidence the one great essential of guilty knowledge is absent; and I therefore ask you to reject the theory of the prosecution altogether. Looking at the case as a whole, I ask you to conclude that even if the person who appeared in the Frieake scheme was the same as wrote the letter from the Charing Cross Hotel, there is still the same deficiency of guilty knowledge on his part. The loan of a key to a brother does not call for any elaborate explanation. One brother talking to another outside the shop at which one of them works does not imply guilty knowledge. Whether you look at the prisoner with respect to the charge of being an accessory before the fact or after the fact, guilty knowledge is still conspicuous by its absence. Man does not lightly shed blood. If there is one crime that men instinctively abhor, it is that of taking life, and, above all, the life of a woman with whom he has lived on terms of intimacy and respect; but what the prosecution ask you to believe is that my client, Thomas Wainwright, has imbrued his hands in the blood of one who never did him the slightest harm, and whose existence produced not the slightest annoyance or trouble to him. It is, say the prosecution, nonsense to account for his writing the letter by brotherly affection. But is it not in a still greater degree nonsense to ask you to believe he has imbrued his hands in the blood of an innocent woman from brotherly affection? The case for the prosecution is that this woman had claims on Henry Wainwright which were so burdensome and impossible, from his impecuniosity, for him to meet, that he does not shrink from this dreadful crime; yet you are to believe, notwithstanding that utter impecuniosity,

Addresses to Jury.

that he was in a condition to bribe his brother to assist in this dreadful deed. They have, however, never shown the passing of any money, not even of a single sum. I know there is the bill spoken of by Lewis, of its acceptance and discounting, but how can you tell the money did not go to the acceptor? I do not think, however, much reliance can be placed on the evidence of Lewis, who evidently gave it with a bias, and blurted out irrelevant things calculated to injure the prisoners. It is strange, however, that if there was any truth in the story of the £300 acceptance, he should never have communicated it to the solicitor of the Treasury, and that it should not have been opened by the Attorney-General.

I have now touched upon almost every point in the case, except the moustache and beard. I propose to call before you Mr. Arkell, a respectable ironmonger in Oxford Street, who will state to you that from the arrangements under which his business is carried on, he is able to say that Thomas Wainwright, who was in his employment in 1874, from March to October, was never absent from his work except for three days in August, when he had a holiday, and his working hours were from 8 a.m. to 8.30 p.m. I don't put it as an alibi, because it is quite possible he might after 8.30 p.m. have been able to reach Sidney Square, and have been present on the night of the disturbance there. Mr. Arkell gives a direct contradiction to the evidence of Miss Wilmore, Mrs. Foster, Mrs. Stanley, and Rogers as to the colour of his hair as compared with that of the man said to be Frieake. I now propose to call only three witnesses—Mr. Arkell, the solicitor, and Mr. Rufer, if he is here; and I think their evidence will tend to satisfy you on many points in this case.

Evidence for Thomas George Wainwright.

ALEXANDER ARKELL, examined by Mr. MOODY—I am in busi- ness as an ironmonger at 291 Oxford Street, close to Davies Street. I knew the prisoner Thomas, who entered my service as shopman on 30th March, 1874, and continued with me until 10th October. I employ various countermen, and I have a sheet on which are entered each day the takings of each counterman. I have the sheet here. Each counterman enters into a separate column his sales. During the time Thomas Wainwright was in my employment he was very regular, except that he was late in the morning. He was absent four or five days, which by reference to my sheet I find to be 11th May, 22nd June, 3rd,

The Wainwrights.

A. Arkell 4th, 5th, and 13th August, and 7th October. 3rd August was the Bank Holiday, the 4th and 5th were holidays I gave. While I was away in August I received a telegram from him from Ramsgate, 3rd August, asking me to let him stay another day. He was not late every morning, but usually late on a Monday. He ought to have been at business at 8 a.m. He left at 8 p.m., when the shop closed. He generally got away at 8.10 or 8.15. During the time he was in my service he wore a full dark moustache, but never a beard, and no whiskers. The colour of the moustache was dark. I am not a locksmith, but I deal in locks. (Padlock and keys handed to witness.) That is about a shilling padlock. They are made in large quantities, and it would be extraordinary to find a key that would not fit it. (Witness turned both keys in the padlock, unlocking with both.) There is no doubt one key fits the lock best, but even that I should not call the proper fit. I am not sure that it was not intended for the lock, but either of them would do equally well.

Cross-examined by the ATTORNEY-GENERAL—Thomas Wainwright was engaged as shop manager. I used occasionally to send him out to collect debts, but not frequently. I had four countermen at the time he was with me, of whom he was one.

Did Thomas Wainwright, on 1st September, only sell five articles? Do you infer from that he was not present all day?—Yes.

On 5th September, I see from your sheets, that while Alfred sold a column full of articles, Thomas Wainwright only sold seven articles. What is your inference from that?—That was Saturday, when we close at five o'clock. Either he was out collecting, or he was dressing the window, when he would not have much to do with the counter.

Was he a good salesman?—I never knew his equal.

I see on 10th September, 1874, the number of articles entered as sold by Thomas Wainwright is about equal to the sales of Alfred. Do you infer from that that the prisoner was away on part of that day?—I think he was there the whole day, but the day may have been wet.

Look again to 11th September. What should you say as to that?—That as far as the till was concerned, it seems to have been one of our worst days. This day might have been a wet day. On this day, I see the sales are small matters, which would be left to younger hands. On that day, no doubt, he would be dressing the window.

How many sales did he make that day?—I see they are 46s. 11d., double any other man's.

178

Evidence for Defence.

Do you say they are greater than any of the others?— **A. Arkell**
Yes; more than double the money of the others.

On 13th August you say he was away all day?—Yes; he
was away altogether, but I find from these sheets he was back on
the 14th. While he was working with me he was living somewhere at Fulham, but I never of my own knowledge knew
where.

Did you discharge him?—Yes, sir. I discharged him for
two reasons. He had been, as I have said, very irregular of
a morning, and it came to my knowledge that he had deserted
his wife. I never spoke to him about living at Parson's
Green, or about Mrs. Raper.

Re-examined—I paid Thomas Wainwright two guineas a
week, besides commission on sales, which amounted to about
50s. a week. He was manager in my absence.

CHARLES GEORGE GRAULIER, examined—I am a solicitor of **C. G. Graulier**
the Supreme Court. Formerly I was an attorney. My offices
are 13 Railway Approach, London Bridge. The prisoner Thomas
was a client of mine. He came first to consult me in February,
1875, at which time he was about to open the Hen and Chickens.
I was employed to draw up an agreement between him and Mr.
Moore, but it was never completed. The lease was not actually
executed in consequence of Mr. Moore not carrying out his part
of the agreement. After the failure of the business at the Hen
and Chickens, I was consulted by Thomas with regard to the
surrender of the premises. I corresponded on the subject with
Mr. Stuckey, the solicitor for the lessor, at Brighton.

I believe no rent had been paid for the Midsummer quarter,
and Mr. Stuckey wrote to me and said that if he accepted the
key the quarter's rent and the costs of the lease should be paid.
I have experienced in such cases that by the time a second
quarter's rent is due the difficulty disappears, when there is
nothing to distrain. The earliest time at which I was spoken
to about the surrender of the premises to Thomas Wainwright
was the beginning of August, or it might have been the last
few days of July. I met him in the street and he spoke to me
about it.

Cross-examined by the ATTORNEY-GENERAL—I have known
Thomas since the beginning of January, 1875. I had never
seen him before that. I have no idea what his private residence
was then. He had started in business then; the agents had
given him possession. He had some goods in the shop. He
told me he lived at the Rosamond, at Fulham. I do not think

179

The Wainwrights.

C. G. Graulier   I wrote to him there, but he told me so that I might communicate with him on hearing from Mr. Stuckey in reference to the lease. The partnership with Mr. Moore went off at the beginning of June, when I was first made acquainted with it.

Re-examined—I wished to communicate with him to let him know about the lessors, and he told me to write to him at the Rosamond, at Fulham. That was all he told me. Beyond that I knew nothing of my own knowledge. I cannot tell whether he was only there on a visit.

Evidence for Thomas George Wainwright closed.

Closing Speech for Thomas George Wainwright.

Mr. Moody   Mr. MOODY said—The witness I have called before you has established the fact that Thomas could not have been aware that the Hen and Chickens was to be made a place of deposit for the body, when he was about to give up the premises. The first inquiries would naturally be made of the last occupier, and a man would hesitate a long time before he submitted to being made the first person to whom attention should be drawn. From the evidence I have called before you, you will gather that there has been no change in the personal appearance of Thomas, and that he had during the whole time spoken of his present dark, full moustache, and therefore could not have passed by the description given by several of the witnesses for the prosecution. If your minds are clear on that point, I again ask you to acquit him entirely of any guilty knowledge with reference to the letter and the spade, and if the writing of the letter were put to him in the way it has been suggested, is it at all probable that a man would suspect his own brother of that which even the relatives did not suspect? The writing of the letter was a matter which one man might well do for another. The charge is that, without motive, he made himself a partner to a scheme of blood. Such a charge is one founded on the grossest improbability. Such a charge should be supported by evidence beyond suspicion, but there no doubt is grave suspicion in the evidence in this case, and I trust you will find yourselves able to say that you think the letter E (from Dover) was written without any guilty knowledge, and it will be your pleasure to say that he is not guilty. In asking you to give this verdict on behalf of Thomas, I may say, although without any authority to do so, I am asking for the same verdict on the part of Henry.

Adjourned till to-morrow.

Eighth Day—Tuesday, 30th November, 1875.

The LORD CHIEF JUSTICE, on taking his seat at a few minutes after 10 a.m., said he had great difficulty in getting into the Court.

Mr. BESLEY, addressing his lordship, said that he had looked over the evidence, and found that it completely bore out his statement in his speech on Monday—that the hair of Harriet Lane was both " curly " and " frizzy."

Closing Speech for the Prosecution.

The ATTORNEY-GENERAL said—The defences of the prisoners have been presented to you by their respective counsel, and it now becomes my duty to reply to the arguments and evidence they have adduced. In the course of that reply it will be necessary for me more or less to comment on the more salient points of the evidence produced both by the prosecution and for the defence. It will be my desire in these comments not to lose sight of the momentous issues involved, not to forget the feelings of the advocate in an earnest desire to sift the evidence as completely as I can, and to aid you in discovering the truth. I will deal with the facts in the order in which they have been presented to you from the beginning. And first as to the case of Henry Wainwright. His counsel (Mr. Besley), in the course of his, in many respects, most able speech, has presented to you a digest of the evidence, and commented upon it very fully, and set before you the defence he makes for his client, and I propose, at the outset, to take a general view of what that defence is. He says that the evidence for the prosecution is incomplete and unsatisfactory—not sufficient to convince your minds that guilt lies at the door of the prisoner he represents. The learned counsel then went on to say there is not sufficient evidence to establish that the body found was that of Harriet Lane. He says no doubt a body was found on the premises of Henry Wainwright, with which he was dealing on 11th September, 1875, under circumstances of grave suspicion, which no doubt called for some explanation on the part

The Attorney-General

181

The Wainwrights.

The Attorney-General of Wainwright, and the explanation he gives is simply that it was not the body of Harriet Lane, but that it might be that of some woman who had received injury at the hands of Wainwright, and who committed suicide on these premises, Wainwright being induced by the horror of the moment to conceal the body lest, if it were discovered on his premises, he might have a charge made against him which it would be difficult to meet. But, on the assumption that the body is that of Harriet Lane, he has given no explanation whatever of the conduct of this man. He has a right to say, if he thinks so, that the evidence is not conclusive enough to bring home guilt to the prisoner, but on the assumption that the body is that of Harriet Lane, there is no explanation and no theory to account for the inference you are invited to draw from the facts presented to your notice. On the other hand, supposing that it is not the body of Harriet Lane, the theory on which he desires you to act upon is that the unfortunate woman, whoever she may have been, met with her death by her own hand, and that Henry Wainwright, under the influence of fear, buried the body in those premises.

Just consider for a moment whether this theory can be tenable. You have the evidence before you of the injury found to have been inflicted upon the body. It is perfectly true that there was a cut in the throat sufficient to destroy life almost instantaneously, for that cut severed the windpipe and all the structures to the vertebræ, and she had two bullets in her head, and a third was lodged in the hair pad. Can you imagine all those injuries to have been inflicted by her own hand? Suppose the cut in the throat was inflicted during life, how would it be possible for her afterwards to discharge these three bullets with such deadly and certain aim? Reverse the case, and suppose the bullets were first discharged, how was it possible for the woman afterwards to inflict the wound in her throat? My learned friend contends that the wound in the throat was not inflicted till after death, but no one has advanced any reason why it should be so inflicted, and there is no evidence of any motive for inflicting it after death.

What have we, then? Why, there is this cut in the throat, and we have it clearly proved that there were two wounds made by a pistol—one behind the ear and another before the ear, made by bullets which had entered and lodged in the woman's brain. In addition to that, you have it that there was a third bullet, which had lodged in the pad, stopped by the mass of hairpins. How would it be possible for a woman who attempted to commit suicide first to discharge a shot into the

Address to Jury.

back of the pad? Could you, gentlemen, do you think, discharge a pistol into the back of your neck, and, if it could be done, do you think any one would do it? That is not the way a woman who wished to destroy herself—by a pistol, mind you—would commit suicide. She would, you may be sure, discharge it into her forehead, her mouth, or her heart, or any part of the body that she could reach with facility, and it is idle to suggest that she would commence at the back of her head. But if she did not so commence, the absurdity becomes greater, for, having two bullets lodged in the brain, she must have then performed the difficult—I was about to suggest impossible—act of discharging the third at the back of her head.

The LORD CHIEF JUSTICE—There is no proof that the shot which lodged behind was fired first, and, of course, it would be physically impossible after two bullets were lodged in the brain, though, of course, it is possible that a person might fire a shot which did not take effect, and then follow it up by another.

The ATTORNEY-GENERAL—Precisely so, my lord. Well, gentlemen, I put it to you—is it physically possible? Try yourselves to turn the muzzle of a revolver to the back of your own heads where that bullet lodged in the pad. If it could be done, is it likely it would be done by a woman? It is the last thing which would occur to her mind. But even if she had done so in this case, and the bullet was arrested in the pad, it must have come with such fearful force against the back of her head as to stun her instantly, and do you think she could then discharge two shots into the brain. Or, taking the reverse case, do you think she not only lodged one bullet in her brain, but followed it up with a second before firing the one which lodged in her pad? Really, gentlemen, you must deal with the facts of this case as you would deal with any other case—by looking upon it with the eye of reason, and I will not insult your reason and outrage your common sense by asking you to assume that the woman committed suicide. If she did not, then at the very threshold this difficulty stares Henry Wainwright in the face.

There is a woman buried at 215 Whitechapel Road, under the floor of the paint room; on 11th September, 1875, he is dealing with the remains; can any one doubt from the evidence that his hand severed the remains into a number of pieces? On the 11th he is taking them to the Hen and Chickens; he is arrested; he is found in possession of the mutilated remains of a woman who has met with her death by foul play, and it is

183

The Wainwrights.

incumbent on him under these circumstances to give you some
explanation, but explanation there is none. If you disregard
the theory of suicide, what explanation does Henry Wainwright
give you of the possession? What, I submit to you, gentlemen
of the jury, is that? If it was not suicide, it was murder, and
no explanation is given by my learned friend who defends Henry
Wainwright. The only defence my learned friend relies on is
that the evidence adduced by the prosecution is unsatisfactory.
What does my learned friend say to show that the evidence is
not satisfactory? After comments, in which I thoroughly
agree, on the unenviable task we have all to perform in this
matter, and after commenting upon the nature of the surgical
evidence in the case, my learned friend complains that the
prosecution have offered no evidence with regard to the early
intimacy or the commencement of the intimacy between Henry
Wainwright and Harriet Lane. He seemed to think I had
promised to trace her from Waltham Abbey, and to give evidence
of her life up to the time she left Mrs. Foster's, in Sidney
Square, on 11th September, 1874. I don't remember making
any such statement. I said I should show she was the daughter
of John Lane, and had been educated and in business there,
and had left to come to London some time in 1872; that she
had formed a connection with Henry Wainwright, and was his
mistress. It was not reasonable to expect the prosecution to
show more than that; and if we had, what advantage would
have resulted from it? That in 1872 this unhappy woman was
the mistress of Henry Wainwright no one can doubt, for we
have him obtaining lodgings for her, acknowledging her, keeping her children as his, and at the places where she was living
it is assumed that Henry Wainwright, who passed under the
assumed name of Percy King, was her husband. It would be
a waste of time, therefore, to go into the origin of the acquaintance which left Harriet Lane, in 1872, the mistress of Henry
Wainwright in London, living in 1873 with Mrs. Wells, and
in 1874 with Mrs. Foster, from whose lodgings she departed
on 11th September, from which time she was never again heard
of alive.

Then my friend deals with the evidence with respect to Henry
Wainwright being in embarrassed circumstances. I advanced
on .the part of the prosecution that in the middle of 1874
Wainwright was in embarrassed circumstances, that he was short
of money, that he had the greatest difficulty in supplying Mrs.
King with the money he was in the habit of giving her; that
he had expenses, it is clear, for he had a wife and family of

Address to Jury.

four or five children living at Tredegar Square. It is clear that in January, 1874, there was a proceeding instituted by Sawyer to obtain a dissolution of partnership, and about the same date there was a petition of Henry Wainwright for the liquidation of his affairs. At a meeting of his creditors it was resolved that a dividend of 12s. in the pound should be received—6s. within a few days after the meeting, 3s. at the end of three months, and 3s. at the end of six months. The first and second instalments were paid, and the third is not paid, so that it is clear that at that time he was obliged to compound with his creditors to get them to agree to a dividend of 12s. in the pound, the third instalment of which he was unable to meet. The evidence does not stop there, for we have the fact that he himself, about July, 1874, was asking his manager, Rogers, to dispose of a revolver. This may have been a trifling subject, but if he had to resort to that means for the purpose of raising money, it is obvious that he was in an embarrassed condition. At an earlier date we have Mrs. King, whom he had undertaken to support, also disposing of her things. If she could have got money from Henry Wainwright it would not have been necessary for her to dispose of her things. But the fact of her doing so at that time must convince you that Wainwright was short of money. I do not think with regard to this part of the case the comments which my learned friend thought proper to make will have any great weight with you.

I now come to another matter to which my learned friend referred—the evidence relating to Frieake. My learned friend said he could not understand why Henry Wainwright should have introduced any one to Harriet Lane under the name of Frieake. If the person whom he did so introduce was not Frieake, what object, says my learned friend, would there be in selecting such an uncommon name as Frieake? Why not select some other name? May not this have been the solution? Edward Frieake, the auctioneer of Coleman Street, was a friend of Henry Wainwright's, and had been for some years. Personally, he was not known to Mrs. King, but it may be, and indeed it is highly probable, that in the course of conversation with Mrs. King, many references may have been made to Edward Frieake, and the friendship that existed may have been described. Therefore, if it was necessary for any purpose to introduce any one to Mrs. King, nothing would be so natural as that the name of this Mr. Frieake, who was known by her to be the friend of Henry Wainwright, should be selected as the person to be represented. But whether it is natural or not, whether it is

The Wainwrights.

probable that he would do so or not, it is clear that Frieake's name was selected, and that some one was introduced to Mrs. King as Frieake.

The Attorney-General went on to show that the suggestion made by the prisoner's counsel—that the person introduced was a real Mr. Frieake, who ultimately succeeded in estranging the affections of Mrs. King from Henry Wainwright—was untenable, and that the terms of the letter written by Mrs. King beginning "My dear Mr. Frieake," and apologising for rude behaviour, were not such as would be written by a woman to a man between whom and herself there existed an undue familiarity, and with whom she was about to go away. Then, he continued, there is the letter from Henry Wainwright himself, to which I shall have occasion again to refer. It is dated 5th September, which, you will remember, is shortly before the 11th. He writes thus to Mrs. King, "Dear Pet,—E. F. is going down at seven to-night. He will give you a call with a message," &c. This friend "E. F." must have been a person in whom Henry Wainwright had the most perfect confidence. Assuming he was not Thomas Wainwright, what happens? We have the fact that Mrs. King leaves her abode in Sidney Square a little after four o'clock on 11th September. According to Henry Wainwright's statement, she finds her way to 215 Whitechapel Road, and is never more seen afterwards. It is suggested she has gone away with Frieake, this man who has been carrying messages between the two. The fact that she found her way to this place on the day named is substantiated by the evidence of Mrs. Taylor, who, when she questioned Henry Wainwright about the absence of her sister, got the reply that on 11th September she left Sidney Square and came to Whitechapel Road. She had then gone with Frieake to the theatre, for he had stayed in the shop until ten o'clock at night, expecting their return; but they did not come back—consequently he concluded that they must have gone off together to Brighton. It may be that the whole is a fabrication, or that the part of the story which states that Mrs. King came down to these premises on that afternoon is as false as the rest of it. Supposing she did not come down, we at all events find this—that the body of a woman was afterwards discovered buried there; that Harriet Lane from that time till this has never been heard of by any of her friends or relatives, and is supposed to have gone off with one named Frieake.

You will remember that Harriet Lane was the mother of two children, borne by her to the man whom she must have once

186

Address to Jury.

loved. These children she was exceedingly fond of. She was the daughter of a man who had not ceased to respect and regard her. Whatever her faults or errors may have been, she was always treated with kindness by the members of her family. She was a well-educated woman. She had all these ties to bind her to those she loved at Waltham. Is it then credible or conceivable that a woman of this kind would leave her home, all those who were dear to her, to go away with a man who must have been almost an absolute stranger to her? Would she—even if she did this—never make any communication to those who were left behind? Would she not have made some communication to those in charge of her children? A woman does not act in the way the gentlemen on the other side would have us believe. None of you can possibly conceive that this woman would have been silent so long as this had she gone with a person named Frieake to Dover or Paris, or anywhere else.

If Frieake was not Thomas Wainwright—and I am now assuming he was not—who was he? One would suppose that if he was intimate enough with Henry Wainwright to be sent by him to carry messages to a woman who was living as Henry Wainwright's wife, and was intimate enough to make arrangements about furniture, to be alluded to in a letter written by Henry Wainwright to Mrs. King, to be allowed to convey Mrs. King to the theatre—then Henry Wainwright knows something about him. What has he ever told anybody who has had anything to do with reference to this case about this Mr. Frieake? That he is not Mr. Frieake of Coleman Street is as clear as the sun at noonday. Then who is he? What description has the prisoner given of him? He said he was a man who used to go to Purcell's—which I take to be some tavern—or to the Philharmonic, or the Nell Gwynn. If there be a Mr. Frieake, is that all the information he can offer about him? It would be idle to suppose that, being on the terms of intimacy which you may infer from the evidence in this case, he can give no further or better account of him than this. Mr. Besley struggled hard to satisfy you—and his observations were of the greatest importance—that Frieake and Thomas Wainwright were not identical, and my friend Mr. Moody, to whose case this was specially referred, has endeavoured to do the same thing in a speech of the greatest ability. This is a matter of the greatest moment, not only to the case of Henry, but to the case of Thomas. If Thomas Wainwright and Mr. Frieake are identical, what a story does it tell! Then you have three Mr. Frieakes to account for. If Thomas Wainwright was the Mr. Frieake

187

The Wainwrights.

who was calling at the lodgings of Mrs. Foster, then you have
the Mr. Frieake of Coleman Street, and another Mr. Frieake,
who, it is suggested, appeared on the scene at the very nick
of time when his presence was required, and about whose history
we are entirely ignorant. Therefore it is of vital importance
for the counsel for Henry to establish, if he can, that Thomas
was not identical with this Mr. Frieake, as much so as for the
counsel for Thomas to establish the same fact.

What evidence have we on the subject of the identity of
Thomas Wainwright with this Mr. Frieake, who was passed off
as such to Mrs. King? You have that of Miss Wilmore, Mrs.
Foster, and Mrs. Stanley. I pass by the evidence of Mrs. Wells,
because I agree to a great extent with what fell from my
learned friend, that there has been no testimony given by her
which should induce you to suppose that the man who was
called Edward was the same person. We have no means of
knowing who he was. The event to which she speaks happened
so long ago that we have no reason to believe that a scheme
was then on foot which would render it necessary for any one
to personate Mr. Frieake. As the story progresses, and when
we come to August and September, we have it clearly proved
that somebody or other was having interviews with Mrs. King
at the lodgings where she then resided, who represented himself to be Frieake. Who was that? I submit to you that this
point is conclusively proved by Harriet Lane's own letter to
Mr. Frieake of Coleman Street. She must have understood
that there was a Mr. Frieake coming to see her, and that he
was of Coleman Street, because she addressed the letter to him
at that place and in that name. That he came not very often,
but on several occasions, is deposed to by Miss Wilmore and
Mrs. Foster; and Mrs. Stanley speaks to one occasion. But it
is true that Miss Wilmore and Mrs. Foster have not identified
the man with absolute certainty. They say, " To the best of
our belief and knowledge he was Thomas Wainwright. He did
not present the appearance Thomas Wainwright now presents.
He had no whiskers "; and they describe his moustache—some
as light and others as a slight one. Their descriptions might
not be accurate, and if they stood alone I should not ask you
to rely upon them; but their testimony does not stand alone,
and I will now refer you to the evidence upon which I rely to
establish the identity of Thomas Wainwright with Edward
Frieake, and that is the testimony of Mrs. Foster, the landlady
of the house where Mrs. King lived. She speaks of two or three
occasions when Frieake came to her house. She believes that

Address to Jury.

the first occasion was towards the end of August or the beginning of September, 1874. She further states that upon one or two occasions the man who came brought with him a bottle of champagne, and that upon one occasion, when he came to see Mrs. King, she was obliged to go to a public-house on the opposite side of the way for the purpose of borrowing three champagne glasses. Now, this is a thing which she would be likely to remember, and probably as champagne was a wine which she seldom or never tasted, she got three champagne glasses with the idea that she would be asked to have some. Well, the champagne was in due time consumed, and she remembers the empty champagne bottle next morning. That is a bit of evidence of a striking character. As to the identity, she only swears that the man was Thomas Wainwright to the best of her belief. But the prosecution have called Mr. Humphries, the landlord of the Princess Royal, the house in question, and he told you that he remembered the two brothers, Thomas and Henry Wainwright, perfectly well; that he had known them for years, and that he recollects them being in his house on one occasion for some time; that during that time they smoked a couple of cigars and drank some soda water and brandy. He further remembers that after they had been there some time Thomas ordered a bottle of champagne, carried it away with him, and shortly afterwards Mrs. Foster or some one else came to his house and borrowed three champagne glasses. Now, if he really does recollect that circumstance, it was the same circumstance as spoken to by Mrs. Foster. Does not this lead irresistibly to the conclusion that the man who took the bottle of champagne over to Mrs. Foster's was Thomas Wainwright? And if he was, it is as clear as anything possibly can be that the man who represented himself to be Frieake was Thomas Wainwright.

The date of that occurrence, according to Mr. Humphries, who spoke from an entry in his diary, was 5th September, 1874. Now, you have had evidence brought before you that Thomas Wainwright was in the employment of Mr. Arkell, an ironmonger of Oxford Street, and his time during the period he was there has been endeavoured to be accounted for. But on 5th September he was not there all day. If you refer to the "sales sheet," which was produced, you will find that, whilst there were many sales effected by the three other countermen on that day, scarcely any article was sold by Thomas Wainwright. Again, 5th September of last year fell on a Saturday, and on that day the shop of Mr. Arkell is closed at

189

The Wainwrights.

five o'clock, instead of eight o'clock, the usual hour on other
days. But there is more than that. We find on this very 5th
September as follows:—" Dear Pet,—E. F. is coming down at
seven to-night. He will give you a call with a message from
me," on that very day, the 5th of September. Now, if Thomas
Wainwright was being passed off to Mrs. King as Frieake, he
must have had some purpose to serve. It is not for me to say
what. It may be that he was intended to satisfy her that he
was about to take her to some residence, and that he was to
provide the furniture for it, or a hundred other reasons may
have been suggested to her mind to account for his visits. You
now have the whole of the incidents which I have narrated
before you, and I say that they all point to the same conclusion,
and I ask, upon that evidence, can you have such doubts as
any reasonable man would entertain that the man who found
his way there was Thomas Wainwright? Everything concurs
to show that he was.

Referring to the evidence given by Mr. Humphries, which
the counsel for the prisoners contended was inaccurate, I am of
opinion that, so far as regarded his statement that the disturbance in the street took place on 5th September, his evidence
was inaccurate. But with regard to the champagne glasses
and Thomas Wainwright taking the champagne, it did not
depend on the evidence of Mr. Humphries alone. You have
had that evidence corroborated, and corroborated in the most
singular and extraordinary manner, by the evidence of Mrs.
Foster. That he might have heard a disturbance was clear,
but not on that day. That a disturbance did take place was
pretty certain, for Mrs. Foster and Miss Wilmore spoke to
it, and, I believe, also Mrs. Stanley. In Harriet Lane's letter
to Mr. Frieake I do not say that the disturbance is alluded
to, and I don't say that the circumstance referred to in the letter
was that disturbance, but it may have been. You have a letter
which is dated Sunday night. You know that on Saturday
Thomas would not be required at his shop in Oxford Street,
and he would be able to be there. The letter says, " I trust
you will pardon me writing to you, but I feel that I ought to
apologise to you for my rude behaviour last night to you."
She proceeds to say she had been very much worried and excited,
and that that must account for her conduct. Thomas might
have been there on the Saturday, and the only thing is that
if you assume that the notice to quit was given on the Saturday,
then you would not have the dates tallying; but if you were
to assume that the notice to quit was given on the Sunday or
Monday—that was, a notice to commence on the Wednesday—

Address to Jury.

that would make it come to 9th September, and the two days which were given extra would bring it to the 11th. The disturbance is spoken to, and as far as the evidence of Mr. Humphries was concerned, he cannot be accurate when he says it took place on the 5th. You must bear in mind the circumstance of the champagne glasses, and you must satisfy yourselves that he is the man.

My learned friend has endeavoured to show that it has not been made out that the chloride of lime was bought on the 10th, or that it was bought by Henry Wainwright. The date of the purchase is, however, fixed by Mr. Baylis's books, and, according to Rogers and Mrs. Rogers, the lime found its way into No. 84 on the afternoon or evening of the 10th, the date being fixed by Mrs. Rogers by the fact that on the morning of the 11th she was delivered of a child.

I now deal with the pistol shots, the evidence with regard to which has been subjected to such severe comment by my learned friend. Now, I do not know that it is important whether the men who heard these pistol shots, or said they heard them, really did hear them or not, because it is obvious that later on, or before, or at that time, a woman died who met her death by two or three pistol shots, and that they were fired in rapid succession. I am not going to ask you to place reliance on this evidence, if it does not deserve to be relied on. The men themselves who deposed to this matter were of good character, and by their demeanour in the witness-box would impress you with the belief that they wished to tell the truth. But, on the other hand, there is a good deal to be said against their evidence, because they said afterwards they remembered three pistol shots fired in rapid succession between the hours of five and seven in the evening, apparently coming from the direction of Henry Wainwright's premises. They say the date of those shots was 11th September, although the figures in the memorandum made by one of them on the completion of certain repairs to a large van of Mr. Martin's looked more like 9 than 11. Then the books showed that Mr. Martin had actually paid a sum of money to Mr. Wiseman on 4th September, and another on the 9th, which together made up the amount of the bill for the little van and the large van. Well, it may be that he paid for the large van before the amount was due, but I don't know whether that is very probable. I should think it rather probable he would not pay until the van had been delivered, and, if so, the testimony of Mr. Wiseman goes to corroborate the testimony of Mr. Martin, and goes to corroborate the evidence of Mrs. Trew.

The Wainwrights.

Taking these matters into consideration, and the fact that
these men said at first they had not heard shots, I do not on
the part of the prosecution ask you to receive their testimony
without doubt, or rely implicitly upon it, although it is due
to them to say that I believe they came into the box to tell you
a truthful story. But exclude their evidence altogether. What,
then? It would be the absence, not of an indispensable link
in the chain, but of an additional one. The shots were fired,
and in rapid succession, into the head of this woman, and I
ask you whether in all probability they were not fired on 11th
September? If not, when were they fired? Where was this
woman on the 11th of September? It was said that Wainwright
gave her £15 to pay her debts, and £10 more for an outfit
to go to Brighton. Where is the evidence of that outfit having
been purchased? And if she were not killed that night, how
was it no one has heard of her? But, again, if that body is not
that of Harriet Lane, she is in all probability alive now. She is
said to have gone away with Frieake to the Continent, but they
must have heard all the circumstances under which these men
are now being tried for their lives, and she at least must have
known that one word from her would clear one whom she once
loved, and loved most tenderly, from peril. There, however,
is the body found, and if that body is Harriet Lane's, she must
have been shot down that night, about the period spoken to.
There is no evidence, at any rate, to show where she is. I
say, therefore, discard the evidence, if you will, of the men
hearing the shots fired, and the case remains as strong as
before, for you cannot doubt that it is the body of Harriet
Lane, and that she met her death by means of the three
chambers of a revolver being fired into her head on 11th
September.

Then the next matters to which I will draw your attention
are the statements of Henry Wainwright to Miss Wilmore, to
Mrs. Taylor, to Fowler (or Eeles), and to Lane, and my learned
friend says they are not proved to be false.

The letter to Miss Wilmore has been proved to be in the
handwriting of Thomas Wainwright from the Charing Cross
Hotel, and in it, under the signature of "T. Frieake," he
said, "We are just off to Dover," and that they were to be
married in a few weeks. Is that letter false or is it not? Is
it not written to put people off the scent at the instigation
of Henry Wainwright by saying, "We are just off to Dover"?
Assume for the moment that the suggestion made had any
foundation in truth—that Frieake had taken her to France.
Why should the prisoner have made all these excuses and

Address to Jury.

explanations? If she had deserted him for a wealthier man, and left her children on his hands, he could not have been to blame. Her connection with him was known to her friends, and why need he have resorted to these suspicious excuses? All he had to do was to tell the simple truth, but instead of that he gets his brother to write this letter, and a more astute or cunning letter could not have been devised to put inquirers off the scent and pacify her friends, and to induce them to be quiet, as, if they were quiet, Frieake promised to marry her. There were also the verbal statements of Miss Wilmore and Taylor, that when shown this letter by them Henry Wainwright went to his desk and produced another which he said he had received, and which was to the same purpose.

But the thing does not stop there, for shortly afterwards three telegrams were received. The letter to which I have just referred paves the way by saying, "We are just off Dover," and these telegrams come from Dover Pier telegraph office, and state, "We are just off to Paris, and intend to have a jolly spree." Who sent those telegrams? Was it Frieake, or was it not rather the man who dictated or wrote that letter? We have the fact of these three telegrams from Dover—one to Miss Wilmore, one to Henry Wainwright, Whitechapel Road, and the third found its way into the district where Parson's Green is situated. Then, again, those telegrams—what tale do they tell? When Miss Wilmore gets hers, she finds her way to Henry Wainwright, and he reads to her another, which he says he has just received, which says, "We are just off to Paris, and intend to have a jolly spree." Now, I ask you, was that not a contrivance to follow up the Charing Cross letter, to satisfy the friends of Harriet Lane and put them off the scent? Then, again, he makes further excuses. He says the woman has been seen by his foreman and by one of his porters. But was that true? We have had the foreman, Rogers, and he tells you he never saw the woman. There is nothing to prevent Henry Wainwright, if the statement is true, calling that workman or porter himself. Then, again, it is pretended that Miss Wilmore saw Mrs. King, and she says herself she did believe she had seen her. But was it not probable that she would entertain such belief? Her mind had been so prepared for it by the statements of Henry Wainwright himself, that when she saw that woman driving in a hansom cab. with a gentleman by her side, near the Bank of England, with hair somewhat of the same colour, she rushes to the conclusion that it is Harriet Lane. But because she supposes that it was Harriet Lane, are you to jump to the conclusion that it was?

o   193

The Wainwrights.

My learned friend then deals with Mr. Rogers, and he asks
you to discredit his testimony, because he says it is untrue;
that it is untrue, because he never mentioned to the coroner,
to the magistrate, or afterwards to the prosecution the statement
he made to my lord when asked as to the contents of the letter
which was handed to him by Henry Wainwright to take to his
wife at Tredegar Square. But do you think he is not to be
believed for that reason? Rogers is a man who had been in
the service of Henry Wainwright, and for years he had been
treated with the greatest possible kindness. Do you think it
possible, having been so treated, that Rogers should be anxious
to state anything damning to the character of his old employer?
You recollect the circumstances of Mrs. King being at No. 84
in a fainting fit, for that was spoken to by Mrs. Rogers.
Rogers was asked about the same affair. He says, "Yes, I
remember being called down to the shop and seeing Henry
Wainwright and Mrs. King there together." He does not
recollect the cries of "Don't! don't," but he comes down and
sees Mrs. King in a state of excitement, and Henry Wainwright
gives him a letter to take to Tredegar Square. Mrs. King
snatches the letter and tears it open, but still Rogers gets away
with it into the street. He says, "Then I was prompted to
look at it, and I saw such nonsense that I did not take it, and
I told Henry Wainwright afterwards that I had not taken it."
He was asked afterwards what were the contents. If he had
been anxious to strain matters against Henry Wainwright, would
he have said what he did? If he were not the witness of truth
he would have given some statement with regard to the contents
of that letter which would have borne more seriously against
the man to whom his testimony was directed. His story was,
" I cannot survive the disgrace . . . you will never see me
any more." Disgrace about what? Not a word about Mrs.
King. I submit to you that when Rogers told you that he was
telling you the truth.

My learned friend next dealt with the period between 1874
and September of this year, and on that he only makes one
remark, and that is with reference to the evidence of the
witness Johnson, who was on the committee of inspection of the
bankruptcy affairs of Henry Wainwright. He says Johnson's
evidence was a mere nothing. But is my learned friend correct
in saying that Johnson's testimony is wholly valueless? You
will remember that in November he was engaged in repairing
No. 215, and, amongst other things, he " stippled " the window
of the warehouse at the back, which was commanded by the

194

Address to Jury.

back window of the house, and especially by the kitchen window. Perhaps Henry Wainwright had good reason for "stippling" the window in November, 1874. Who can tell? The theory of the prosecution is that in the paint room at the end of the premises there was this dreadful secret—a woman lying buried, whose body it was necessary for Henry Wainwright to get rid of. Would it do, then, for him to have that paint room and the door of the paint room commanded by the eyes of any one looking from the kitchen window?

The LORD CHIEF JUSTICE—It occurs to me that, as long as there were people in the house, he would not have cut through the joists, on account of the noise it would make.

The ATTORNEY-GENERAL—My theory is that the joists were cut through long before, my lord. We have this fact, that the window was "stippled" by the instructions of Henry Wainwright, but I did not call Johnson to prove that. I called him because his name was mentioned by Henry Wainwright, who, in speaking to Stokes at the time of the removal of the remains, said, "I wonder whether old Johnson is on the look-out."

Next we come to my learned friend's remarks about what happened on 11th September. On the 10th preparations had been made for the removal of the body. The cloth, the cord, the chopper, the hand-spade, had been bought, and it is clear that some conversation took place between Stokes and Henry Wainwright, who was contemplating how he should dispose of these implements after he had done with them. On the 11th there is no doubt that he and Stokes were together, that Stokes carried away the parcels, and that Henry Wainwright and Alice Day found their way with them to the Hen and Chickens. It has been said, "If Henry Wainwright was conscious of guilt, why did he employ Stokes? and, if Thomas Wainwright was implicated, why did he not do what Stokes did?" Henry Wainwright might well have supposed if he or his brother were seen carrying the parcels away a suspicion would attach to them which would not attach to the man who was employed by Mr. Martin if he was seen doing it. Is it not reasonable that persons engaged in wicked transactions should make a mistake? It was a grievous mistake he made, for if he had not allowed Stokes to remain while he went for the cab he might have got the body safely to its destination. Then it is said, if he was conscious of guilt, why did he take up with Alice Day? But might not even that be for the purpose of averting suspicion? Here is a man in possession of the mutilated remains of a murdered woman, a man

195

The Wainwrights.

who, when he is arrested, said to the police officers, "Say
nothing, and here is £50 each for you"; and again, when the
parcels are about to be opened, he says, "Don't touch it, for
God's sake, and I will make it £200." Is not that the conduct
of a man conscious of guilt? A man goes to the police station,
and, after having had plenty of time for consideration, says
that some gentleman whom he had met in a public-house had
offered him £3 to carry the parcels to the Borough. Is a man
who gives such an explanation to the police officer a man who
is not conscious of guilt?

Then my friend comes to the identity of the body, and upon
this part of the case he lays the greatest possible stress. We
say, on the part of the prosecution, that this woman was
Harriet Lane, and we say that for a variety of reasons—many
of which my friend has endeavoured to scout—we say that that
was Harriet Lane, because she was a woman about twenty-four
years of age, that her height was 5 feet or thereabouts, that
her build was slight, and her hands and feet were small, that
she had light hair, that she had one decayed tooth (only one),
and that in a peculiar position, that she had a scar on the right
leg, and that, besides these distinctive marks on the body, she
was a woman who might have borne children. She had a
wedding ring and keeper, was dressed in a dress trimmed with
large jet buttons, and similar buttons were found where the
woman was found; she had also a hair pad made in a peculiar
way, to which she attached her hair by means of a great quantity of hairpins, and to which was attached a piece of ribbon
velvet. Now, all those distinctive features were to be found
in Harriet Lane, and they are all, with one exception, to be found
on the dead woman. My friend says, taken individually, they
are not matters to which you would attach much importance.
Perhaps not; but put them together, and do you expect to find
in two women an exact correspondence in all these things? It
is said that Harriet Lane was a little taller than Mrs. Allen,
her sister, but the photograph which will be placed before you
will enable you to judge of the difference. The height of Mrs.
Allen was 5 feet and one-eighth of an inch, and the dead woman,
after the parts had been put together, measured only a little
less. I have drawn your attention to the way in which that
difference may be accounted for. We have had before you
surgeons of eminence—Dr. Bond and Mr. Larkin—for the prosecution, who say that after death has taken place for some considerable time the cartilages which intervene between the bones
will shrink.

Address to Jury.

The LORD CHIEF JUSTICE—I don't think either of the surgeons, on examination and cross-examination, was asked whether bones would shrink. I am not sufficiently familiar with the subject to be able to form an opinion. Mr. Besley, with some cogency, made that the foundation of his argument.

The ATTORNEY-GENERAL—In life the bones are not close together. A cartilage intervenes, and those are the subjects that shrink. Mr. Larkin and Mr. Bond gave this opinion, which Dr. Meadows and Mr. Aubyn did not venture to contradict. Then you must consider whether these bones or limbs could be placed exactly in the same position as in life after they had been hacked and severed in the most unscientific way. With reference to the slight make, there is no question about that. The hair is described as light auburn, with a golden tinge about it. Some witnesses, I am informed, said it was "frizzy." By looking at the photograph of Harriet Lane your attention may be directed to the manner in which, at the time it was taken, she wore her hair over a pad. This may lead you to the conclusion that it was wavy, or, if you like, "frizzy." The hair was said to have been bleached by the chloride of lime. But no one will say that this agent destroys entirely the colour of hair, or that in this instance the entire quantity of hair was impregnated with it. Taken from the grave, it presented a solid, dull appearance, but when washed it showed a lighter aspect, such as it has.

The Attorney-General then alluded to the decayed tooth, and, coming to the evidence that the body found was that of a woman who had borne children, said he would not ask them to place too much importance on the statement, but there was this fact, that the woman, like Harriet Lane, had a wedding ring and a keeper on her finger, so that, although she was not married, she passed as a married woman.

He next alluded to the scar on the leg, which Mr. Aubyn could not deny was found on the place described. That gentleman had said he found a scar on the other leg, but on being further questioned, he would not swear whether it was a mark caused by decomposition. And how was it found? By candle-light on the day just before the woman was placed in the grave. This witness fixed the age of the deceased between twenty-five and thirty years, but he got into such confusion with regard to his reasons for fixing the limit at twenty-five that he (the Attorney-General) did not think they would attach much importance to his evidence in regard to the body which he examined. His friend said that, although the wedding ring and keeper were found, yet no furrow on the finger of the dead

197

The Wainwrights.

woman could be discovered to show that she had worn these
articles. The surgeons for the prosecution say that they should
not expect to find such a furrow, as the fingers were in so
advanced a stage of decomposition that even had the ring been
worn regularly it could not have been discovered. But we
find that for some time before 11th September, 1874, the ring
was not worn, but was in pawn. Other evidences as to identity
were found in the fact of a jet button, such as were worn by
Harriet Lane, being found in the rubbish near the grave,
and that the ears of the body were pierced for earrings.
Harriet Lane, it was proved, was in the habit of wearing a
peculiar pad, and a similar pad was found on the body.

But the identity does not rest here, because again I have
to call your attention to the very great importance, not only
as to the evidence of facts which has been given, but also upon
those matters which must exist, but which have not been dis-
closed—I mean, if this pad is not the pad of Harriet Lane,
whose pad is it? If it is not the body of Harriet Lane, well,
then Harriet Lane went away with Frieake, or with somebody
else. Harriet Lane is alive now in all human probability, and
so is Frieake. But Harriet Lane has never been heard of since
11th September, 1874. We have no news of her; but, on the
other hand, on 11th September in this year, exactly twelve
months after Harriet Lane found her way from Sidney Square
to Whitechapel Road, we have this terrible discovery of Henry
Wainwright in possession of the mutilated remains of a woman
who evidently came to her death by foul play. Why is she
silent, except because she is dead?

Gentlemen, these are the facts in relation to the identity
of the body with that of Harriet Lane which my learned friend
commented upon, except that he dealt with the second count
in the indictment, which alleges, for obvious reasons, that the
body found and the woman murdered is that of a woman whose
name is unknown. I have already commented upon the
theory of my friend with regard to that portion of the case.
His theory is that it is the body of somebody else who committed suicide. I say that such a theory is an insult to your
reason; but whether it is so or not, what account has Henry
Wainwright given with respect to that woman? He must know
all about her. In his breast all knowledge in relation to her
must lie; but he has given no account of her, either through
his own mouth or by his counsel.

I regret that no question was asked with respect to the
bones, but I don't suggest that there would be shrinking of
them. I do, however, suggest that there would be shrinking

198

Address to Jury.

of the cartilages. If you are to come to the conclusion that the body was that of a woman only 4 feet 11 inches in height, it is clear that she could not be the woman who was nearly the same height as Mrs. Allen. This, therefore, is matter of grave importance to consider, whether the evidence of Mr. Bond with regard to the shrinking of the cartilages is correct, and whether that is sufficient to account for the difference in the height. I submit to you that it does, and I think it right to draw your attention to the very terms of the evidence. [The learned counsel here read the evidence of Mr. Bond, wherein he described the manner in which the cartilages shrank.] Mr. Bond put it as the contraction, or disappearance, as it were, of the intervertebral cartilages which exist between the numerous bones of the spine. Then, again, the shortening may have been contributed to by the cutting up of the body. If that question has been set at rest by that evidence—and it has not been contradicted by Mr. Meadows and Mr. Aubyn—it brings the height of Harriet Lane to as nearly as possible that which she was described to have been. Then you have the correspondence in height as well as in other particulars, and it would be a most extraordinary thing that you should find a correspondence between the body discovered and the woman missing, and yet get no explanation of the whereabouts of the woman.

Having said this much, I now pass on from the case of the prosecution as presented to you against Henry Wainwright to the case which for the prosecution I present to you against Thomas. As I said in opening the case, the character of the evidence is the same, although the amount of evidence is very different. Still, it will be your bounden duty to consider the evidence laid before you as pressing against Thomas with the greatest care—on the one hand that justice shall not be defeated by your giving effect to any doubt not worthy of your attention, and care on the other hand that the interest of the prisoner shall not suffer. The evidence against Thomas begins with the allegation that he for some reason or other—it may be from affection for his brother, from a desire to serve his brother, or for some less worthy motive—lent himself to a plot which had been invented by his brother to pass himself as Edward Frieake, who was the friend of Henry Wainwright. You may ask, what was to be gained by such a plot? That is not for me to say. But if I show that such a scheme was on foot, I shall ask you to infer something. It may be that Harriet Lane was to be soothed or conciliated, or to be persuaded that some place would be obtained for her,

The Wainwrights.

and that steps were being taken for the purpose of obtaining
it. It may be that what was intended amounted at the outset
to no more than that. It may be that there was a deeper
design, and that a plot was intended for the purpose of getting
Harriet Lane to go to the place where her destruction was
effected. It may be that there was a design or plan adopted
for the purpose of persuading Harriet Lane that money was
to be obtained through the medium of Mr. Frieake—money
to be used for the purpose of providing her with a suitable
residence. That is the suggestion I find, and it is entitled to
your grave attention and consideration.

But, as I said before, if there was this arrangement, scheme,
or contrivance, and if I show you that it existed, there must
have been some reason for it, and some object intended by it.
Can you have a doubt as to its existence? I submit to you
from the evidence of Mrs. Foster that there can be no question
that the Frieake who called there was the only Frieake of whom
we have any intelligible account. Harriet Lane no doubt
thought that Mr. Frieake, the auctioneer of Coleman Street,
was this Frieake, and this I take to be clear evidence, even to
demonstration, from the letter which she wrote to him, and
which I have already read. As to that letter, I shall call
your attention specially to the words, "I have well considered
the subject we spoke of, and think if Harry and yourself
would see me to-morrow evening, we may be able to arrange
matters satisfactorily." It is clear from this that something
had been going on in the shape of an arrangement, an arrangement to which Harriet Lane, Henry Wainwright, and this man
Frieake were to be parties. It is evident from the letter that
Harriet Lane had been introduced to Frieake, and that the
latter had called upon her at her lodgings is pretty clear,
but not absolutely so. We gather also from this letter, which
speaks volumes on this point, that Frieake had been kind to
her, and this surely implies previous acquaintanceship of some
extent. She refers to having " behaved unladylike," and
may this not have been the night spoken to by Mrs. Foster?
I do not say so, but perhaps there are reasons for believing it
was. This letter was received in the due course of post by
Frieake, the auctioneer of Coleman Street, who naturally was
perfectly astonished at its contents. If Thomas Wainwright
was Frieake, he would be free from his business on Saturday,
and would be able to go to this place. But I shall leave this
part of the case until later on. At present I say that this
letter should be sufficient to satisfy any reasonable mind that
there had been a Frieake who was introduced to Harriet Lane
as the auctioneer of Coleman Street.

Address to Jury.

The Attorney-General

Mrs. Foster says that this Frieake came to her house to see about furniture which he was going to get for Mrs. King, and get her opinion on the colours she would like, and so forth. This shows that something was being instilled into this woman's mind which led her to believe that she was to be established in another home, or to have, possibly, a home of her own.

I ask you, then, is it not clear that some scheme was on foot, and that it was that some person, under the name of Frieake, should personate Mr. Frieake, the auctioneer of Coleman Street? I put it to you—I am not desirous of pressing it unduly—if Thomas Wainwright was the Mr. Frieake who had gone to those lodgings, then he must have known that it was not the woman's intention to abscond at all. Would he not ask Henry Wainwright, "How is it you ask me to put my name to such a tissue of lies? What is your motive? Where is Mrs. King? Satisfy me that Mrs. King is alive, satisfy me that Mrs. King is being cared for; satisfy me that there is some shadow of foundation in this story, and I will do it." It is strange that even a brother's love or a brother's affection should have led him to commit to writing words which convey the idea that this woman, who he had no reason to believe had designedly separated herself from her friends, had gone away, never to return.

Regarding the letters and telegrams, you are entitled to connect the two things together, and to assume that there was a plot between the two brothers prior to September. Who sent those Dover telegrams? It was either Thomas or Henry, both of whom knew that this woman was missing, and I say that it must have been Thomas. It is curious that these telegrams should have been sent, and I don't know that I can suggest any reason which would account for them.

We do not hear anything more against Thomas till we come to the time he is engaged in getting a lease of the Hen and Chickens in the Borough in October, 1874. He left the service of Mr. Arkell, Oxford Street, and towards the end of the year we find him borrowing money from Mr. Lewis on a draft accepted by his brother. As far as we know, he got the money, Henry being responsible for its being paid out of a sum of £300 he expected to receive when his claim on the insurance company was settled. Mr. Lewis seems not only to have taken a bill of sale on the ironmonger's goods in the shop at the Hen and Chickens, but he placed an attachment on that sum.

The LORD CHIEF JUSTICE—It must have been an existing debt, and not a promise for which the acceptance was given, otherwise there could have been no attachment.

201

The Wainwrights.

The ATTORNEY-GENERAL—If there were any existing debt it could not have been a bribe, and I therefore say no more about that. As regards the key, the only cogent fact to which I will draw your attention is that Thomas obtained the key from Mr. Lewis, and it was afterwards found in the possession of Henry Wainwright when he went to the Hen and Chickens to deposit the body of the woman on 11th September, 1875. The next piece of evidence affecting Thomas is that on 10th September, 1875, while Henry was buying the cloth and the rope he was buying the chopper and the spade. We have now to deal with the question whether this was Thomas. Mr. Arkell, his employer, deposed that he attended pretty regularly to his business, but he was absent on a number of occasions, as was shown by the small number of sales he had effected; and then Mr. Arkell's shop closed at five on a Saturday, and 5th September was a Saturday, so that there was nothing to prevent Thomas from getting to the residence of Mrs. Foster in Sidney Square on that day. With reference to the matter of the champagne glasses, Mr. Humphries has an entry in his diary to fix the date.

The LORD CHIEF JUSTICE—It strikes me, Mr. Attorney-General, that it is not at all impossible he may have made that entry when the glasses were returned, which would make all the difference.

Mr. BESLEY—I am sure your lordship will forgive me for interrupting, but my memory is that there was to be a change of managers on 8th September, and that Mr. Humphries on that day found the glasses were short, which led him to infer that he sent for the glasses, which were lent on the preceding 5th.

The LORD CHIEF JUSTICE—No, I did not hear that.

The ATTORNEY-GENERAL—If 5th September was the day on which he saw Henry and Thomas, it must be the date on which the champagne glasses were supplied. Now, it may be said, as your lordship has said, that he may be inaccurate as to the date on which the two brothers were there, but it is a circumstance not unworthy of your attention that on the very day that Mr. Humphries speaks of the brothers being present at his house, on that very day, Henry Wainwright sends the letter to Harriet Lane which commences "Dear Pet."

If Thomas was Frieake, what was he playing the part of Frieake for? Was there some plot or conspiracy against this unhappy woman? What was his motive, and by what reasons was he actuated? Affection and friendship may actuate one

202

Address to Jury.

man to serve his brother, while upon another such motives would have no effect, but the chance of obtaining a sum of money may have effect.

On 10th September, 1874, Henry Wainwright is known to have purchased some chloride of lime, but there is no connection with Thomas Wainwright in that matter, and we have the fact that Thomas did not appear again on the scene until the writing of that letter which bears no date, but which is addressed from the Charing Cross Hotel. That letter is admitted to be in his handwriting. On the subject of that letter let me draw your attention to the theory of my friend Mr. Moody, that if there had been any—I am assuming that Thomas Wainwright was Frieake—if there was any contrivance or scheme by those two brothers, it was a scheme under which Mrs. King should be persuaded that Mr. Frieake, the friend of Henry, was obtaining in some way, or about to obtain, a loan wherewith to purchase furniture for her new lodgings. Therefore, if that be so, there was no idea that Mrs. King should disappear with Wainwright, certainly no idea that she could disappear with Mr. Frieake, and to be separated from her friends, to lose sight of her children, or to be estranged from those who were dear to her. That is what would be in the mind of the man who wrote this letter. He would know he had been playing a part to pacify and soothe Mrs. King, but not having any criminality in it, and when he was asked to write this letter which conveyed to Miss Wilmore that she was to break with her old friend, and was not to come back again, was he an innocent man?

The LORD CHIEF JUSTICE—Why not? I mean with reference to the consciousness of guilt.

The ATTORNEY-GENERAL—Why, he should not write it because he knew he was the man who had been passed off as Mr. Frieake, and that this was a lie about her going off with him. He must have known it was not her intention to withdraw herself from her friends and her children. It was not her intention to discard all her intimates and connections, her friends and acquaintances, for the future. If there was another Frieake, and Henry had come to Thomas and said, "This poor Mrs. King has absconded, and has gone away with Frieake, a friend of mine, and she will not come back, and I am anxious to satisfy her friends that they may not bore me any longer with their inquiries," he might then have written such a letter as this. I ask you if you can understand it—I do not ask myself if I can understand it. Why, if she had gone away, in a moment he could have exculpated himself by speaking the truth; but if there was

The Wainwrights.

another Mr. Frieake, I might understand, and you might understand, that Thomas could have written this letter. But if Thomas was Mr. Frieake, then you have Mr. Frieake, of Coleman Street, who had nothing to do with this matter; you have Thomas, the known Mr. Frieake, who had nothing to do with the elopement of Mrs. King; and in order to understand that, you have to understand that there was another and a third Mr. Frieake, about whom we can learn nothing, as far as I know—a man who had been a friend of Henry Wainwright, a companion of Henry, trusted by Henry with the negotiation of an agreement with Mrs. King, who was living under his protection as his wife, but about whom Henry Wainwright could have given a satisfactory account. It is useless to support even the minor charge, unless there is good reason for believing that he was aiding and assisting his brother to escape from the consequences of his crime.

Let us then consider what must be done between the purchase of the spade and the chopper and the brothers being together on the morning of the 11th. The work of removing the remains and cutting up the body could not have been done by Henry alone in the short time he had at his disposal. I would remark that there is a bit of evidence tending to show that Henry Wainwright could not do this alone, because you will remember there was found on the floor of the warehouse by the police not only the axe and shovel and pieces of American cloth and rope, but there was also found a knife, which has been described to you, which is called a pocket knife.

Mr. MOODY—A very common one.

The ATTORNEY-GENERAL—A very common knife, I hear my learned friend Mr. Moody say, and a very common knife it is, I admit; but was it Henry Wainwright's knife? Because if it were, he must have had two, for when he was searched by the police there was found amongst many other things a pocket knife. Then comes the question, was he doing the work alone, and, if not, who could be with him? Can you conceive any one else being with him except the man who had written at his suggestion the letter from Charing Cross station? Thomas Wainwright was seen the next day with Henry Wainwright close to Mr. Martin's shop, and appeared to be ill, and had shaved off his moustache. You must say what in your judgment this all points to. Then, again, it is undoubted that the body was being removed by Henry Wainwright to the Hen and Chickens, where it appears there was the very receptacle which one would choose for depositing, at all events for a short time,

204

Address to Jury.

the remains of that unfortunate woman, and these premises were in Thomas's occupation.

You have heard the indictment under which Thomas is charged with being a party to this crime, and under that part of the indictment it will be open for you to find him guilty of being accessory before the fact. There is a separate count for aiding and assisting his brother after the murder which has been committed, and in disposing of the remains, or, in fact, of assisting his brother to evade justice. These are the facts which I have to lay before you against Thomas Wainwright. Although these charges are of the gravest character, the first being looked upon as bad as actual murder itself, and in fact it assumes the shape of a charge of murder, of course you would not dream of convicting any man of such a crime except upon the most clear and convincing proof. You must ask yourselves whether the proof that has been offered to you is sufficient to satisfy your minds that Thomas Wainwright was guilty of either of these offences. As I put in my opening, so I put to you again now, one of the main questions seems to be whether the explanation which he gave, or the explanation which is given for him before you, is such an explanation as can be offered to reasonable minds, or such as reasonable minds can be convinced is consistent with innocence. If it is, he is entitled to your verdict of acquittal; if it is not, I am sure you will not hesitate for a moment in fulfilling your duty.

Adjourned till to-morrow.

Charge to the Jury.

Lord Chief Justice

LORD CHIEF JUSTICE COCKBURN said—Gentlemen of the jury, I am quite sure there needs no exhortation from me to ensure your careful attention to the facts of the case, which I am about to bring before you. You have shown throughout the deepest appreciation of the magnitude and importance of this great trial, and you have given to it unqualified and unceasing attention, which must have been eminently satisfactory to all who desire that you should arrive at a just and righteous decision.

We start at the outset of the inquiry with a fact of primary importance. On 11th September the prisoner Henry Wainwright was found in possession of the mangled body of a woman. It was found that those remains had recently been severed by some blunt instrument. It was discovered that they had been recently taken from a grave, dug evidently for the purpose of concealment, in premises which had been occupied by the prisoner. It was discovered that the remains of the woman so found in the possession of the prisoner had been murdered by some one. You have to inquire whether the life thus taken by foul means was taken by the prisoner at the bar.

In this case there can be no doubt that the life of the deceased was taken by violence. The whole question turns on the point—was it the prisoner at the bar by whose hand that life was taken? It is alleged on the part of the prosecution that the remains found in the possession of the prisoner were those of Harriet Louisa Lane, who, as we all know now, was for some time his mistress. Evidence has been brought to satisfy you of the fact that these remains once constituted the body of Harriet Louisa Lane. Of the value of that evidence and the effect of it you are to form your own judgment; but I am bound to tell you that if you should be of opinion that the prisoner took the life of the person whose body he was dealing with, even though the proof of identity should fail, it will then be your duty to convict him. It is not necessary in a charge of murder that the identity of the person killed should be established; the law throws its protection alike around the

206

Lord Chief Justice Cockburn.

Charge to the Jury.

unknown and the known as far as it can, and makes him who Lord Chief Justice takes human life amenable to its penalties.   If, then, it is shown that the life of the veriest stranger or outcast has been taken, he who takes it will be as responsible as though it was the life of the highest in the land.

Although the proposition is unquestionably true, in such a case as this, where the murderer has not been taken red-handed with the blood of his victim upon him and the instrument of death in his hand, where the evidence is almost entirely circumstantial, it is of importance that the identity of the person murdered should be established, in order to discover the existence of some motive for taking that life. Happily men do not ordinarily commit crime without some motive, though in every instance that motive is inadequate to the crime of murder.   There are, however, minds on which motives, however inadequate, will sometimes operate to produce crime; and therefore, in this case, where the evidence is entirely of a circumstantial character, the question whether these were the remains of Harriet Louisa Lane becomes of great moment, and one on which you will have to exercise your judgment to the best of your ability.

The evidence to establish the remains with Harriet Louisa Lane is of a twofold character.   It is partly direct, such as a comparison of the remains with the personal appearance and marks of the missing woman, or the finding of articles of her dress in the grave.   It is also based upon the facts and the history of the case itself.   I will state as succinctly as I can, but omitting nothing you ought to know, what those incidents are.   Harriet Louisa Lane was the youngest of seven living daughters of Mr. John Lane, of Waltham Cross.   She must have been, about the time she became missing, of the age of twenty-four.   It appears that she was apprenticed to Mrs. Gray, milliner, of Waltham Cross, and had a fellow-apprentice whose name is intimately connected with this inquiry—I mean Ellen Wilmore.   When the term of her apprenticeship expired in the end of 1870, or the beginning of 1871, she came to London.   She appears to have been a person who for her class had had a rather superior education.   We are told that she attempted to set up in some business as a milliner at Waltham Cross, which came to nothing.   The first that we really know of her after she came to London is that she had become the mistress of Henry Wainwright, and had borne a child.   After she came to London she renewed her acquaintance with Ellen Wilmore, who at first supposed she was the wife of the man whose assumed name, " King," she had assumed.   They were

207

The Wainwrights.

both going by the name of King—he Percy, and she Mrs. King. Miss Wilmore says that in August, 1872, Mrs. King was delivered of a child, the acknowledged child of Henry Wainwright. We do not know where she was living during the first part of her intimacy with the prisoner, but in October, 1873, lodgings were taken for her at the house of Mrs. Wells, St. Peter Street, Hackney Road. The prisoner Henry Wainwright took her to the apartments himself. At this time a child was born, and was in the care of Miss Wilmore, who, at the instance of the mother, took it at the age of three months, the prisoner Henry Wainwright paying £1 a week for its maintenance. It appears from Mrs. Wells's evidence that during the time Mrs. King was staying at her house he was in the habit of visiting her from time to time and of staying for a considerable time on several occasions. She remained there until the end of April or the beginning of May, 1874, and in the course of that stay she was delivered of a child. Now, that was the child of the prisoner Henry Wainwright, for he visited her shortly after her confinement, and on various other occasions. During that time we hear no complaints of want of pecuniary supplies; everything seems to have gone on smoothly.

She left in the early part of May to go to other lodgings, which had been taken for her by Henry Wainwright at the house of Mrs. Foster, 3 Sidney Square. Mrs. Foster had apartments to let, and Wainwright calls and looks at them, and inquires whether she would take a lady with a nurse and two children. Mrs. Foster made the natural inquiry whether the lady was his wife, and she received an answer which for the time satisfied her on that point, and she agreed to let the apartments. The next morning he brought Mrs. King to look at the apartments, and, she approving, they were taken. The prisoner had mentioned the night before to Mrs. Foster that he was a traveller, that his business took him very much away from London, and that as a consequence he could come but seldom to see Mrs. King. In fact, from the time he took her to see the apartments to the time she left he never once slept there. He directed Rogers, who appeared to have been the means of communication between him and Mrs. King, to go in the evening, take a cab, and take her and the nurse and children to the new lodgings in Sidney Square, which Rogers accordingly did.

Here, then, we have her settled in the month of May at Mrs. Foster's, and here begins a new phase, as it were, in this mystery. Up to this time things had gone on smoothly with her. There were no complaints of want of money, no dissensions

208

Charge to the Jury.

or discord between the parties. But very soon after Mrs. King had gone to live at Mrs. Foster's we find pecuniary difficulties arising. As early as 20th May we find her resorting to pledging her things. She begins by pledging that which a woman who is a wife, or even only passes as one, usually keeps to the last, viz., the wedding ring which she was in the habit of wearing. Down to 11th September, a memorable day in the history of this case, we find from Miss Wilmore's statement that she had parted with everything she could spare, even to her very linen, to the pawnbrokers. Now, it would be wrong to ascribe that to any intention on the part of Henry Wainwright to desert this woman, or to fail to maintain her as far as he could. I think we must look for the cause of it to the alteration which had taken place in his circumstances, an alteration which it is important to bear in mind in more respects than one.

As early as the end of 1873 Henry Wainwright, who appears at one time to have carried on a flourishing business, got into difficulties. He had dissolved partnership with his brother William, with whom for a long time he had carried on the business. I suppose, then, for the purpose of bringing capital into the business, he took into partnership a Mr. Sawyer, in November, 1873, but Mr. Sawyer soon became dissatisfied with the state of things which he found. He thought he had been deceived and duped, for he repudiated the partnership, threw affairs into Chancery, and obtained a dissolution of the partnership on 8th June, 1874, getting himself appointed receiver to get in the assets and liquidate as far as he could the partnership debts. He took possession of the premises, and remained in possession till the ensuing July, so that it will be easily understood that it must have been a serious interruption and detriment to the business of Henry Wainwright. In the meantime, the partnership with Sawyer being dissolved, the prisoner was pressed by his own immediate creditors, and was obliged to have recourse to a liquidation. On 15th May a meeting of creditors took place at which it was resolved that they would accept a composition of 12s. in the pound, the terms being that 6s. should be paid down in a week, 3s. at the expiry of three months, and 3s. more at the expiry of six months. Wainwright at this time owed over £3250, independent of a considerable debt to his brother William. The 6s. should have been paid in the course of a week, but it was not paid till the month of July, at which time £787 6s. 8d. appears to have been received by the trustees on the part of the creditors. The second instalment of 3s. in the pound is said to have been paid a long time

The Wainwrights.

afterwards, while the last instalment never has been paid at all.

It is plain, under these circumstances, that Henry Wainwright was at this period in a state of great pecuniary difficulty, otherwise the instalment would not have stood over. No doubt it was a matter of difficulty with him to find money to meet the demands upon him. He is therefore in this position: he is involved in pecuniary embarrassments, has engagements to meet in order to keep off actual bankruptcy of a kind which would embarrass him very much indeed. He has, besides the demands of his creditors, to keep up his own establishment in Tredegar Square, where he has a wife and five children to maintain; and last comes this unfortunate Harriet Lane, who appears to have had no resources of her own, and whose tendency does not appear to have been to have recourse to her own exertion to maintain herself and her children, and who was dependent on him, and looked to him, and to him alone, for her maintenance, and who before that, by his liberality or extravagance, had received as much as £5 a week—a considerable sum for a man in his position.

In this state of things we may rightly suppose that a woman who found herself in such a position of need would be perpetually urging the man, to whom she thought she had a right to look, to find her the means of subsistence. On one occasion we find he can only manage to send her a couple of pounds, at which she is indignant, and throws them upon the table with expressions of dissatisfaction. Rogers tells us that in July or August she was at the shop at least a dozen times, and Mrs. Rogers says she was there twenty times. Scenes of anger appear to have occurred between them; and on one occasion Rogers saw them at the other end of the shop gesticulating violently, and on another occasion Mrs. Rogers heard loud talking as of people quarrelling. Besides that, there takes place a scene which is not immaterial, if you believe the evidence. Some time in August Mrs. King's necessities must have been very pressing, for all her things were in pawn; and one evening Mrs. Rogers, who was at the top of the stairs, heard the voice of a woman exclaim, "Oh, don't! oh, don't!" Immediately afterwards Mrs. Rogers' husband is called downstairs, and Wainwright gives him a letter addressed to his wife at Tredegar Square, which he tells him to take there. Mrs. King makes a snatch at the letter and endeavours to get it out of Rogers' hand, but Rogers holds it fast, and the result is that it is torn across. In that condition Rogers takes it, but he says he

Charge to the Jury.

thought he would look at the letter before he took it, and he tells you he found it contained strong language to this effect, "I can't survive the disgrace and exposure. . . . You will never see me more." Afterwards it occurred to him that this letter had only been given to him for the purpose of producing some effect on the mind of Mrs. King, and that it was not intended that he should take it, or, at all events, that it was a foolish thing on the part of Wainwright, if he had written this letter under excitement, to send it to his wife. Under these circumstances, he thought he had better not deliver it, and he therefore took the earliest opportunity of throwing the letter into the fire. He having gone out, Mrs. Rogers tells us that she heard the door slam shortly afterwards; there is a ring at the bell, and on going downstairs, she looked into the shop, and there saw a woman lying upon the floor, and that woman she found was Mrs. King. She opens the door, and the prisoner comes in, and she tells him that Mrs. King is lying on the floor. He goes up to her and says, "Oh, she has fainted. Get me some vinegar." Mrs. Rogers gets the vinegar, and he says to her, "That will do. I will take care of her." Soon afterwards they are heard to go out.

You are asked by the learned counsel for the prisoner Henry Wainwright not to believe the statement of Rogers and Mrs. Rogers, and, if that statement be untrue, they have committed the most vile and wicked perjury. But with what motive? There does not appear to be the slightest feeling of resentment towards Henry Wainwright; and yet, if they have invented this story, they have come here, not to further the interests of one party at the cost of another in a civil suit, but for the purpose, as far as in them lay, of giving evidence whereby the conviction of Henry Wainwright of the crime of murder shall be established. Now, what is there to lead us to believe that they have been guilty of this awful crime? I confess I do not see it. All I can say is that, if such a scene happened, it shows what was the unfortunate position of the two parties.

Besides this, there appears to have been constant communication between the two—application for money which the prisoner had not the means to supply. It is said that this state of things supplies a motive operating on the mind of Henry Wainwright, and there is no doubt she must have been a heavy burden upon him, a burden not easy to be got rid of, and one which would cling to him for years to come. There can be little doubt that she was in his estimation a constant source of danger. He had not the money to satisfy her, and she was apt

211

The Wainwrights.

to be ill-tempered. It is no wonder, when she found herself in such a position, she was apt to be ill-tempered, and on more than one occasion she showed this. There would be no knowing what a woman under such circumstances, if she happened to get a little too much drink, might do in the way of creating a disturbance, and possibly lead to an exposure which might reach the ears of Wainwright's wife, who up to this time knew nothing of the secret correspondence with the woman who passed as Mrs. King. Thus he lived, as it were, on the edge of a volcano that might at any moment have exploded, and led to disastrous consequences as regarded both his domestic life and his public life, because he was carrying on business amidst respectable tradesmen, who were well acquainted with him, so that to have a woman coming to his place of business and beginning a disturbance there, and clamouring and making her position relative to himself known, could not, of course, help being distressing and annoying in the extreme. Hence it is, although such a reason for desiring to get rid of her is frightfully inadequate when we consider the enormity of the crime with which he is charged, that we are still afforded some explanation of the circumstances which are to follow hereafter.

I now come to the Frieake episode. It is a very curious part of the history, and one which requires very careful attention. It appears that during the latter part of Mrs. King's stay at Mrs. Foster's a person passing by the name of Edward Frieake becomes intimate with her. There is some reason to think that Edward Frieake becomes intimate with her. There is some reason to think that Edward Frieake had been introduced to her at an earlier period, when she was staying with Mrs. Wells, for she tells us that shortly after Christmas, 1873, when King happened on one occasion to come to see his alleged sister-in-law, Mrs. King, he brought with him a stranger, who was shown into the parlour downstairs, while King went upstairs to visit Mrs. King. After a short time he opened the door of Mrs. King's apartment, and called at the top of the stairs, "Edward, come up; I want you," upon which the stranger went upstairs, probably for the purpose of being introduced. He stayed only a short time, and came down again, taking his seat again in the parlour, and remained there during the continuance of the visit to the lady upstairs, which appears to have lasted from an hour to an hour and a half. Mrs. Wells had thus an opportunity of seeing the stranger, and she is a witness to his identity.

212

Charge to the Jury.

Nothing more is heard of Frieake or his connections with Mrs. King until some time in the month of August. Then he appears to have visited her on two or three occasions, at all events, at the house of Mrs. Foster. This lady tells us that Mrs. King told her she expected a gentleman to call upon her on a particular day, that he was a friend, that he had promised to furnish two rooms for her, and that he was coming in order to see if they could agree about the carpet. The gentleman came that evening. Mrs. King met him on the stairs, and he at once passed into her room. On another occasion the same gentleman came, and then gave his name as Frieake. Mrs. Foster went upstairs and announced him, he following. When he was announced, Miss Wilmore, who was in the room, left the room. As she was going out he went in, and she had thus an opportunity of seeing him.

On another occasion we have the story about the champagne, a not unimportant one, because it tends to fix the identity of the person who was passing under the name of Frieake. It seems that upon the occasion of one visit of this gentleman he brought a pint bottle of champagne, and Mrs. Foster tells us that Mrs. King asked her for some champagne glasses. Mrs. Foster did not happen to have such things, but she goes across to the Princess Royal, the public-house, asks for three champagne glasses, and they are lent her. Mr. Humphries, the landlord of the public-house, fixes the 5th September for the occasion upon which the two brothers were at the Princess Royal for an hour or an hour and a half. After they had been there for some time Thomas Wainwright asks for a pint bottle of champagne. He gets it, goes out, and shortly afterwards in comes Mrs. Foster to borrow the champagne glasses. From this we may infer that the man who took away the pint bottle of champagne was the man who made his appearance on the other side of the square at No. 3 with a pint bottle of champagne. Humphries goes on to say that some person came back and called for a quart bottle of champagne, which he took away. He fixes these two events as having happened on one and the same evening, namely, 5th September, 1874. His reason for fixing the date on that day is that, upon being asked to lend the champagne glasses, he found that his own establishment was short of them, and he enters a minute in his book of the day's proceedings to direct his manager to get more champagne glasses, in order that they may not be short of them.

The Wainwrights.

Lord Chief Justice Now, the question presents itself, who was this person taking the name of Edward Frieake? Was he the undoubted Edward Frieake, the auctioneer who lived at Coleman Street? It is quite clear Mrs. King thought so, because, having had a dispute with the supposed Edward Frieake—having behaved, as she says, rudely to him, and shown temper to him—she afterwards felt ashamed, and she sat in her room and wrote him a letter. That letter finds its way to the counting-house or place of business of the undoubted Edward Frieake. Therefore we can come to no other conclusion than that Mrs. King herself was allowed to suppose that the E. Frieake to whom she had been introduced by Henry Wainwright was his old friend E. Frieake, the auctioneer.

Now comes the question, what was the purpose of this introduction and of these negotiations taking place between E. Frieake and Mrs. King It is one of the mysterious parts of this case—one as to which, having turned it over in my mind again and again, I cannot find any satisfactory solution for. The counsel for the Crown, in order to involve Thomas Wainwright in the charge of being an accessory before the murder, which they say was afterwards committed by Henry Wainwright, make this the basis and the ground work of their case, and the way in which they put it is this—Henry Wainwright had at this time got tired of this woman, and meditated getting rid of her by murder, but inasmuch as if she were to disappear without any ostensible cause inquiries would be made about her, in reply to which it would be necessary to have some explanation and excuse ready, he accordingly introduced to her his brother, or somebody else, by the name of Frieake, in order that when she was got rid of by violence, it might be said that she had gone off with Frieake. Well, that is a very strong assumption, and unless it is the only hypothesis upon which this transaction can be accounted for, it is a very strong thing to assume that long before the disappearance of Harriet Lane, these two brothers had concocted this iniquitous scheme. Even if you should be of opinion that this adoption of the name of Frieake was a deception, and that it was practised by Thomas Wainwright at the instance and instigation and with the connivance of his brother, do you see your way to the conclusion that either of the brothers at that time had in his mind that the woman should afterwards be murdered, and the name of Frieake then used again in order to account for her disappearance, by saying that she had gone off with this Mr. Frieake? If you cannot arrive at that conclusion, if you feel that it is

214

Charge to the Jury.

impossible with every possible explanation before you to stand on that as secure ground, then the case against Thomas Wainwright as accessory before the fact fails, and as far as that which it has been suggested was done by him with a view to the future crime he was meditating, and which he carried into effect, fails also.

At this time it was quite evident some change was contemplated. Miss Wilmore was to take the children, but for that purpose money was wanted. There was a terrible pressure on Henry. He had made a composition which had swallowed up £700 or £800, and money for some of the creditors was not forthcoming. Miss Wilmore, too, was paid in advance. Matters, however, became precipitated by the disturbance in the street. One evening between ten and eleven o'clock Mrs. Foster was disturbed by a knock at the door, and went downstairs. She there found a neighbour, who told her there was Mrs. King in the street with two gentlemen—one Mr. King and the other the one known as Mr. Frieake. She found her lodger under the influence of drink, wrangling with the men, and collecting a crowd in the street, to the surprise of every one. Mrs. Foster did her best to get Mrs. King indoors, but the latter turned fiercely on the former with the accusation of interfering between her and her husband. Upon this Mrs. Foster went in and shut the door. Soon after this a knock came again, and she found Mrs. King had been brought to the door by the two gentlemen, but instead of going in she suddenly turned round and ran after the two men. Miss Wilmore then went out to try and get her in, which she at length did, but she was in such a state of excitement that she had to sit up with her all night. This was not satisfactory to Mrs. Foster, as the person making the disturbance must be known to the neighbours as her lodger, and by this time probably she was not unwilling to get rid of her tenant. There is nothing so unsatisfactory to a lodging-house keeper as that their tenants should suffer from want of money, and this poor lady had before been unable to pay her rent. Accordingly the next day she gives Mrs. King a week's notice to quit. We do not know the day on which that notice was given, but we know that it expired on 9th September. On that day Mrs. King should have left, but she had not received money to pay her way out. She owed rent, and she owed bills in the neighbourhood, and was in a state of destitution, as all her clothes had been pawned, and Mrs. Foster was induced to allow her two days more. We may suppose that Henry Wainwright had a hard struggle to find the money, but he managed to get it on the 10th, and on that day he sent her £15.

215

The Wainwrights.

On the 11th Mrs. King proceeded to settle her affairs. She
paid her rent and her debts, and Miss Wilmore got her things
out of pawn. Mrs. King took one of her dresses, a grey silk,
to wear that day, and she trimmed it with some black jet
buttons, which were bought in the neighbourhood. She sewed
them on her dress, and it turned out that of those purchased
there were a couple of buttons above what was required. Miss
Wilmore put them into a little stay-box, and those play a not
unimportant part in this drama. All the other things are
placed in a large wooden box and portmanteau and a band-box,
and the stay-box inside the large one. She had taken a place
at No. 6 The Grove, Stratford, where Miss Wilmore was to live
with the children, and where the boxes were to go. All this
being done, and these arrangements made, she went out, taking
nothing with her but the clothes she wore and her rings, which
had been got out of pawn, and a nightdress. Having put up
that single article, Miss Wilmore locked up the box and gave
her the key. They took leave of each other, and Mrs. King
went away. She was in good health and in good spirits, which
was not surprising; but from that hour to this she has never
been heard of alive.

About this date of the 11th September, the day of her
disappearance, there was buried in the prisoner's premises, or
rather, to speak more correctly, in premises which had been
occupied by the prisoner Henry Wainwright, and of which he
still had control and the key, the body of a woman which
corresponds in many, if not in all, particulars with the woman
who had disappeared. A twelvemonth afterwards by a strange
coincidence in date the prisoner Henry Wainwright is found
removing from the grave in which this body had been placed
its remains to another place of concealment. Now, it is alleged
that the body so interred in premises under the control of Henry
Wainwright was the body of the woman Harriet Lane. It is
certain that the body thus found was the body of a person
whose life had been taken by violence. It is alleged that the
prisoner took that life. That is the theory of the prosecution,
and I shall call your attention presently to the evidence as to
the identity of the remains which the prisoner is found removing
with the dead body of Harriet Lane.

When Harriet Lane left 3 Sidney Square, she must have left
in the mind of Miss Wilmore the impression that she was only
going away for a day or two, and she was therefore disturbed
when Saturday, Sunday, and Monday came without any tidings.
On the Tuesday she went to Henry Wainwright's place, and he

Charge to the Jury.

told her that she had gone to Brighton. Well, now, gentlemen, you must just see for a moment whether the facts stated by the prisoner are probable. He had had difficulty in getting together the £15 necessary to pay her expenses at Sidney Square, and even that had not been enough, for Miss Wilmore had had to advance £2 to make up the necessary amount to pay everything, and get all her things out of pawn. Now, inasmuch as she had got her things out of pawn, she did not want money to buy others, and it does strike me as rather unlikely that he, a man in pecuniary embarrassment, should be supplying her with an additional £10 for such a purpose. Then, when Mrs. Taylor went to the prisoner Henry's place and asked about her sister, the prisoner repeated what he had said to Miss Wilmore—that he had given Mrs. King £15 for her lodgings and £10 for an outfit. Now the observation presents itself, is it a likely thing to have occurred? However, it might have happened, and don't let us press anything too strongly against the prisoner.

According to Miss Wilmore, up to this time there had been no mention of the name of Frieake, and it is certain that at the first interview the name of Frieake had not been mentioned. There seems a doubt in the statement of Mrs. Taylor whether it was not mentioned at the interview she had for the first time with the prisoner. There is some little confusion as to this, and no wonder, considering the great number of interviews which took place. According to Miss Wilmore's account, the name of Frieake was not mentioned until a subsequent occasion, when she saw the prisoner Henry Wainwright standing, I think, at the door of his shop. As she passed she stopped, and said, "I have not heard of Mrs. King; have you?" and he said, "I have. She has gone off with my friend Frieake, an auctioneer, who has lately come into a large property." Upon a subsequent occasion the two women, Wilmore and Taylor, agree to go and see Henry Wainwright, and on that occasion the name of Frieake is brought about with additional emphasis.

With regard to the letters that passed, there is no doubt that the one from the Charing Cross Hotel to Miss Wilmore was written by Thomas. The name is not spelt as Frieake spells his name, as one of the vowels is omitted. Well, now, there is no doubt that that was craftily devised, because it not only cut Harriet Lane off from all further communication with her friends, but it gave an apparent reason why she should acquiesce in that which was most repugnant to her feelings. She evidently

The Wainwrights.

Lord Chief
Justice was a person of a friendly and amiable disposition; she was
attached to her family and friends, and was in the habit of
visiting them, though I cannot suppose a woman who gives
up her children, as she did, to a friend to be kept, could be very
sensitive of the feelings of a mother. Still, she was fond of
her children, and nothing would be less likely than that she
should allow any great length of time to pass without inquiring
about them. If it could be put in this way : here was a man
who is prepared, not only to maintain her, but to marry her
if she cuts off all connection with those associated with her by
blood or friendship; a woman might yield to such a thing. If
the letter was a false one, and was used for the purpose of
deceiving, it was most artfully devised. On Miss Wilmore going
in the morning to Wainwright and showing him the letter, he
produced a similar one, and on 17th October Miss Wilmore
received a telegram, which she showed to Mrs. Taylor, and the
two women went to Wainwright and showed it to him. "Oh,"
he says, "I have received one, too." He fetches it out, saying,
"It came from Teddy Frieake at Dover," and he then showed
the contents of it to them, which appeared to be in exactly
the same terms as the other. Now comes the question—from
whom came those telegrams? The letter dated Charing Cross
Hotel is undoubtedly in the handwriting of Thomas Wainwright.
No one who has compared the genuine writing with the letter
can entertain the shadow of a doubt about it. Nor, indeed, did
his counsel seek to deny it. We may therefore assume that the
other letter, written to Henry Wainwright, was in his handwriting. I don't think it very material whether it was or was
not; whether the parts in this deception were performed by
two or three persons, seems to be a matter of little moment.
The telegrams from Dover are in the name of Frieake, and one
of them was sent to Miss Wilmore, one to Wainwright at the
East End, and one to Wainwright at Fulham, where we know
Thomas Wainwright had some intimate friends with whom
he was in the habit of staying. If it were not for the circumstance that one of the three was addressed to Wainwright in
the Fulham district, one could entertain little doubt that Thomas
Wainwright, having lent himself to the scheme of deception,
went down to Dover and telegraphed from there in the name of
Frieake; but then there is the improbability of Thomas Wainwright, if he were at Dover, telegraphing to any one of the
name of Wainwright at Parson's Green, because it is not shown
that his wife or any one of the same name was there. As I
said before, I don't think it matters much whether these letters

218

Charge to the Jury.

and telegrams were sent by one and the same person or by two distinct persons, as they were clearly carrying out a scheme which was to prevent inquiry as to what had become of the woman.

We will pass by that part for a moment and go on with the further interviews. Mrs. Taylor tells us that after this she had a further interview with Wainwright. She asked him if he had heard anything, and he said, "Nothing further. When they have had their frolic out, they will come back." He also said, "Should she return, I would not take to her. Would you blame me?" And, says Mrs. Taylor, "I can't blame you under the circumstances," showing that Mrs. Taylor was impressed with the notion that she had gone off with Frieake.

So matters remained with regard to the two women; but it happened that Mrs. Taylor had a friend in the person of a man named Eeles, and Eeles was the inquiry officer for a charitable institution. The interview between Eeles, who had assumed the name of Fowler, and Wainwright was interrupted by an officer of the Sun Fire Office, who was investigating the honesty of a claim by the prisoner for compensation on account of the premises No. 84, which had been burned down in the previous November.

His lordship went on to state the nature of the conversation which afterwards took place between these two men, and also between Mr. Eeles and Mr. Frieake. Mr. Frieake, he said, feels uncomfortable about this affair; he is engaged to a young lady he is about to marry, and that he should have been stated to have gone off with another woman would naturally disgust him considerably. The two make their way to Henry Wainwright, and ask to see him. Eeles says, "I have brought Mr. Frieake himself," and Wainwright replies, "Oh! that is not the Mr. Frieake I mean; it is a totally different person." So Mr. Frieake says, "What does this mean? I am afraid you are getting me into a mess I know nothing of. It may be the ruin of my happiness. It not only affects my business, but I am going to be married, and if this comes to the ears of the young lady to whom I am to be married, it may destroy my happiness for life." Wainwright says, "Don't be uneasy. It is not you. I never meant you." Frieake then answers, "Do you mean to say there is another Teddy Frieake who has the same name, or who assumes the name I possess?" The prisoner says, "It is a man I have known for some time. He is a billiard player I have seen at Purcell's, Fenchurch Street, at the Philharmonic, and at the Nell Gwynne. He is the man." Mr. Frieake thereupon said, "Do you mean there is another

219

The Wainwrights.

man called Teddy Frieake in London? Mine is a very uncommon name," and he then makes an observation about the peculiar way his name is spelt, and that it was not like the ordinary names to which we are daily used. Then Henry described this Teddy Frieake as being a man with a slight dark moustache, and said this affair would only be got up to extort money from him. Mr. Frieake remembers then that he had received a letter in the preceding August with the name of King subscribed to it, and when, shortly afterwards, Eeles calls again with Mr. Lane, the father, he produces it. With this letter they all go to Wainwright and show it to him, and point out the particular part of it in which the writer says, " I have well considered the subject you spoke of, and if Harry and yourself see me to-morrow evening, we may be able to arrange matters satisfactorily," the name Harry obviously referring to Henry Wainwright. They ask him to explain that passage, but he says he cannot, and then the father makes a strong appeal to him, if he knows where his daughter is, to tell him, or if she be dead, to no longer keep him in suspense, but let him know the worst. Wainwright says he knows no more than he has told—namely, that he believes she has gone off with Frieake.

Now, were those statements true, or were they not? Was this statement that she had gone off with Frieake founded either on fact or on anything which Wainwright believed, or was the whole, from beginning to end, mere invention? One cannot shut one's eyes to the fact that his statements were conflicting. If there be a Frieake such as the prisoner has represented really existing, unless we suppose him to be in the distant regions of Australia, he cannot fail to have heard of this inquiry. He cannot fail to know that at this moment the life of Henry Wainwright is hanging in the balance, and that he can at once exculpate him, and by coming forward can save him. It is true he might think it would involve him in some obloquy and disgrace if he admitted taking off this woman, but what man would shrink from encountering such exposure in order to save the life of a fellow-creature from being unjustly sacrificed? Can you doubt that if this Frieake really existed he either would have been called or some reason given to account for his absence? If this man formerly frequented some particular billiard saloon, there must be some people who would have known him, and if he had suddenly disappeared, and they had been called and said, " Oh, yes; there was such a man ; we knew he was Edward Frieake, but he has disappeared," why, that simple fact proved, although

˙Charge to the Jury.

the prisoner might not have been able to prove where he was, would have done more to extricate him from the circumstances which now militate against him than even the most eloquent and able speech of the most able member of the bar.

Even supposing that at the end you should be of opinion that this statement that she had gone off with Frieake was a falsehood, and that the man was a mere creation of the brain, it does not follow that Henry Wainwright is guilty. It may be that he adopted this fraud and deception for reasons which I have already alluded to, but you must take it as a fact that at the time when inquiries were being made about the missing Mrs. King, Henry Wainwright was making these excuses for her absence.

Well now, gentlemen, I have brought the case down to the point of the charge of murder against the prisoner Henry Wainwright. You will remember that these inquiries after Harriet Lane were discontinued somewhere early in the year 1875, and old Lane and Eeles had gone for the last time to see Henry Wainwright. The deception, if deception it was, which had been carried out through these letters and telegrams had produced its effect—inquiries were baffled. In the meantime the remains of a woman were lying in the back premises of 215 Whitechapel Road, silently undergoing that gradual decay which is the eventual and inevitable destiny of the human substance when life has fled. In the back premises of Henry Wainwright the remains of a woman, as I have already said, corresponding in many, if not all, particulars with those of the missing Harriet Lane, were lying, and there they might have rested until now, or perhaps until the further progress of decomposition had prevented every possible means of identification, until every means by which identity could be ascertained had passed away, but for circumstances arising out of the pecuniary embarrassments of Henry Wainwright, a state of things to which it is necessary to call your particular attention.

The learned judge then detailed the pecuniary embarrassments which led to the premises at No. 215 being taken possession of by Mr. Behrend, and advertised for sale. In that hour, he continued, the possibility of access to those premises would have been cut off. So things stood, and you will easily understand that, if the body of this woman had been committed to that grave by Henry Wainwright, and if the body should be found, it would become manifest upon investigation that the person whose body it was had come to her death by violence, and the premises having been his in which it was found, he might stand in a very awkward position; and as the premises

The Wainwrights.

were exposed for sale, and might at any moment be given up to a purchaser, and inasmuch as, after that, if anything should be observed about the floor and it should be proposed to take it up—if any of those accidental circumstances happened, and the discovery of the body should be made, it would be very awkward indeed for him. Accordingly, he made up his mind to remove the body to the Hen and Chickens. which had been occupied by his brother Thomas, but was at that time empty, and in the cellar of which the body might be buried.

It seems clear from what followed that the prisoner Henry Wainwright made up his mind to hide the body. In order to do that it was necessary to divide the body into parts. You cannot carry with any degree of safety, either in a cab or by any other mode, a dead body along the streets of London. The police, who are a vigilant set of fellows, would watch any parcel of a suspicious kind of appearance. Therefore Henry Wainwright made up his mind not only to exhume the body, but to cut it up into parts, so that it might be packed and concealed with greater security. He goes to work to provide himself with the necessary implements. In the first place, it was necessary to have an instrument with which to dig up the body; in the second place, it was necessary to have an instrument with which to divide it; then he must have some material in which to pack it; then he must have some rope with which to tie it; and we find that on the 10th, the day before the murder was discovered, he purchased 3 yards of American leather, he purchased some rope, he purchased a hatchet, a wood chopper or small hatchet, and the spade, through the intervention of his brother, whom he employed for the purpose. On the 10th he has some conversation with the young man Stokes. Stokes had known him for many years, worked for him when Henry Wainwright was in business himself; for at this time, you will recollect, he had ceased to carry on business, and had become the manager of Mr. Martin. Stokes tells him that he has bought a chain for some use he had for it at Mr. Martin's. "Ah!" says Henry Wainwright, "that will be very useful. By the by, I have got something which I think would be very useful if we want it in the premises. I have got a spade and a chopper I should be glad to get rid of. I wish you would suggest to Mr. Martin to buy them. Offer them to Martin; say they are yours, don't say they are mine. Ask him to buy them, and I daresay he will buy them." It certainly does strike one as a strange thing to do, that a man who has a spade and chopper to sell, which have been applied

222

Charge to the Jury.

for the purpose for which these had been applied, should, by going to this man, be making evidence against himself by thus disposing of them. That is in his favour, and ought to be mentioned to you. Well, Stokes does not say no to this proposal.

Then in the course of the Saturday afternoon—this was on the Friday—the afternoon of Saturday is the afternoon on which they close the shop somewhat earlier—he asks Stokes to fetch down certain parcels which he said had been there a fortnight. Now, it is quite clear he did not put them there a fortnight before. It is perfectly clear that the body was taken out of the grave the night before. It is perfectly clear that it was cut up—I don't say the night before, but some time in the day or evening before—and it is quite clear that it was hacked to pieces and put into the American cloth, if not the night before, at all events within the then last twenty-four hours. It remains to ask—why should he tell this man the parcels had been put there a fortnight before? However prone men may be to have recourse to lies, they seldom do so unless they have some need for them.

His lordship then went into the circumstances which led to the discovery of the contents of the parcels by Stokes, and the manner in which he called the attention of the police to the prisoner Henry at the Hen and Chickens. Cox, the policeman, had gone to the cab and saw the woman Alice Day in it, and, a third policeman coming up, he gave the cab into his charge, and went after Wainwright just in time to assist the other policeman, Turner, in pushing him inside the door. Turner then said, "Do you live here? I thought Lewis was on these premises?" The prisoner replied, "So he was; and, if you'll go with me to Lewis, he will tell you so in a moment; but you ask no questions, and I will give you £50." The police declined the offer, and asked what he had done with the other parcel, upon which he said he had taken it upstairs. Cox went to see, but had not got far when Turner called him back, having noticed it lying at the top of the stairs leading to the cellar. Cox then said, "Let us see what is in it," and put it on a counter. Then the prisoner burst out into a fervent ejaculation, "For God's sake, don't touch it." But they opened it, and saw that it contained human remains. The prisoner then asked them to let him go, and he would give them £100 or £200. The police then took him and the parcels back to the cab, placed them in it, and drove to the police station. There Inspector Fox received them, and by his direction the parcels were taken into the yard and

The Wainwrights.

opened. They were found to contain the fragments of a human body, severed from each other in a rude way by an axe or chopper. The head was severed from the trunk, and so were the four limbs. The legs had been divided at the knees, but the feet remained attached to the legs. The hands were severed at the wrists. The body had thus been broken into ten pieces. Inspector Fox asked the prisoner where he got the parcels, and he said that a gentleman had given them to him. When asked his address, he gave that of Mr. Martin, adding that, if Mr. Martin was sent for, the prisoner would be willing to give a full account of how he became possessed of this body. Accordingly, Mr. Martin was sent for, and he came over in the evening.

In the meantime Inspector Fox went off with Stokes to 215 Whitechapel Road, and, obtaining the assistance of another policeman, Newman, and a lantern, the first thing they found was a spade and a hatchet or chopper. The spade was lying exposed, but the chopper was wrapped up in a piece of newspaper. The chopper appeared to have some matter attached to it, which created the unpleasant smell that comes from animal remains in a state of decomposition. The spade, when examined, was found to have been recently used, and it had human hairs sticking to it. The officers then searched, and by the light they carried they perceived, on looking closely, that at the back part of the warehouse, which had formerly been the paint room, a portion of the floor seemed raised from its proper level. They also found that from that peculiar spot there proceeded a very strong smell. They then tore up the flooring, and under it they found the grave in which this body had been beyond all question placed, and from which it had been recently disinterred. In the earth of this grave the officers found mixed a quantity of chloride of lime. The next day further researches were made, and other things were discovered.

So matters stood on 11th September, when the remains were removed from No. 215 by the prisoner Henry Wainwright. They had been cut to pieces by some rough instrument, and a chopper was found, which would be just the sort of instrument with which such work could be done. The chopper had matter, apparently human remains, adhering to it, and that chopper had been got the day before by the prisoner Thomas Wainwright, and no doubt had been passed to Henry. Besides this chopper they found a spade, with which the grave had been opened. Finding this spade, it was seen that it had human hair adhering to it. This, and the fact that the chopper

224

Charge to the Jury.

and the spade had been purchased by the brother for the prisoner Henry Wainwright, taken together with the whole circumstances, cannot, I think, leave any doubt in the mind of any one that the body between the 10th and the 11th had been disinterred, and that it had been chopped up by the prisoner. There was the chopper, there were the different parts of the body severed one from the other, and the stones of the yard of the warehouse on which the body had been cut up bore witness to the fact, for there were pieces chipped out quite recently, which could only have been effected by such an instrument. Therefore we have facts on evidence which cannot leave the shadow of a doubt in the mind of any reasonable or rational man that the prisoner Henry Wainwright took up the body from the place where it had been hidden, that he cut it to pieces, and removed it from the place which had evidently been its hiding-place to another.

I will now bring to your recollection the statement made by Henry Wainwright at the police office. You know he had desired that Mr. Martin should be sent for. He came, and then the prisoner makes the following statement·—" A gentleman known to me for some time by meeting him at public-houses asked me if I wished to earn a pound or two. I said, ' Yes, I am always ready to make money,' or something of that sort. He said, ' I can put a sovereign or two in your way.' I inquired, ' How?' He said, ' By taking two parcels over to the Borough.' I said it was a big price for so small a job. He said, ' Take them over; ask no questions; and here's a couple of sovereigns for you.' I said, ' If you make it £5 I will.' He then agreed to give me £3, and told me to take them to the Hen and Chickens, an empty house in the Borough. He brought them to me, put them on the pavement, and I brought them over. That is my account of the possession of these parcels."

I need not point out that that statement was altogether untrue. At that time the prisoner did not know that Stokes had discovered his secret, and had revealed it, nor was he aware that Stokes had come to the station, and was in communication with the office, or he probably would not have ventured the statement, which required only Stokes's evidence at once to destroy.

Now, gentlemen, I enter upon another part of the case. The woman was found with two bullets in her brain, and one lodged in the pad she wore at the back of her head. Besides that, there was a cut extending from the centre of the throat across to the angle of the lower jaw, which had severed all

Q

The Wainwrights.

the vessels and tissues, and had gone right through to the vertebræ of the neck, and which, therefore, must have been a cut which required very considerable force. The great probability is that the murderer, finding that the first shot did not take effect, brought the pistol round, fired it again, just behind the right ear, and then, not certain that even that would effectually and at once destroy life, fired a third shot. Then we have the cut across the throat. Well, then, we start with the fact that by some cause, either the combined pistol shots and the cut in the throat, or by either of them singly, life was taken; and the question arises, by whom was the act done? If you are satisfied that the person whose remains were found was killed by murderous violence, and you find these remains in the hands of the prisoner Henry Wainwright, what is the presumption that fairly and properly arises, when you find the body in the hands of an individual who is concealing it? Must not in all common sense the presumption be that he who is in possession of the body was the murderer, unless he can give you some reasonable explanation of circumstances so fraught with suspicion, and leading, according to all practical reasoning, to such presumption? What was the place from which this body was taken? Not its proper and natural grave, but a secret grave in these premises. Can it be reasonably doubted that the grave was made for the purpose of concealing that body from the sight of human eye and human knowledge?

I listened with painful anxiety to the address of the counsel for Henry Wainwright to hear if he could offer any explanation which would be satisfactory to thinking men to account for his taking up that body from the grave in which it had been deposited to transfer it to another place, it being plain that the purpose of the transfer was for the concealment of the corpse. One explanation, if explanation it can be called, was offered; it was the vague, and what under the circumstances I must call the wild suggestion, that the woman whose body was found had committed suicide. I pointed out to you yesterday that it is impossible to suppose that a person who was going to shoot herself—a woman with a quantity of hair at the back of her head, should begin by firing at that part. Certainly it is possible, but not likely; and I think it is far more reasonable that the shot was fired from behind with the belief that the bullet would penetrate the skull by a person approaching from behind, rather than a person intending to shoot herself pointing the pistol at a point where the shot would be less likely to penetrate.

Charge to the Jury.

Then there is another fact. This is one of three bullets, and it has been said that if it did not take life instantaneously she might have cut her throat afterwards. It might be so. But every one knows that if you fire a bullet into the brain it will cause death. Here there were two bullets in the brain. Then we have the gash in the throat. If the surgeons are right in saying that that was not done at the cutting up of the body, but was done at the time, although it might not have been done during life, it is quite clear that a person killing herself by a pistol bullet could not cut her own throat afterwards. Gentlemen, you must form your own judgment whether you think this could by any human possibility have been a case of suicide.

There is a further observation; if it was a case of suicide, the person committing the rash and fatal deed must be provided with the instrument with which this was done. The body was buried in the warehouse of No. 215, which was at the time empty, no one living in it. If this woman destroyed herself by those shots, she must have taken the revolver or pistol there with her. If, indeed, the death had occurred at No. 84, where the prisoner kept a revolver, it might have been said that the revolver happened to be lying there, and happening to be charged, this woman in a moment of distraction seized the weapon and fired. But it was not done at No. 84, where the revolver was, but at No. 215, where the revolver was not. As I said, whoever took that revolver there, the person who fired it must have taken it. Whoever took it there cannot have taken it in order that suicide might be committed. Under those circumstances, are you of opinion that this was a case of suicide? If not, we have to inquire further whose hand it was.

Now, I approach a very important point in this case. What were the personal characteristics of Harriet Lane? Slender build, slender limbs; small hands and feet, but not too small for her stature and weight. The remains of the body found in like manner indicated all these points. The next point is the comparison of the hair. There is no doubt, making some little allowance for exposure and the effects of chloride of lime, the hair of the remains is the colour of that of Harriet Lane. Then are there any marks which may assist us? First, there is the decayed tooth. It has been proved abundantly that Harriet Lane had a tooth next the eye tooth which was decayed and eaten away almost to the bone, and, being next the eye tooth, when she laughed or smiled strongly this tooth was perceptible. When we see a beautiful mouth of teeth,

227

The Wainwrights.

and one of them is decayed and black, the disfigurement is always observed; and so, when these remains were shown to the witnesses for identification, they at once looked for the decayed tooth. When her father came to view the body and had seen it, a profound emotion overcame him, and he at once said it was his daughter. But you must not attach any importance to such a circumstance, or that there is any instinctive impulse which may be depended upon in such a case. We must have something more substantial and more certain; and so, when the old man was asked if his daughter had any marks on her body, he at once said she had the scar of a burn, which was caused by a poker falling out of the fire. The surgeons had not perceived this. The body was covered with a greasy exudation, which did not make it very pleasant to handle; but when they heard that Harriet Lane had a scar, they looked for it, and, sure enough, they found it. When the grease was removed there was the scar.

Now, is there anything else which makes the inference drawn from these facts, if conclusive, nugatory? Harriet Lane had had two children, and it, of course, becomes an important inquiry whether the remains were those of a woman who had borne children or not. We have the evidence of Mr. Larkin and of Mr. Bond in the affirmative.

Let me now come to a second heading of the evidence, and that is her dress. Harriet Lane was in the habit of wearing a pad, made out of the rolls which we see in the shop windows, fixed on the back of her head, and on this she was in the habit of sticking an immense quantity of hairpins and frizzing her hair over this pad. A pad was found attached to the head of the deceased woman, and it corresponds in colour. Mr. Larkin, who undid it and took the bullet out of it, says that it was filled '' with an immense quantity of hairpins,'' sufficient to turn the bullet—at all events, to diminish its force and prevent it penetrating the head. That, again, is worthy of consideration. There was a velvet band found. Harriet Lane used to wear a velvet band, and though a particular velvet band cannot be identified as compared with another, here you have all these various items corresponding in the two cases. Then we come to a by no means unimportant article, namely, the two jet buttons. Miss Wilmore told you that on the day Harriet Lane went away from Sidney Square she had a dress to which was attached a long series of black jet buttons, and that two which were not required were put away into the stay-box. Well, two black jet buttons were found on the ash heap at No. 215, within

Charge to the Jury.

two yards of the grave from which the body was disinterred. When these are compared with the buttons from the stay-box there is the most perfect similarity found between them. They are, in fact, evidently buttons of the same manufacture.

That is the dismal evidence offered to you to satisfy you that this was her body. Besides that, there is what I may call the indirect evidence—that is, the general considerations resulting from the history of the case. Of course, the most important of those circumstances is the fact that Harriet Lane had disappeared. She was attached to her relatives and friends. She was to some extent fond of her children; but from 11th September to the present she has never inquired after relatives, friends, or children. Where is she? That question is very properly asked, and unless you can suppose her to be somewhere where the tidings of this trial cannot reach her, it is impossible to suppose that she would allow the man with whom she had lived on conjugal terms, and the father of her two children, to suffer what may be the fatal consequences of her disappearance. One can conceive no motive for conduct so unnatural as that she should not come forward if she is alive. It is said that she may be in the wilds of Australia; but is it at all likely, so long as it could be supposed that she had gone away with Edward Frieake, and that Frieake had made the condition of his maintaining her in affluence and comfort, that she should cut off all connection with her relatives, friends, and children? One can understand that worldly interests may have predominated over natural affection. Therefore if we can believe that there was an Edward Frieake with whom she had gone off who made that condition, she might have cut herself off from all her friends. If you should come to the conclusion that Frieake was a delusion, what motive could have pressed upon her mind to induce her to avoid all communication with her friends? That makes the theory of Frieake one of the material matters of the case. If this woman had been killed by some one else, the prisoner would not have been at the trouble of burying her in the first instance, or of removing her after.

Now, I come to the case against the prisoner in the event of your being of opinion that this was the body of Harriet Lane. In the first place, we found that this body was originally buried upon the premises belonging to the prisoner, or which had belonged to him, and over which he retained control. What is the fair and legitimate inference to be drawn upon the body being there? Is it not that the body was killed there? For if it was not killed there, why should it be taken there to be

The Wainwrights.

buried? Why should the danger and suspicion be incurred?
But if it was killed there, there was every reason why it should
be buried there, because there would have been the same danger
of transferring the body to another place. On the day before
Harriet Lane disappeared, the prisoner purchased a quantity of
chloride of lime. A grave is found full of chloride of lime; a
body is found covered with it. Where did the chloride of lime
come from? By whom was it used? It must have been used by
the person who buried her. Was it the prisoner? If so, he
was the person who buried her. If it was not so used, what
became of it? He said it was to go to Southend, and the learned
counsel for the defence said the prisoner's books were to be had,
and it was possible, if they looked therein, a customer for the
chloride of lime would be found at Southend. But, alas! if
this had been sent to a customer at Southend, it would have
been easy to evoke the assistance of that customer, and if there
were any entry in the books, is it probable that any one would
have known that better than the man who entered it? We
could have had these books before us, and so have got rid of the
truth of the terrible fact that chloride of lime was purchased
on the 10th, and that the body buried in the prisoner's premises
is alleged to be the person who disappeared on the 11th.

Now comes this additional question of the method of her
death. She was killed by having three shots fired. She in all
human probability would not have had an instrument by which
those shots could have been fired. Were they fired from a
revolver? A single pistol, you know, would hardly have
served the purpose of firing three shots, not even if it were a
double-barrelled one, because it would have to be reloaded.
The probability is that these three shots were fired in succession. Unfortunately, we are aware the prisoner had a revolver,
and we know that under the stress of circumstances in July he
wanted to pawn it for so small a sum as 50s., and could not get
that amount, and the revolver was put back into his desk.
We know also that he possessed cartridges, so that he had the
means of killing this woman in the way she appears to have been
killed. Three shots were fired, and Harriet Lane disappeared
on the same day upon which it was alleged these shots were
discharged.

Putting these facts together, they certainly are formidable,
and the more so if it can be shown with certainty that the
dates of the shots and the disappearance were the same. The
evidence of the two Kays and Wiseman went to establish that
proposition.

230

Mr. Douglas Straight.

Charge to the Jury.

Do all the facts which I have at too great length and too great minuteness brought to your attention lead to the conclusion that this woman, who was murdered by some one, fell by the hand of the prisoner? If upon that consideration you entertain any reasonable doubt, it is your duty to give Henry Wainwright the benefit of that doubt. If it be one which you feel, as rational, thinking minds, you cannot reasonably entertain, if the facts taken together lead you irresistibly to the conclusion that the woman fell by the prisoner Henry Wainwright's hand, then, sad and painful as may be the duty, you, upon the oath you have taken truly to try between the Crown and the prisoner at the bar, must do that duty sternly and unflinchingly.

I have now some final observations to make upon the case of the other prisoner Thomas Wainwright. It would be dangerous, indeed, from the circumstances to which I have called your attention, to infer that Thomas Wainwright entered into a scheme with his brother to pave the way for the destruction of this woman; and unless you see your way clearly to the double fact that when the character of Frieake was first assumed, the brother contemplated the subsequent murder, and also that Thomas Wainwright entered into a scheme with him, and promised him his assistance in order to lead people to think that by first assuming the name of Frieake, and getting up an intimacy with her under that name, in order that when she was afterwards destroyed it might be said that she had gone off " on the spree " with Frieake, there is an end of that part of the case, and you cannot find him guilty of being an accessory before the murder. Then comes the question—and a very serious one for him—whether he was an accessory after the fact? That rests upon two or three considerations. In the first place, it is quite clear that he lent himself to a scheme for turning aside inquiry by pretending that she had gone off; but it does not necessarily follow, even assuming that by this time Henry Wainwright had destroyed the woman, that Thomas was aware of the fact. You must be satisfied that in all these things in which he is implicated he was aware that murder had been committed, and that he intended to assist his brother in concealing that fact. If the evidence leads you irresistibly to that conclusion, of course that must be your verdict; but, as I said before, you must be clearly of opinion that he was not the mere creature and innocent tool of his brother, and that he had full knowledge of the guilt of his brother, supposing that guilt to be established. In order to find him guilty of being an accessory after the fact, you must feel certain that he knew of the murder,

231

The Wainwrights.

and lent himself to the assistance of his brother, in order to
avert from the head of that unfortunate man the consequences
which would attach to the discovery. Now, here you must
pause to consider whether you think the evidence before you is
sufficient to lead you to the conclusion that he knew of the
murder. If you think he did, you must find him guilty; but,
on the other hand, if you entertain any rational doubt on the
matter, you must give him the benefit of the doubt, and say he
is not guilty.

Gentlemen of the jury, the case is now in your hands. Of
one thing I am quite certain, and that is, that you
will discharge your duty to the best of your ability, and to
the satisfaction of your consciences. You will let the
world know that never did a jury give more devoted and un-
divided attention to a case than you have done during this protracted trial, with a desire to arrive at a just and righteous
conclusion.

The jury retired to consider their verdict at 3.45.

Verdict and Sentence.

The jury returned into Court at 4.38, and, having taken
their seats, they were called upon by Mr. Avory, the Clerk of
Arraigns, to answer to their names. This ceremony having
been completed, Mr. Avory put the question—"Have you
agreed upon your verdict?" to which the formal reply was
given, "We have."

Mr. AVORY—Do you find that the prisoner Henry Wainwright is guilty or not guilty of the indictment, which charges
him with wilful murder?

The FOREMAN—We do all say he is guilty.

Mr. AVORY—Do you say that Thomas Wainwright is guilty
of being an accessory before or after the fact?

The FOREMAN—Not guilty before, but guilty after.

Mr. AVORY—And that, you say, is the verdict of you all?

The FOREMAN—It is.

The LORD CHIEF JUSTICE—Call upon them.

Mr. AVORY—Prisoner at the bar, you have been indicted for
the crime of wilful murder, and to that indictment you have
pleaded not guilty, and have thrown yourself upon your
country. That country has found you guilty. What have you
to say why judgment should not be pronounced against you?

Verdict and Sentence.

HENRY WAINWRIGHT—I should like to make one or two observations, and they shall be very short indeed. I have first to express my deep obligation for the untiring energy and ability of my counsel during this protracted trial. I thank him, and all who have assisted him, deeply. My thanks are due to the very many friends who have, with such promptitude and alacrity, come forward to give me their valuable and substantial assistance. I have not been able to reply to all the persons——

The LORD CHIEF JUSTICE—I cannot allow you to make a speech. You can only reply to the question whether you have anything to say why sentence should not be passed.

HENRY WAINWRIGHT—Then I will only say, standing as I do now upon the brink of eternity and in the presence of the God before whom I shall shortly appear, that I swear that I am not the murderer of the remains found in my possession. I swear that I have not buried these remains, and the proof that I did not exhume those mutilated remains has been proved before you by witnesses. I have been guilty of great immorality; I have been guilty of many indiscretions; but for the crime of which I have been brought in guilty I leave this dock with a calm and quiet conscience. My lord, I thank you for your kindness in allowing me to say these few words.

The LORD CHIEF JUSTICE—Prisoner at the bar, you have been found guilty, in my opinion upon the clearest and most conclusive evidence, of the murder of Harriet Louisa Lane, which has been laid to your charge. No one, I think, who has heard this trial can entertain the slightest shadow of a doubt of your guilt, and I can only deplore that, standing as you surely are upon the brink of eternity, you should have called God to witness the rash assertion which has just issued from your lips. There can be no doubt that you took the life of this poor woman, who had been on the closest and most intimate terms of familiarity and affection with you, who had been the mother of your children. You inveigled her into the lone warehouse. The revolver was not there before, but it must have been taken for the purpose, and with that she was slain. The grave was dug there for her remains, which were those you were removing when you were arrested; and about that no one can entertain the shadow of a doubt. It was a barbarous, cruel, inhuman, and cowardly act. I do not wish to say anything to aggravate the position in which you stand, nor dwell upon the enormity of your guilt, further than by way of rousing you to a sense of the position which you now occupy, in which the hope of earthly mercy is

The Wainwrights.

cut off. The only hope and consolation you can have is in the future, where truth cannot be mistaken, where no assertion of yours will stand you in any stead, though where, if you seek for mercy, it must be through sincere repentance for the crime which you have undoubtedly committed. I have to warn you against any delusive hope of mercy here as long as the law exists which says that he who takes the life of a fellow-creature with malicious aforethought shall answer for it with his own. This is a case to which it would be impossible that mercy could be extended; therefore, prepare for the doom which awaits you. I have now only to pass upon you the dreadful sentence of the law, which is that you be taken from hence to the place whence you came, thence to a legal place of execution, to be there hanged by the neck till you shall be dead; that your body be buried within the precincts of the gaol in which you shall be last confined after your conviction; and may the Lord have mercy upon your soul.

Thomas George Wainwright, the jury have, in my opinion correctly, acquitted you of the heavier crime of having entered into the scheme conceived by your brother with the view to the murder of Harriet Lane. Their opinion, and they have pronounced it by their verdict, is that, having become aware of the crime committed by your brother, you lent yourself to assist him in its concealment. No fraternal affection, no regard or sympathy which one brother should have for another, can excuse you in the eyes of the law for assisting him in his endeavour to escape the consequences of justice. Your offence, although lighter, and one far short of being an accessory before the act, is one which ought to be punished with proper severity; for through the concealment of such crimes they have sometimes been perpetrated with impunity and safety, and human life thereby endangered. I am ready to believe that you were actuated under the influence which your brother had over you, without which you might not have done what you did. I have taken that into consideration, as I believe you to have been his dupe and his tool, and he has in some degree your crime to answer for practically as well as his own. You yielded weakly and wrongly to his influence and his greater age; but although that does not in any way mitigate the character of the offence, I think, on the whole, that justice will not be satisfied with a less punishment than I am about to inflict. The sentence of the Court is that you be imprisoned and kept in penal servitude for seven years.

After the prisoners had been removed from the bar, the LORD CHIEF JUSTICE said—I think it right to exercise a power

Verdict and Sentence.

which I have vested in me, sitting here upon this trial, by Act
of Parliament, to order that a reward be given from the proper
fund to the man Stokes. His conduct and his energy on the
occasion of these remains being removed from Whitechapel
to the Borough, and his perseverance in following up the cab
in which those remains were being conveyed, have in reality
led to the discovery of this crime and the conviction of the
offenders concerned in it. I shall direct, therefore, that he
shall receive from the proper fund the sum of £30.

Lightning Source UK Ltd.
Milton Keynes UK
UKOW01f1914260717
306122UK00010B/546/P